NATO
ENLARGEMENT

NATO ENLARGEMENT

Illusions and Reality

EDITED BY TED GALEN CARPENTER
AND BARBARA CONRY

CATO
INSTITUTE
Washington, D.C.

Library of Congress Cataloging-in-Publication Data

NATO enlargement : illusions and reality / edited by Ted Galen
Carpenter and Barbara Conry
   p. cm.
Includes bibliographical references (p.   ) and index.
ISBN 1-882577-58-2 — ISBN 1-882577-59-0 (pbk.)
   1. North Atlantic Treaty Organization. 2. National Security—Europe.
3. Russia (Federation)—Foreign relations. I. Carpenter, Ted Galen.
II. Conry, Barbara.
UA646.3.N2425 1998
355′.031091821—DC21   97-52330
                                                   CIP

CATO INSTITUTE
1000 Massachusetts Ave., N.W.
Washington, D.C. 20001

To Brian and all the American children of his generation who might someday have to fight in a war caused by the decision to expand NATO.

Contents

Acknowledgments

This book is the outgrowth of a June 1997 Cato Institute conference, attended by more than 200 people, on NATO expansion. Many individuals deserve appreciation for helping to make that event such a success. We wish to thank Edward H. Crane and William A. Niskanen, respectively president and chairman of the Cato Institute, for their consistent and enthusiastic support of the conference and the subsequent book. Julie Briggs, Heather Anttila, Andrew Stone, and other members of the Institute's administrative staff did an excellent job of handling the conference's many logistical requirements. Lea Abdnor and Peggy Ellis performed the crucial task of promoting the event to members of Congress and their staffs. Adam Garfinkle, Peter Ackerman, and Ivan Eland generously donated their time to moderate the various panels. We wish to express our special appreciation to Sen. Kay Bailey Hutchison for taking time from her extraordinarily busy schedule to deliver an incisive luncheon address.

An additional debt of gratitude is owed to those who have helped to make this book possible. David Boaz, Cato's executive vice president, presided over the project with patience and offered a variety of useful suggestions. David Lampo, the Institute's director of publications, helped to keep us on schedule with periodic—and sometimes insistent—reminders of deadlines. Jeanne Hill, Carrie Lips, and Emily P. Smith labored long and diligently to incorporate the revisions made by the authors. Pavel Kislitsyn, Laura Dykes, and Dale Henry spent many hours tracking down sometimes elusive sources for the various chapters. Marian Council designed an appealing cover.

Our copyeditor, Elizabeth W. Kaplan, has done her usual meticulous job of improving the manuscript and preparing it for publication. Any errors that may have escaped her rigorous screening are solely the responsibility of the editors.

Most of all, we want to thank the authors for their cooperation and enthusiasm. It has been a pleasure to work with them, and we believe that our collective endeavor has produced a book that addresses the real implications of NATO expansion and serves to clear away the many creative illusions produced by proponents of enlargement.

Introduction

The decision to expand NATO by inviting Poland, the Czech Republic, and Hungary to join the alliance is a fateful undertaking. Advocates of enlargement insist that it will foster cooperation, consolidate democracy, and promote stability throughout Europe. But an enlarged NATO is a dubious idea. Instead of healing the wounds of the Cold War, it threatens to create a new division of Europe. Even worse, it will establish expensive, dangerous, and probably unsustainable security obligations for the United States.

There are four major drawbacks to NATO enlargement. One is that, if enlargement is not merely an empty political gesture but is intended to provide meaningful security to the new member states, it is certain to be expensive. A 1996 study by the Congressional Budget Office concluded that the costs could run as high as $125 billion by 2012. Subsequent RAND Corporation and Pentagon studies have produced far lower figures, but those calculations are based on the assumption that Europe's security environment will remain quiescent for at least the next 15 years. They further assume that an enlarged NATO can meet its obligations merely by upgrading Central European defenses and by creating a small rapid-reaction force. The RAND analysts estimate the probable costs of enlargement at between $30 billion and $52 billion over 10 to 15 years. The Pentagon's figures are even lower—$27 billion to $35 billion.[1]

Basing cost projections on a rosy scenario is dubious methodology. There is no guarantee that Europe's strategic environment will remain placid for 15 years. One need only recall how different that environment looked 15 years ago to appreciate how rapidly radical transformations can occur.

The comment of a "senior U.S. official" following the release of the Pentagon report reveals much about the underlying motives of advocates of NATO enlargement. "There was a strong political imperative to low-ball the figures," admitted the official. "Everybody realized the main priority was to keep costs down to reassure Congress, as well as the Russians."[2]

If the overall cost projections in the RAND and Pentagon studies are excessively sanguine, the assumption that the European countries will pay the overwhelming majority of those costs is even worse. Poland, Hungary, and the Czech Republic face daunting financial problems that make it difficult for them to spend additional billions of dollars on bringing their military forces up to NATO standards. All three countries are under pressure from the International Monetary Fund to reduce their budget deficits. Moreover, there is a dearth of domestic support for undertaking expensive military burdens, even if the costs were theoretically affordable.

Prospects for generous funding by the current European members of NATO are no better. The West European countries have slashed their military spending, in some cases at a rate even greater than that of the United States, since the end of the Cold War. There is no evidence that such trends will be reversed to fund NATO's enlargement. Indeed, both the British and the French governments have recently announced plans to further cut defense expenditures and reduce the size of their militaries.

The public in several West European countries seems preoccupied with thwarting efforts to trim their bloated welfare states. German chancellor Helmut Kohl has encountered ferocious opposition to his efforts to scale back domestic welfare programs. The situation in France is even more volatile. The attempt by newly elected French president Jacques Chirac to make modest cuts in such programs provoked mass demonstrations, eventually impelling Chirac to seek the resignation of the cabinet minister responsible for the austerity plan. Chirac's effort to placate an angry populace proved insufficient, however, as French voters elected a Socialist parliamentary majority in the spring of 1997.

Given such political realities, it is naive to assume that there will be a groundswell of public support for increased military outlays to bring the Central European states into NATO. Moreover, the West European political elites show no inclination to challenge public opinion on this issue. Indeed, within hours of the decision at the Madrid summit in July to expand the alliance, Chirac stated bluntly that France would not contribute a single franc to pay for enlargement.

West Europeans across the political spectrum have stated privately, and sometimes publicly, that NATO enlargement is primarily a U.S. initiative and that Washington should therefore pay for it.

The conclusion of Walther Stuetzle, a former senior defense planner for the German government, seems prophetic. "So who will pick up the tab? I think that it will have to be the United States."[3] It is not a minor concern. American taxpayers could be on the hook for an additional $25 billion to $35 billion over the next 10 to 12 years—even if one accepts the extraordinarily low RAND and Pentagon projections. The burden could be more than $100 billion if the more realistic (in fact, conservative) CBO numbers are correct.

Those who believe that NATO enlargement can be done "on the cheap" ignore the fact that the new members are expecting reliable security guarantees, not just the honor of alliance membership. That leads to the second problem with enlargement: the United States will be assuming extremely dangerous obligations if it is serious about providing protection. Russia has important strategic, economic, and cultural interests throughout much of Eastern Europe going back generations and, in some cases, centuries. It also has a daunting array of grievances, some spurious, some legitimate, with its various neighbors. Extending security commitments to nations in what Moscow regards as its geopolitical "back yard" virtually invites a challenge at some point. Although that may not be an immediate danger, given the disarray in the Russian military, one cannot assume that Russia will remain weak forever.

A Russian challenge, now or in the future, would create a horrific dilemma for the United States. Washington would have to renege on treaty obligations to its new allies or risk war with a nuclear-armed great power. The first option would leave American credibility in tatters; the second might leave America itself in ruins.

Enlargement enthusiasts habitually downplay the extent of America's risk exposure. But the United States, if it is serious about its commitments and is not bluffing, must be willing to do whatever is necessary to defend its new allies—including shielding those countries with the U.S. strategic nuclear arsenal. Indeed, it would be difficult to mount an effective conventional defense of the easternmost members of an expanded NATO against a capable adversary. That is especially true if NATO goes beyond the first round and brings in the Baltic states—which both President Clinton and Secretary of State Madeleine Albright have implied will happen someday. Most military experts believe that the Baltic republics cannot be defended by conventional means. The only alternative would be a U.S. nuclear guarantee, with all the risks that course implies.

The third problem with enlargement, closely related to the second, is that the alliance could become entangled in parochial disputes among the Central and East European states. Article 5 of the North Atlantic Treaty obligates the United States and its allies to help a fellow member repel aggression from *any* source—not just a great power with hegemonic aspirations. That is a matter of concern since there are several potential flashpoints along the alliance's revised security frontier. Hungary has problems with three neighboring states—Serbia, Slovakia, and Romania—about the treatment of ethnic Hungarians in those countries. Although Hungary has signed paper accords with Slovakia and Romania, there is little evidence that the underlying grievances have been resolved. There is not even a paper accord with Serbia, where tensions involving the mistreated Hungarian minority in the province of Vojvodina are approaching the boiling point.[4]

Even more worrisome is that part of NATO's eastern frontier would be the border between Poland and Belarus. The political situation in the latter country is ominous. Ruled by the autocratic and eccentric Alexander Lukashenko, and having one of the weakest economies in Europe, Belarus is a political volcano waiting to erupt. There is considerable danger in having the United States obligated to protect Poland if trouble breaks out along the Polish-Belarusan border—especially since Belarus is increasingly a political and military client of Russia.[5]

At the very least, an expanded NATO could entangle the United States in an assortment of Bosnia-style peacekeeping missions. The Clinton administration explicitly sees peacekeeping as a crucial—perhaps even the principal—function of an expanded NATO. According to the president, NATO is now an organization "adapted to its new crisis management and peacekeeping missions."[6] Both the Senate and the American people should ponder whether involving U.S. forces in such ventures is truly in America's best interest.

Advocates of enlargement believe that, in the president's words, "NATO can do for Europe's East what it did for Europe's West at the end of World War II—provide a secure climate where freedom, democracy, and prosperity can flourish."[7] Even if one accepts the argument that NATO was crucial in pacifying and stabilizing Western Europe, there is little prospect of comparable success in Eastern Europe. Many of the sources of conflict in Western Europe had been ebbing long before the creation of NATO. The Anglo-French antagonism, the complicated dynastic rivalries, and a host of other issues that once plagued the western portion of the Continent had already receded into history. The principal remaining source of tension—the Franco-German territorial feud over Alsace-Lorraine—had also been decisively resolved with Germany's crushing defeat in World War II.

By contrast, Eastern Europe remains a cauldron of boundary disputes, ethnic and religious rivalries, and fragile, unstable political and economic systems. The process of nation building in Eastern Europe today resembles that in Western Europe two or three centuries ago, with all the attendant turbulence. Clinton's attempt to recreate Washington's West European policy of the late 1940s in a volatile Eastern Europe is dangerously misguided. America is far more likely to become entangled in Eastern Europe's problems than it is to be the region's savior.

Finally, there is the probable adverse impact of NATO enlargement on Russia's political development and relations with the West. There is a conceptual contradiction at the heart of the campaign for enlargement. Some prominent advocates of NATO expansion, most notably Henry Kissinger and Zbigniew Brzezinski, seem motivated by an animus toward Russia. To that faction of the pro-enlargement camp, a larger NATO is primarily an insurance policy against any revival of Russian imperial ambitions. If a second cold war emerges, they would rather have the democratic West's defense line on the border between Poland and Belarus than between Germany and Poland. They especially want to be certain that the alliance would have the strategic depth that it lacked throughout the Cold War.

But other advocates of expansion, including most members of the Clinton administration, strongly (and apparently sincerely) reject the concept of an enlarged NATO as an anti-Russian measure. They believe that expanding the alliance must have the objective of fostering the political and economic integration of all of Europe, including Russia. Indeed, they have argued that in time Russian leaders will come to see an enlarged NATO as beneficial to Russia's interests, since it will help prevent instability in historically volatile Central and Eastern Europe.

It is increasingly evident, however, that Russia's opinion leaders are suspicious of the motives for NATO enlargement, despite the soothing words of the Clinton administration. That should concern all Americans who grasp the importance of cordial U.S.-Russian relations to continued peace in the world.

The enlargement issue undermines pro-Western democrats in Russia and plays into the hands of Communists and ultranationalists. Clinton administration officials and other supporters of NATO expansion profess to be baffled at the hostile reaction of Russians across the political spectrum. But even democratically inclined Russians find it difficult to countenance a powerful, U.S.-led military alliance perched on their country's western frontier. The few political figures who fail to oppose enlargement are excoriated by their opponents as stooges of foreign powers. Given the fragility of Russian democracy, that development is exceedingly worrisome. Just as the foolish "war guilt" clause in the Versailles Treaty after World War I undermined domestic support for Germany's democratic Weimar Republic, and eventually helped bring the Nazis to power, NATO enlargement could fatally wound democracy in Russia.

The expansion of NATO also threatens to poison Russia's relations with the West even if a democratic regime retains control. We should not accord excessive importance to the willingness of Russian president Boris Yeltsin to sign the Founding Act on Mutual Relations, Cooperation and Security between NATO and the Russian Federation. Russian leaders understood that, given their country's weakened condition, they could not block the first stage of enlargement. Therefore, they adopted a strategy to make the best of a bad situation and limit the damage to Russia's interests. The rhetoric coming from Moscow suggests a continuing seething resentment about the West's determination to expand NATO and a growing determination to prevent any further rounds of enlargement. The danger is that, when Russia recovers economically and militarily, Russians will remember that the West exploited their country's temporary weakness to establish a dominant position in Central and Eastern Europe and seek to overturn that outcome.

Moscow can take several unpleasant countermeasures even in the short term. Prospects for a START III nuclear arms agreement to further reduce the Russian and U.S. arsenals are likely to be an early casualty of NATO enlargement. Even the fate of the START II agreement in the Duma is uncertain. Moscow also has an incentive to seek closer strategic relationships with Iran, China, and other powers outside Europe. There are already ominous signs of a Moscow-Beijing axis. Russian and Chinese leaders speak of a "strategic partnership" between the two countries, and China is now Russia's largest arms customer.

As NATO expands eastward, Russia can also seek to create its own political-military bloc among those nations left out of the alliance. Moscow is already vigorously courting such countries as Slovakia and Bulgaria. The 1997 union agreement between Russia and Belarus may be the first tangible step toward establishing an anti-NATO bloc. It is revealing that although the reformers in Yeltsin's government vehemently (and successfully) opposed the economic integration provisions in the draft accord, they mounted no comparable opposition to the provisions outlining military cooperation. From Moscow's perspective, Belarus is an important security buffer between an expanded NATO and Russia. It also could become a forward staging area for Russia's forces if relations between Moscow and the Western alliance deteriorated.

Some proponents of enlargement argue that, whatever the costs and risks of expanding the alliance eastward, they pale in comparison with those that would exist if the United States were drawn into yet another massive European war. But U.S. policy should not be based on the need to prevent such a highly improbable event. As several of the authors in this collection point out, there is no European power today or in the foreseeable future that has either the intention or the ability to replicate the campaigns for continental hegemony undertaken by Nazi Germany and the Soviet Union—or even the more limited bid for preeminence made by Wilhelmine Germany in 1914.

From the standpoint of American interests, what matters in Europe is the conduct of the handful of major powers. As long as those states remain at peace with one another, and no menacing would-be hegemonic power emerges, there is no credible danger to America's security. Events involving small countries in Central and Eastern Europe may create annoyances, but they will not affect European stability or the overall configuration of power on the Continent. In that vein, Britain's ambassador to the United States, John Kerr, admitted with surprising candor that "the war in Bosnia could rumble on for years without directly impinging on the security of Western Europe."[8]

U.S. policymakers must learn to distinguish between parochial squabbles and serious threats. The belief that it is impossible to tolerate any episode of instability anywhere in Europe because it will eventually draw in the United States is fallacious. Yet the case for NATO expansion reflects the historical analysis of former national security adviser Anthony Lake. According to Lake, "If there is one thing this century teaches us, it is that America cannot ignore conflicts in Europe."[9] Lake and other advocates of NATO enlargement miss the crucial point that both of the armed conflicts in Europe in which the United States ultimately intervened were wars involving all of Europe's great powers. Such serious disruptions of the international system had the potential to place important American interests at risk.

Not every conflict that has erupted in Europe, or is likely to in the future, has wider strategic implications. There is no validity to the notion that limited struggles, especially those involving small powers in peripheral regions, are destined to escalate to continental conflagrations that will drag in the United States. Ironically, expanding the alliance may increase rather than decrease the danger of a major war, since it will almost certainly exacerbate tensions with one European great power: Russia.

The contributors to this volume hold a variety of views about future U.S. policy toward NATO. Some of them argue that the alliance—in its traditional form—still plays an important role in Europe's security and advances American interests by providing an institutional expression of transatlantic solidarity. Others conclude that NATO is a Cold War relic that encourages an unhealthy European reliance on the United States to manage Europe's security affairs. They believe that alternative security institutions, directed by the Europeans themselves, should be created or strengthened to deal with the Continent's problems in the post–Cold War era. The various authors are united, however, in their belief that the expansion of NATO is a disastrously misguided initiative.

The book is divided into four sections: "Problems of Cost and Credibility," "NATO Enlargement and Russia's Relations with the West," "Ins and Outs: Creating a New Division of Europe," and "Alternatives to an Enlarged NATO."

In Part I, "Problems of Cost and Credibility," Ted Galen Carpenter points out that what the Clinton administration touts as a "new"

NATO is actually a confusing hybrid that ignores the fundamental differences between a collective security organization and a traditional military alliance. Blurring that distinction obscures the fact that NATO enlargement obligates the United States to use any means necessary to defend new members from any adversary—an inherently risky and expensive proposition. Carpenter warns that an enlarged NATO would be simultaneously provocative and lacking in credibility.

William Hyland traces the historical evolution of NATO in chapter 2 and notes that it is both unusual and unwise for an alliance with no clear mission and drastically reduced capabilities to extend significant new security commitments. Bringing new members into the alliance would greatly enlarge NATO's security frontiers. Current members, who have reduced the size of their militaries since the end of the Cold War, would probably be unable to fulfill new security obligations without creating massive reserve forces and generally bolstering their defense capabilities. Absent such enhancements, NATO enlargement is a meaningless gesture that fails to address the need for a new approach to European security in the post–Cold War era, according to Hyland.

In chapter 3, Alan Tonelson criticizes the strategic incoherence that has driven NATO enlargement. Many proponents of enlargement have set forth unexceptionable goals—such as peace, stability, and prosperity in Europe—but they have not considered key issues of cost, risk, and feasibility or whether NATO enlargement is even relevant to achieving their objectives. The resulting mismatch between means and ends creates the likelihood that expanding NATO will make Europe less, not more, stable over the long term, Tonelson argues.

Christopher Layne notes in chapter 4 that two broad strategic rationales—counterhegemony and regional stability—have historically driven U.S. military engagement in Europe. In the post–Cold War era, however, neither rationale applies. He argues that in the absence of a major hegemonic threat in Europe, there are no interests that merit risking U.S. blood and treasure. European security should instead be the province of the Europeans, Layne asserts.

In chapter 5, Benjamin Schwarz characterizes NATO enlargement as a logical extension of the U.S. empire. Washington is prepared to assume the immense costs and risks of NATO expansion as a means of exercising American global leadership. Schwarz warns that such a strategy entails literally infinite costs and risks and urges greater public debate of Washington's commitment to a global *pax Americana* and the inevitable expansion of U.S. security commitments that policy entails.

Barbara Conry examines potential conflicts involving the Czech Republic, Hungary, and Poland in chapter 6. Many proponents of enlargement contend that NATO expansion will pacify Central and Eastern Europe much as NATO facilitated the Franco-German rapprochement after World War II. Conry argues that potential conflicts in Central and Eastern Europe today, however, are unlikely to be greatly dampened by NATO. Conflicts involving new NATO members are more likely to become perennial headaches for the alliance, much as disputes between Greece and Turkey have long plagued NATO.

In Section II, "NATO Enlargement and Russia's Relations with the West," Susan Eisenhower details the erosion of trust between Russia and the West in recent years. She contends that at the end of the Cold War Moscow made a series of unilateral concessions based on the expectation that postcommunist Russia would be welcomed as part of the West. As Russian-Western relations have chilled, however, Russian resentment has increased markedly. Moscow may perceive NATO enlargement as the ultimate betrayal, according to Eisenhower, which would undermine both Russian-Western relations and democratic elements within Russia.

Jonathan Dean argues in chapter 8 that the Founding Act is a good idea on its own merits but that NATO enlargement obliterates the benefits that act would otherwise have. Although Russia might in time become reconciled to a modest enlargement limited to the three countries invited at the Madrid summit, Dean contends that it is clear that NATO intends to expand further. Given those circumstances, he views comprehensive enlargement—eventually including Russia—as less dangerous than an alliance that extends beyond the Czech Republic, Hungary, and Poland but excludes Russia.

In chapter 9, Stanley Kober draws parallels between events surrounding NATO enlargement and events that led up to World War I. Moscow perceives NATO enlargement as a Western effort to take advantage of Russian weakness to permanently exclude Russia from Europe. Kober notes that Russia has already taken defensive steps in response—including initiating a strategic rapprochement with China—and expresses concern that the provocations, miscalculations, and entangling effects of an outdated alliance could play themselves out once again at the close of the 20th century.

In chapter 10, Anatol Lieven dismisses the notion that the Founding Act significantly eased Russia's objections to NATO expansion and laments the West's willingness to allow empty rhetoric to obscure significant—and dangerous—issues. He notes with concern the reflexive anti-Russian sentiment among some influential members of the American foreign policy community, who appear intent on denying Moscow any interest—even a legitimate interest—in developments outside Russia's borders. Efforts to deny Russia the prerogatives of a normal great power may well eventually have explosive results, Lieven cautions.

In Section III, "Ins and Outs: Creating a New Division of Europe," Hugh De Santis points out the potentially destabilizing consequences of NATO enlargement. Those include the risk that the "failed suitors" denied membership in the first round of expansion will reverse their progress toward liberalization; that those countries will turn away from the West, perhaps joining an informal Russian sphere of influence; or that enlargement will redivide Europe into clearly defined rival geostrategic blocs. Avoiding such pitfalls, De Santis explains, will depend not only on the alliance's adroit management of the challenges ahead but also on the actions of the United States, Russia, the West European nations, and other players.

James Chace makes the case in chapter 12 that history has established inclusiveness, even of former enemies, as a cardinal principle of a peaceful European system. Current NATO enlargement schemes, which exclude Russia, violate that principle. Chace argues in favor of a European security organization that would include both the United States and Russia. He warns that excluding Russia from the European system would redivide Europe and thus invite disastrous consequences.

In chapter 13, Owen Harries criticizes realists who advocate NATO enlargement on the basis of the conviction that Russia is inherently expansionist. He recalls that the United States during the Cold War always insisted that its opposition was directed against the Soviet regime and ideology, not the Russian nation and people. Failing to make that distinction today, and expanding what amounts to the

American empire up to the Russian border, is dangerous, Harries warns.

In chapter 14, Eugene Carroll contends that the muddled arguments for enlarging NATO confuse military initiatives, political objectives, and economic goals. He argues that there is no major threat to Europe today, and that expanding the alliance at this point is likely to redivide Europe and thereby create a threat that would otherwise not exist. Carroll warns that leaving Russia on the outside of a redivided Europe will force Moscow to explore other means of shoring up Russian security, which could have serious—and dangerous—implications for the United States.

In Section IV, "Alternatives to an Enlarged NATO," Doug Bandow argues that NATO in its present form is a relic of the Cold War that should be disbanded rather than expanded. The United States has no vital interests at stake that justify keeping large numbers of U.S. troops permanently stationed on the Continent. Given Europe's immense collective economic and human resources, European security should become a European responsibility, Bandow contends.

In chapter 16, Jonathan Clarke makes the case for an alternative to NATO that builds on the alliance's unique strengths but features an updated organization, doctrine, and membership to reflect changed strategic circumstances. Such a structure must be inclusive, and it should emphasize mediation and small peacekeeping operations over security guarantees. The Organization for Security and Cooperation in Europe, Clarke suggests, may be a starting point.

Amos Perlmutter, in chapter 17, argues that a "Middleuropa" security structure would better advance U.S., West European, and Central and East European security interests than would an enlarged NATO. Such a structure would allow the Central and East European countries to meet their defense needs—perhaps with parallel ties to the West and to Russia—without redividing Europe. That security arrangement, together with an expanded European Union to further Central and East European economic and political development, could potentially form the basis of a stable and secure Europe.

In chapter 18, Ronald Steel contends that Washington's enthusiasm for NATO enlargement is based largely on the fear that the alliance will become irrelevant—and that U.S. influence will therefore be reduced—unless NATO takes on new missions and new members. He argues that enlargement will actually contribute to, not forestall, the waning of American influence on the Continent. NATO enlargement will bridge the historic divide between Eastern and Western Europe and thus provide the impetus for the creation of a new European entity, which would make the U.S. role in Europe increasingly superfluous.

In the concluding chapter, Stanley Kober warns that the expansion of NATO is based on the fallacious assumption, embraced especially by Secretary of State Madeleine Albright, that the United States can convert NATO into an effective collective security organization for imposing peace and freedom in Eastern Europe. Kober argues that the United States should, instead, lead by example and foster the emergence of stable democratic systems, based on individual rights rather than group identity politics, in the former Soviet bloc, thereby reducing the likelihood of armed conflict. Membership in NATO will have little impact on whether such systems develop.

The analyses presented in this book constitute an important contribution to a debate that, for practical purposes, is just beginning, despite the Clinton administration's premature (and foolhardy) insistence that NATO issue formal invitations to the Czech Republic, Hungary, and Poland at the Madrid summit. Although NATO enlargement has received considerable media attention and has been a subject of discussion in foreign policy circles, the debate has not yet progressed beyond the preliminary stages. Key issues—including the strategic rationale for NATO enlargement, whether security guarantees to new member states can be made credible, and who will pay for enlargement—remain unresolved.

It will be the special responsibility of the U.S. Senate to see that such critical matters are addressed in a serious fashion during the ratification debate. NATO enlargement is a pivotal national security issue that will shape U.S. foreign policy and the European security system for decades to come. By examining the many pitfalls associated with extending U.S. security guarantees into Central and Eastern Europe, the authors in this volume seek to advance the emerging public and congressional debate.

Notes

1. Congressional Budget Office, "The Costs of Expanding the NATO Alliance," March 1996; Ronald D. Asmus, Richard L. Kugler, and F. Stephen Larrabee, "What Will NATO Enlargement Cost?" *Survival* 38, no. 3 (Autumn 1996): 5–26; and U.S.

Department of Defense, "Report to the Congress on the Enlargement of NATO: Rationale, Benefits, Costs and Implications," February 1997.

2. Quoted in William Drozdiak, "NATO Expansion 'On the Cheap' May Have Surcharge," *Washington Post*, March 12, 1997, p. A1.

3. Quoted in ibid.

4. Ted Galen Carpenter and Pavel Kislitsyn, "NATO Expansion Flashpoint No. 2: The Border between Hungary and Serbia," Cato Institute Foreign Policy Briefing no. 45, November 24, 1997.

5. See Ted Galen Carpenter and Andrew Stone, "NATO Expansion Flashpoint No. 1: The Border between Poland and Belarus," Cato Institute Foreign Policy Briefing no. 44, September 16, 1997.

6. White House, Office of the Press Secretary, "Remarks by President Clinton, French President Chirac, Russia President Yeltsin, and NATO Secretary General Solana at NATO/Russia Founding Act Signing Ceremony, Elysée Palace, Paris, France, May 27, 1997," pp. 1–2.

7. White House, Office of the Press Secretary, "Remarks by the President at the United States Military Academy Commencement, West Point, New York, May 31, 1997," p. 4.

8. Quoted in Stephen Chapman, "Will Bosnia Save NATO—Or Destroy It?" *Chicago Tribune*, November 23, 1995, p. A27.

9. Anthony Lake, "Bosnia: America's Interests and America's Role," Remarks at Johns Hopkins University, Baltimore, Maryland, April 7, 1994, White House, Press Office, p. 1.

PART I

PROBLEMS OF COST AND CREDIBILITY

1. Strategic Evasions and the Drive for NATO Enlargement

Ted Galen Carpenter

When NATO leaders met in Madrid in July 1997, they invited three Central European nations—Poland, Hungary, and the Czech Republic—to join the alliance. Advocates of NATO enlargement insist that adding new members will foster cooperation and promote stability throughout Europe. It is more likely to create a new division of Europe and dangerous security obligations for the United States.

Proponents of enlargement insist that a "new" NATO—something more akin to a Euro-Atlantic collective security organization than to a traditional military alliance—is evolving. That "spin" is increasingly evident in President Clinton's comments. "NATO, initially conceived to face a clear-cut and massive threat, is now a lighter, more flexible organization adapted to its new crisis management and peacekeeping missions. This alliance that is renovating itself is no longer that of the Cold War."[1]

Such remarks reveal an ignorance of the profound differences between collective security organizations and military alliances, which are collective *defense* organizations. The former have two noticeable characteristics. They tend to be ineffectual "talk shops" rather than serious security mechanisms; the League of Nations and the United Nations are classic examples. They also, by definition, must be as inclusive as possible. Alliances, on the other hand, are selective and exclusionary; they are invariably directed (either implicitly or explicitly) against an identifiable adversary.

NATO cannot become a collective security organization unless it admits virtually all European nations—which would make it nearly congruent with the Organization for Security and Cooperation in Europe. But not all European nations will be admitted; after the first round of enlargement, there will still be as many European countries left outside NATO's tent as there will be on the inside. What the Clinton administration is apparently attempting to do is create a weird hybrid entity—part traditional alliance and part collective security organization. That objective is apparent from another Clinton comment: "We are building a new NATO. It will remain the strongest alliance in history, with smaller, more flexible forces, prepared to fight for our defense, but also trained for peacekeeping." He added, "It will be an alliance directed no longer against a hostile bloc of nations, but instead designed to advance the security of every democracy in Europe—NATO's old members, new members, and nonmembers alike."[2]

That statement reflects a dangerous conceptual muddle. The American people are likely to end up with the worst of both worlds: a NATO that periodically becomes entangled in messy, Bosnia-style peacekeeping missions in disputes that have little, if any, relevance to vital American interests and a NATO that is obligated to protect Central and East European nations from any threat posed by their great power neighbor, Russia.

Both scenarios are worrisome. There is little doubt that the Clinton foreign policy team sees the Bosnia mission as a model for future NATO enterprises. One "carrot" held out by Secretary of State Madeleine Albright to gain Russian acceptance of NATO's enlargement was a proposal to create a permanent joint brigade, similar to that sent to Bosnia to enforce the Dayton accords, for European peacekeeping missions. (Albright's motto seems to be, "Let a hundred Bosnia missions bloom.")

The prospect of U.S. and other NATO troops being used as armed social workers is bad enough, but the other scenario is even more troubling. For all the propaganda about the new NATO and its more political orientation, NATO remains first and foremost a military alliance to protect its members from armed attack. Although the organization does have a political dimension, it never has been exclusively—or even primarily—a political association. If NATO moves eastward, the United States and the other current members will be undertaking new and potentially far-reaching security obligations. No amount of "feel-good" rhetoric about encouraging stability and fostering democracy should be allowed to disguise that reality. Even Clinton belatedly acknowledged the point during his May 31, 1997, commencement address to graduates at West Point: "In the years ahead, it means that you could be asked to put your lives on the line for a new NATO member, just as today you can be called upon to defend the freedom of our allies in Western Europe."[3]

Fear of Russia

It may be true that the Central and East European countries do not view NATO in exclusively military terms. There are indications that several governments consider inclusion in the alliance important evidence that their nations are finally and irrevocably part of "the West."[4] Some of those countries may also see NATO membership as a way of entering other important Western institutions—especially the European Union with all its economic benefits—through the back door. Nevertheless, the core objective of the countries seeking NATO membership is unambiguous: they want the protection of the alliance's security guarantees.

During the initial post–Cold War years, most Central and East European leaders avoided publicly identifying specific potential enemies, preferring instead to cite general security concerns. Laslo Kovacs, chairman of the Hungarian parliament's Foreign Affairs Committee, typified the tendency to address the issue obliquely when he stated, "The security risk we now face stems from the instability of the region rather than a traditional military threat."[5]

That was always a vacuous, if not dishonest, formulation, yet it is routinely echoed by American advocates of NATO expansion. Security threats are not akin to a force of nature that can arise unpredictably and strike at random. They emanate from specific sources—usually a revisionist state or an insurgent movement. Citing "instability" as the primary problem facing post–Cold War Europe begs the question of who is likely to cause instability.

Ominous political developments in Russia have changed the tone of statements from Central and East European capitals. Although there are still diplomatic circumlocutions about NATO's guarding against the vague specter of instability, officials increasingly have a definite security threat in mind. Indicative of the new attitude was the statement in February 1997 by Zbigniew Siemiatowski, a close adviser to Polish president Aleksander Kwasniewski, that denounced "Russian provocations" and clearly regarded Moscow as a security threat to his country.[6]

There is a subtle but important conflict between the agendas of Western proponents of expansion and the Central and East European governments that seek to join NATO. The former portray enlargement primarily as a political exercise to enhance European "stability." The latter regard NATO as a lifeguard to protect their independence from potential adversaries—especially a revanchist Russia.

19

To those governments and populations, NATO's great appeal is precisely the obligations of mutual assistance set out in article 5 of its charter. Apprehensive Central and East European nations want reliable protection, not merely membership in a political association and "consultations" in the event of trouble. It is also apparent that at least some officials see article 5 as a specific guarantee of *U.S. protection.*[7]

Such desires on the part of Russia's former Warsaw Pact allies create difficult enough problems. Similar goals on the part of several former Soviet republics are even more troublesome, since NATO's acquiescence would require an alliance presence in Russia's "near abroad"—a step that influential Russians across the political spectrum have made clear would be highly provocative. That is not merely a hypothetical problem; the three Baltic states express the same eagerness as Poland, Hungary, the Czech Republic, and other Russian neighbors for NATO membership and article 5 guarantees. Moreover, the Baltic republics are receiving support from some Central European countries (especially Poland), at least a few West European officials, and influential Americans both in and out of Congress.[8]

Credibility Problems

It is not at all clear how security guarantees to the Central and East European countries can be made credible. Most proponents of new NATO missions in Eastern Europe act as though there is no serious prospect that the security promises embodied in article 5 will ever have to be honored, even as they insist that alliance security commitments will somehow deter aggression and enhance the stability of the region. Such a position is inconsistent if not disingenuous. Either the alliance intends to afford the nations of Eastern Europe reliable protection against "aggression," or it does not.[9] If the former is true, the commitment involves significant costs and risks—including the prospect of a confrontation with a nuclear-armed great power. If the latter is the case, NATO's leaders are engaging in an act of deceit that could prove fatal to any East European nation foolish enough to rely on the alliance. A retreat under pressure would also devastate NATO's credibility (and the credibility of NATO's leader, the United States) on other issues. It is a problem that simply cannot be finessed, however much advocates of enlargement may try.

To be effective, a military alliance must be a credible security shield, not merely a psychological security blanket. Expansion based on the latter assumption is little more than an irresponsible bluff that Russia, given its extensive interests in Eastern Europe, might someday decide to call.

Indeed, it could be argued that as NATO expands eastward the risk of a collision with Russia might be even greater than it was during the Cold War. Three factors are especially important in determining whether extended deterrence—attempting to deter an attack on an ally or a client—is likely to succeed: the balance of military forces between the guarantor power and the potential challenging power, the importance of the stakes to the protector, and the importance of the stakes to the challenger. Advocates of widespread U.S. security guarantees to allies and "friends" habitually focus on the first factor, but the other two are also crucial. Indeed, the relationship of the latter two might justifiably be termed the "balance of fervor."

America's explicit security guarantees during the Cold War were largely limited to areas of substantial economic and strategic importance. Western Europe was always at the top of that list; the region was considered crucial to America's own security and economic well-being, and U.S. policymakers were determined to prevent that power center from coming under the control of the USSR. (It is useful to recall that the U.S.-led NATO did not go beyond that objective and interfere when Moscow used force on three occasions to restore order in its East European empire—East Germany, 1953; Hungary, 1956; and Czechoslovakia, 1968.) Given Western Europe's importance to the United States, it was credible to leaders in the Kremlin that the United States would be willing to incur significant risks—even the possibility of a major war with nuclear implications—to thwart Soviet conquest of the region.

Conversely, while Western Europe would have undoubtedly been a significant strategic and economic prize for the Soviet Union, the area was not essential to Moscow. There was, therefore, a definite limit to the risks the Kremlin was willing to run to gain dominion. Although Soviet leaders could never be sure that the United States would really go to war on behalf of its allies, challenging the commitment would have been an extraordinarily reckless gamble.

The balance of fervor is substantially different when it comes to NATO's enlargement into Central—to say nothing of Eastern—Europe. Russians of nearly every political persuasion regard that move as an unwarranted intrusion into Russia's geopolitical "back yard." That point is especially worrisome given the desire of the more aggressive proponents of NATO enlargement to incorporate the Baltic states. Relations between Russia and several of its neighbors are tense, as disputes continue over boundaries, resources, and the treatment of Russian minorities in the other independent republics of the former Soviet Union.

Moreover, the greater role played by nationalist sentiments and democratic politics in post-Soviet Russia may make Moscow's foreign policy more unpredictable than it was during the Soviet era. Political leaders who are accountable to a demanding electorate, and who are themselves not steeped in the Leninist dogma of historical inevitability, are more likely than were their predecessors to react to perceived provocations—especially when matters of national pride are involved. Retaliation for the mistreatment of Russian citizens of neighboring states, problems with transit rights to the military enclave of Kaliningrad (which borders on Poland), or any number of other issues could spark an incident between Russia and NATO.

The point is, not that Russia will become a relentlessly expansionist aggressor, but that it is likely to act as great powers have acted throughout history, and that creates the potential for trouble if NATO insists on a presence in Eastern Europe. A great power typically seeks a preeminent role in its immediate region, carves out a sphere of influence or security zone, and refuses to tolerate unfriendly behavior on the part of smaller neighbors.

Sops to Russia

We should not be lulled into complacency by Russian president Boris Yeltsin's willingness to sign the Founding Act on Relations, Cooperation and Security between NATO and the Russian Federation. Russian leaders understand that, given their country's weakened condition, they cannot block the first round of enlargement. They have, therefore, adopted a strategy to, in Foreign Minister Yevgeny Primakov's words, "limit the damage to Russia's interests." Moscow's underlying objective is to raise the political costs of the initial round of enlargement enough that there will never be a subsequent round that might bring the alliance into Russia's near abroad, especially the Baltic region.[10]

It is unlikely that the Yeltsin government achieved that objective with the negotiation of the Founding Act. Indeed, both Clinton and Albright have recently emphasized that the first round of enlargement will not be the last.[11] Albright added, in an unmistakable reference to the Baltic republics, that "no European democracy will be excluded because of where it sits on the map."[12] The concessions given to Russia in the Founding Act were little more than sops, despite Yeltsin's best effort to portray them as meaningful. Russia will have a seat at a new "permanent joint council" at which alliance policies are discussed, but Moscow will not have a vote, much less a veto, on NATO decisions.[13] (Moscow's status seems akin to that of delegates from Guam and other U.S. territories, who have speaking privileges but no vote in the U.S. House of Representatives.) NATO has also formalized its policy that the alliance has "no intention, no plan, and no reason" to deploy nuclear weapons in the new member states.[14] With regard to conventional forces, NATO "reiterates that in the current and foreseeable security environment, the Alliance will carry out its collective defense and other missions by ensuring the necessary interoperability, integration, and capability for reinforcement rather than by additional permanent stationing of substantial combat forces."[15]

Such "pledges" contain massive loopholes. To start with, it is not clear what is meant by "substantial" combat forces; that elastic term would seem to allow NATO to choose virtually any number it deemed appropriate. Moreover, "intentions and plans" can be changed at any time. The advent of a crisis somewhere in Eastern Europe might create the "reason" for altering plans and deploying conventional forces, and perhaps even nuclear weapons.[16] Indeed, there would be enormous pressure to deploy significant NATO assets to provide a tangible display of the alliance's resolve and to reassure an uneasy front-line member.

The concessions given to Russia in the Founding Act do not constitute meaningful, binding restrictions on NATO's conduct. The danger, of course, is that the Russian political elite and public will eventually see the sops for what they are. When Russia recovers economically and militarily, Russians will likely remember how the

West exploited their country's temporary weakness to establish hegemony in Central and Eastern Europe, and they will seek to overturn it.

Ominous Signs

Even now Moscow can take (and in some cases is taking) several worrisome countermeasures. They include efforts to strengthen ties with powers outside Europe, most notably the new "strategic partnership" between Russia and China.[17] The Yeltsin government has also pointedly refused to adopt a "no first use" doctrine with regard to nuclear weapons.[18] Indeed, given the country's financial straits, a heavy reliance on nuclear weapons may be tempting as a cost-effective response to NATO's approach to Russia's border. As the alliance expands eastward, Russia may also seek to create its own political-military bloc among those nations that are not included on the roster of new NATO members. The agreement between Russia and Belarus, which seems so contrary to Russia's political and economic interests, suggests an intention to construct such a bloc. From Moscow's perspective, Belarus is a security buffer between an expanded NATO and Russia—and a potential forward staging area for Russian forces.

The possibility of a deterioration of relations between Russia and an enlarged NATO is reason for apprehension. Unlike the situation during the Cold War, there is no Iron Curtain dividing Europe into clear spheres of influence. Instead, Eastern Europe is one vast gray zone between Russia and the West. One ought to contemplate, for example, the numerous possibilities for friction between Poland and neighboring Belarus—which is increasingly a Russian satellite ruled by the volatile and eccentric Alexander Lukashenko.

Wishful Thinking by Advocates of Enlargement

Advocates of NATO enlargement minimize or ignore the realities of international politics—as though the end of the Cold War has magically invalidated centuries of consistent patterns of interaction between states in the international system. Enlargement enthusiasts also disregard long-standing requisites of deterrence as they spin their ethereal designs for a "new NATO" that will bring peace and prosperity to all of Europe.

A prime example of that approach is a study of the probable costs of NATO enlargement by RAND Corporation scholars Ronald D. Asmus, Richard L. Kugler, and F. Stephen Larrabee. "NATO enlargement is not *currently* threat-driven; rather it is part of an overall strategy of projecting stability and unifying Europe," they emphasize. The strategic requirements of enlargement are moderate "and will remain so *barring a future deterioration in Europe's strategic environment.*" They argue further that an enlarged NATO can meet those requirements merely by upgrading East-Central European defenses and by preparing current NATO forces to project power to the region in case of crisis. "There is no requirement today for deploying large numbers of NATO combat forces in those countries."[19]

The RAND trio steadfastly ignores unpleasant possibilities. Contrasting their cost estimates with those of the Congressional Budget Office (especially the latter's high-end estimate of more than $120 billion by 2012), Asmus, Kugler, and Larrabee contend that the CBO's estimates "are mostly driven by a postulated NATO strategy of preparing for war against Russia." In contrast, their approach "is anchored in the premise of avoiding confrontation with Russia, not preparing for a new Russian threat."[20]

That comes perilously close to wishing a problem out of existence. To be sure, Russia is not the only conceivable threat to the security of the Central European states. Hungary, in particular, could eventually have problems with at least two neighbors, Romania and Serbia, especially over the treatment of Hungarian minorities in those countries. Nevertheless, if a *serious* security threat emerges, NATO military planners know it will come from Russia.

Even a partially recovered Russia could deploy sizable military assets on its western frontier (and perhaps in Belarus as well). And the task of countering that development—of providing the new NATO members with effective, credible protection—would be difficult. The RAND authors assume that a NATO "rapid-reaction" force consisting of five divisions (approximately 80,000 troops) and five aircraft wings (350 planes) would make the new security commitments credible. It is highly doubtful that a force of that size—even taking into account NATO's probable edge in quality and training—would be sufficient to bolster the defenses of the new Central European members against a concerted Russian buildup. Indeed, 80,000 troops smacks of tokenism. NATO sent nearly that many personnel to police the Dayton accords in Bosnia—after a cease-fire was in place.

Tripwire Forces and the Requisites of Deterrence

The RAND trio and others who argue that NATO can extend its commitments eastward without having to deploy conventional forces in the new member states also ignore the virtual consensus found in a vast array of literature on deterrence. Lawrence Freedman, professor of war studies at King's College in London, emphasized that the deployment of ground forces in a state that might be the target of aggression is the sine qua non of extended deterrence.[21] Glenn Snyder, one of the intellectual fathers of modern deterrence theory, made a similar point nearly three decades earlier, stressing that, in extended-deterrence situations, deployment of the defender's forces is one of the most powerful factors in ensuring success, because those deployments are a highly visible signal that the defender is serious.[22]

McGeorge Bundy, national security adviser in the Kennedy and Johnson administrations, stated that the credibility of deterrence in Europe during the Cold War was not due merely to NATO defense doctrine or the existence of large numbers of American nuclear warheads. What mattered more was "the American military presence there and the American political commitment that it represents and reinforces." Indeed, Bundy acknowledged, "A defense based on nuclear weapons alone would not sustain the self-confidence of Western Europe; it would not persuade those nearest the Soviet Union that no Kremlin leader would be tempted to try for easy pickings. Conventional forces are indispensable."[23]

Such considerations were not confined to Europe at the height of Cold War tensions. They have a much wider applicability. Political scientist Paul K. Huth notes the danger when such tangible signs of determination are not present.

> The political commitment represented by an alliance may be discounted by an adversary unless the defender also has a credible military option for protecting its protégé. Alliance ties are not likely to enhance the credibility of extended-general deterrence unless peacetime military cooperation between the allies includes the deployment of forces from the stronger power on the territory of the weaker power.

The deterrent value of an alliance commitment cannot be
separated from the analysis of the immediate balance of
forces and the importance of a tripwire force in position for
the defender.[24]

Those who adopt the sanguine view that NATO enlargement can
take place without tangible indicators of military commitment being
given to the new members have the daunting task of explaining
why such long-standing verities of deterrence theory have suddenly
become invalid. It will hardly be surprising if the East Europeans
eventually seek NATO tripwire forces. One of the earliest and most
consistent aspirations of the West European members of NATO was
to obtain and keep a U.S. troop presence on the Continent.[25] Without
that presence, European leaders stated privately (and sometimes
publicly), they could never be certain that the United States would
honor its pledge to defend their countries if war actually broke out.
Not only did the allied governments want U.S. forces stationed in
Europe, they wanted them deployed in forward positions so that
they would be certain to be caught up in the initial stages of a
conflict. A constant feature of the transatlantic security relationship
was the West European effort to deny U.S. policymakers the luxury
of choice.[26] If the West Europeans were unwilling to trust the U.S.
treaty commitment to aid them, despite the importance to America's
own security of keeping Western Europe out of Moscow's orbit, the
East Europeans, who recognize that their region has never been as
important to the United States, would have an even greater reason
to want the tangible reassurance provided by a NATO tripwire force
that included U.S. military personnel.

The rationale of those who insist that such a deployment will be
unnecessary needs to be something more than the fact that Russia
is currently too weak to pose a credible (conventional) military threat
to the alliance's new members. That may be true, but one can scarcely
assume that Russia will never recover militarily. If such a recovery
takes place, will advocates of enlargement then argue that the United
States must move to shore up NATO's eastern flank—even if the
costs and risks are high—lest inaction fatally undermine the alliance's cohesion and credibility?

Clinton tacitly acknowledged that the kind of military assets
needed to deter an attack on new members will not be materially
different from those needed to perform that mission on behalf of

the West Europeans during the Cold War. "Enlargement requires that we extend to new members our Alliance's most solemn security pledge, to treat an attack against one as an attack against all. We have always made the pledge credible through the deployment of our troops and the deterrence of our nuclear weapons."[27] It is notable that the president did not contend or even imply that the means of making the pledge credible would change—an omission that should reinforce skepticism about how new the "new NATO" really is.

America's Risk Exposure

In examining the requisites of deterrence and the critical role played by both the balance of forces and the balance of fervor, it is imperative to understand the extent of America's prospective risk exposure in an enlarged NATO. The United States is not merely pledging to contribute troops to a NATO rapid-reaction force in the event of trouble; it is promising to do whatever is necessary to defend its new allies. That includes shielding those countries with the U.S. strategic nuclear arsenal. Indeed, it would be difficult to mount an effective conventional defense of the easternmost members of an expanded NATO against a capable adversary. That is especially true if NATO goes beyond the first round of expansion and brings in the Baltic states. Most military experts believe that there is *no* way to defend the Baltic republics by conventional means. The only way to defend them is with a U.S. nuclear guarantee.

Such grave risks should never be incurred except to defend America's vital security interests. Proponents of enlargement must show why the nations of Central and Eastern Europe are so important to America's security and well-being that U.S. leaders are justified in putting not only the lives of American troops but the existence of American cities at risk.

Advocates of enlargement sometimes act as though a bigger NATO is merely an institutional mechanism whereby everyone can gather in the center of Europe for a group hug. It is not. It is an unnecessary, expensive, and provocative initiative with perilous implications. The only question is whether NATO enlargement will turn out to be a farce or a tragedy.

Notes

1. White House, Office of the Press Secretary, "Remarks by President Clinton, French President Chirac, Russian President Yeltsin, and NATO Secretary General

Solana at NATO/Russia Founding Act Signing Ceremony, Elysée Palace, Paris, France, May 27, 1997," pp. 1–2.

2. Ibid., p. 6.

3. White House, Office of the Press Secretary, "Remarks by the President at the United States Military Academy Commencement, West Point, New York, May 31, 1997," p. 5.

4. That motive was evident in the informal remarks of Czech prime minister Václav Klaus at a Cato Institute luncheon on December 4, 1995. See also the interview with Tibor Tóth, deputy state secretary for international affairs in Hungary's Ministry of Defense, *Jane's Defence Weekly*, February 7, 1996, p. 32.

5. Quoted in Celia Woodard, "Hungary Winces As West Defers Its NATO Membership," *Christian Science Monitor*, October 28, 1993, p. 3. See also Pavel Bratinka, "The Challenge of Liberation: The View from the Czech Republic," Svetoslav Bombik, "Returning to Civilization: The View from Slovakia," Jerzy Marek Nowakowski, "In Search of a Strategic Home: The View from Poland," and Tamas Waschler, "Where There's a Will . . . : The View from Hungary," in *NATO: The Case for Enlargement* (London: Institute for European Defence and Strategic Studies, 1993), pp. 13–35.

6. Christine Spolar, "Polish Official's Comments about Russia Draw Fire," *Washington Post*, February 23, 1997, p. A21.

7. See, for example, "Bucharest Treads Line between Moscow, West," Interview with Romanian foreign minister Teodor Melescanu, *Washington Times*, February 6, 1996, p. A12.

8. Chrystia Freeland, "Poland and Lithuania Fuel NATO Row," *Financial Times*, September 18, 1995, p. 2; "Foreign Minister, Danish Counterpart on EU, NATO," Tallinn Radio Network, September 19, 1995, *Foreign Broadcast Information Service Daily Report—Central Eurasia*, September 20, 1995, p. 101; "Officials Comment on U.S. Security Act," Tallinn BNS, February 17, 1995, *Foreign Broadcast Information Service Daily Report—Central Eurasia*, February 21, 1995, p. 100; "Latvia Welcome in NATO, Oslo Leader Says," *International Herald Tribune*, April 24, 1996, p. 5; George Melloan, "If Russia Wants Another Cold War, Fine," *Wall Street Journal*, September 18, 1995, p. A19; Christopher Cox, "Freedom in Europe for All," *Washington Times*, February 4, 1997, p. A19; and William Safire, "Clinton's Good Deed," *New York Times*, May 7, 1997, p. A35. Indeed, legislation introduced by Republican leaders in the House of Representatives explicitly endorses NATO membership for the Baltic states—as well as Romania and Slovenia.

For a detailed argument in favor of offering NATO membership to the Baltic republics, see Vejas Gabriel Liulevicius, "As Go the Baltics, So Goes Europe," *Orbis* 39 (Summer 1995): 387–402.

9. On the improbability of NATO's willingness to wage war to defend the nations of Central and Eastern Europe, see Stephen Blank, "New Challenges to European Security," *Strategic Review* 8, no. 3 (Summer 1994): 40–49.

10. For a remarkably candid admission of that strategy by Sergei Karaganov, director of the Institute of Europe and a member of Yeltsin's presidential advisory council, see his comments quoted in Michael Dobbs and David Hoffman, "Yeltsin Stands Firm against Larger NATO," *Washington Post*, February 22, 1997, p. A1.

11. For Clinton's comments, see White House, Office of the Press Secretary, "Remarks by the President at Commemorative Event for the 50th Anniversary of the Marshall Plan, Hall of Knights, Binnenhof, The Hague, Netherlands, May 28, 1997," pp. 4, 6.

12. Quoted in Michael Dobbs, "U.S. Indicates Preference for Just 3 New NATO States," *Washington Post*, May 30, 1997, p. A30.

13. U.S. Department of State, "Founding Act on Mutual Relations, Cooperation and Security between NATO and the Russian Federation," Paris, May 27, 1997, pp. 3–5.

14. Ibid., p. 7.

15. Ibid., p. 8.

16. Deputy Secretary of State Strobe Talbott has confirmed as much. In a May 20 speech to the Atlantic Council, Talbott stated that the pledges could be changed if a new threat emerged in Eastern Europe. "Talbott: New Threat Could Alter NATO Pledges," Reuters, May 20, 1997.

17. For a discussion of Moscow's countermoves, see Ted Galen Carpenter, "Wishful Thinking and Strategic Evasions: The Campaign for NATO Enlargement," in *NATO and the Quest for Post–Cold War Security*, ed. Clay Clemons (New York: Macmillan, 1997).

18. David Hoffman, "Yeltsin Approves Doctrine of Nuclear First Use if Attacked," *Washington Post*, May 10, 1997, p. A21.

19. Ronald D. Asmus, Richard L. Kugler, and F. Stephen Larrabee, "What Will NATO Enlargement Cost?" *Survival* 38, no. 3 (Autumn 1996): 7. Emphasis added.

20. Ibid.

21. Lawrence Freedman, "I Exist, Therefore I Deter," *International Security* 13, no. 1 (Summer 1988): 194–95.

22. Glenn Snyder, *Deterrence and Defense* (Princeton, N.J.: Princeton University Press, 1961), p. 254.

23. McGeorge Bundy, *Danger and Survival: Choices about the Bomb in the First Fifty Years* (New York: Random House, 1988), p. 599.

24. Paul K. Huth, *Extended Deterrence and the Prevention of War* (New Haven, Conn.: Yale University Press, 1988), p. 215.

25. For discussions of this point, see Lawrence S. Kaplan, *NATO and the United States: The Enduring Alliance* (Boston: Twayne, 1988), passim; Christopher Layne, "Atlanticism without NATO," *Foreign Policy* 67 (Summer 1987): 22–45; Ted Galen Carpenter, "United States NATO Policy at the Crossroads: The Great Debate of 1950–1951," *International History Review* 8 (August 1986): 389–415; and Ted Galen Carpenter, "Competing Agendas: America, Europe, and a Troubled NATO Partnership," in *NATO at 40: Confronting a Changing World*, ed. Ted Galen Carpenter (Lexington, Mass.: Lexington Books, 1990), pp. 29–42.

26. Christopher Layne, "Continental Divide; Time to Disengage in Europe," *National Interest* 13 (Fall 1988): 13–27; and Layne, "Atlanticism without NATO."

27. White House, "Remarks by the President at the United States Military Academy Commencement," p. 5.

2. NATO's Incredible Shrinking Defense

William G. Hyland

The leaders of NATO are creating a transatlantic monstrosity worthy of Mary Shelley. The Atlantic alliance is being buried. In its place, NATO, led by the Clinton administration, is stitching together a Frankenstinian horror: a military alliance with no clear enemy, a military alliance with rapidly diminishing capabilities but expanding geographical commitments, a military alliance that can no longer credibly defend its members, a military alliance that will degenerate into little more than a political club of first- and second-class members plus a list of applicants that may never be allowed to join.

How did this weird concoction come about? The expansion of NATO is, in part, a desperate but flawed effort to salvage an alliance that no longer has a clear mission. It also reflects the residue of anti-Russian sentiment that continues to animate American officials in and out of power. Mainly, it is the result of the fumbling policies of the Clinton administration in refusing to address forthrightly NATO's future in 1993.

Oddly enough, the debate over NATO expansion thus far has seemed more like a discussion at a graduate seminar than a flesh-and-blood shootout over the future of American foreign policy. The United States is on the verge of undertaking profound new military commitments, but the Pentagon is virtually silent, Congress disinterested, and the public apathetic. Perhaps all of that will change when the costs of NATO expansion are publicized. But even the cost estimates are in dispute (as usual). The ultimate cost depends on assumptions about the backup forces that will be earmarked to reinforce the militaries of the new members. The only thing that is certain, as one German official said, is that the United States will have to pick up the tab.[1]

Some History

It was often said that NATO was created to bring the Americans in, keep the Russians out, and keep the Germans down. For the

Europeans, NATO's original purpose was, indeed, to bring the Americans in.[2] It was the Truman administration that produced the concept of an Atlantic alliance in secret talks in Washington in the spring of 1948.[3] Restoring European confidence, however, was not a sufficiently strong rationale to overcome isolationist opposition to an "entangling alliance." In the United States the focus was on NATO's second objective: to deter Soviet aggression—in other words to keep the Russians out. (The third aim, to keep the Germans "down," was gradually reinterpreted. Instead of seeking to forever suppress Germany, the new objective was to tie it into a multilateral European institution, allowing its recovery, though not yet its full integration, let alone its rearmament.)

The American commitment was the product of a bipartisan collaboration between Sen. Arthur Vandenberg, the Republican chairman of the Senate Foreign Relations Committee, and Under Secretary of State Robert Lovett. The Vandenberg Resolution of June 11, 1948, opened the door to the treaty negotiations and eventually permitted the United States to turn its back on isolationism and join an "entangling" alliance for the first time since the American Revolution.

Vandenberg and the Truman administration assumed that the American initiative would encourage the Europeans to unite and make a major effort in their own defense. After 10 years or so, Europe would have recovered; therefore, American participation in a regional defense treaty would, like the Marshall Plan, be only a stopgap. The Europeans proposed a treaty for 50 years; the American side countered with a 20-year treaty that would be renewable.[4] Moreover, no substantial number of new American troops would be required in Europe. When asked if joining NATO meant sending American troops to Europe, Secretary of State Dean Acheson responded with a resounding no.

The Korean War changed everything. The new U.S. commitment to NATO was challenged in Congress when, despite Acheson's assurance, President Truman proposed sending four to six divisions to Europe, in the wake of the Korean attack. That proposal was opposed mainly by Republicans, although the political lines were never very clear-cut. The Great Debate of 1951, as it was called, was the last hurrah of the isolationists. The outcome was a strong affirmation of both the NATO treaty and the commitment of American ground forces. Subsequent challenges to NATO were over the size and armament of the American troop contingent. Even during those periodic debates, U.S. participation in the alliance was never seriously questioned.

Post–Cold War NATO

Even though there was a recurring debate about how to ease tensions during the Cold War, there was virtually no planning for a post–Cold War security order in Europe. After the collapse of the Soviet Union's East European empire, there was a ragged, piecemeal settlement. Its chief features were (a) the reunification of Germany, (b) the reduction and limitation of strategic armaments and conventional arms in Europe, and (c) a significant revision of Western (NATO) military doctrine and strategy.

The result was a new geopolitical and military order in Europe. The expansion of NATO threatens to upset that settlement.

The German Settlement

One of the great nightmares of the post–World War II period was that Germany would reemerge as a unified but neutral state maneuvering once again between East and West. When the prospect of genuine movement on the German question arose, both Britain and France adopted policies designed to forestall reunification. They both went so far as to argue for an interim period of "stabilization," even though that meant perpetuating the Warsaw Pact. The Americans and West German chancellor Helmut Kohl saw the opportunity for a unified Germany and seized it.

The Bush administration, however, insisted that a united Germany would have to be a member of NATO. The United States was willing to treat East German territory as a special zone for an interim period; the only German troops there would be "border guards" not assigned to NATO. The Soviet forces in East Germany would remain for five years, and thereafter no foreign troops would be "stationed" in eastern Germany.

Those concessions were justified as necessary to take into account "legitimate" Soviet security concerns. It was implicitly recognized that the advance of NATO might, in fact, threaten Soviet security. No explicit guarantee against NATO expansion was given, nor was one demanded by Soviet president Mikhail Gorbachev. Opinions differ on how far the Bush administration went in reassuring Moscow that NATO would not expand. But the import of the negotiations was that after the withdrawal of Soviet troops from Germany, NATO would not expand beyond eastern Germany.[5]

The Military Settlement

After 1989 NATO had no clear military role, and soon it sought a new out-of-area mission. In the Gulf War NATO was helpful but not central. For a time it appeared that NATO's European members would create a new role for the alliance as Europe's policeman in the Yugoslavian crisis. The result of the Yugoslavian adventure was the demise of the old NATO: first it was exposed as a paper tiger in various half-hearted bombing missions; then it was reduced to being an arm of the feckless United Nations; finally it was rescued by an American-sponsored de facto partition of Bosnia and relegated to a peacekeeping operation in the Balkans. NATO's involvement in the Yugoslavian conflict has been a repudiation of the original treaty's aims and, indeed, a repudiation of the basis on which the treaty was ratified by the Senate. Skepticism about the new peace-keeping mission was evident in the congressional debates over sending American forces into Bosnia.

The old NATO was buried more ceremoniously by the creation of a new military balance in Europe, codified in the Conventional Forces in Europe agreement. The CFE created a new military regime of limited armaments in a region from the Atlantic to the Urals. In effect, it ended any concept of two blocs. It also greatly reduced the potential for a surprise attack with conventional forces.

Strategic Revision

Perhaps even more significant has been the radical shift in NATO's military doctrine and strategy. For most of the alliance's existence, NATO's military doctrine rested on the two pillars of "forward defense" and "flexible response." A commitment to defend as far "forward" as possible was adopted out of deference to the Germans, who could not sustain an alliance doctrine that counseled an immediate retreat across the Rhine. Recognizing that a conventional defense of the central front would be difficult if not impossible, NATO adopted the doctrine of flexible response, a euphemism for the use of nuclear weapons and, in particular, for the first use of such weapons.

In an effort to reassure Gorbachev of NATO's benign intentions, those doctrines were radically altered at NATO summits in July 1990 and November 1991. The new doctrines officially dropped the concept of forward defense in favor of a "reduced forward presence" and modified "flexible response" to reflect a "reduced reliance on nuclear weapons," which became "truly weapons of last resort."[6]

In July 1990 all of the Warsaw Pact members were invited to set up liaison missions at NATO headquarters, further eroding the structure of two distinct competing blocs. At the same time, NATO leaders were undermining the founding principles of the alliance. As British prime minister Margaret Thatcher put it in a message to President George Bush, "What is the point of defence and security if we are letting those who were so recently our bitter foes—and at worst could become so again—so close to the innermost councils of our defense and preparedness?"[7]

In short, by the time the Warsaw Pact and the USSR disappeared, NATO had reduced its defense establishments, limited its armaments, and diluted its defense doctrines. It also had dissipated its forces and energies in a Balkan sideshow. Given those developments, it made little sense at that moment for NATO to expand its security responsibilities to the states of the former Warsaw Pact.

NATO Expansion

The Bush administration dodged the issue of NATO expansion by creating a hollow shell called the North Atlantic Consultative Council. That action opened the door to an expansion of NATO, but at no point did the Bush administration suggest formal inclusion of the former Warsaw Pact countries in NATO. Indeed, the administration seemed to signal the opposite: that NATO would not expand.

The Clinton administration thus inherited no clear commitment and could have rested on Bush's circumvention. The Clinton administration, however, equivocated over NATO's expansion. At first the issue was brushed aside. Secretary of State Warren Christopher stated at a June 10, 1993, NATO meeting in Athens that "at an appropriate time, we may choose to enlarge NATO membership. But that is *not now on the agenda.*"[8] In response to growing political pressures in Europe, the administration insisted that it would not draw a new line of division in Europe. It then sought to put off the entire question by inventing a compromise, the half-baked Partnership for Peace, an "evolutionary process of expansion" that would be "non-discriminatory and inclusive" but not tied to a specific timetable or specific criteria for membership. The effect was to postpone expansion for at least four years.[9]

But little was done by Washington in the interim to counter growing Russian objections to NATO expansion. The "inclusive" expansion was narrowed down to the so-called Visegrad countries—Poland, Hungary, and Czechoslovakia (before its breakup)—with vague promises that other new members would be added later. By 1996 the original arguments justifying the creation of NATO in the 1940s—reassurance and deterrence—were increasingly invoked to justify its expansion.

Nevertheless, new members cannot become truly integrated into NATO because they cannot be credibly defended. Any credible defense of Poland or the Czech Republic would require a massive commitment of ground forces, if not stationed in those countries, then quickly available from reserves. The doctrine of forward defense, however, has been abandoned. At the Helsinki summit (March 1997) between Clinton and Boris Yeltsin, when the Russian president voiced his concern that NATO enlargement would lead to a potentially threatening buildup of "permanently stationed" combat forces of NATO near Russia, Clinton stressed that the alliance "contemplated nothing of the kind."[10] Those concessions were subsequently incorporated into the Founding Act on Mutual Relations, Cooperation and Security between NATO and the Russian Federation, signed in Paris in May 1997.

If the defense of its new members is to be seriously contemplated, expansion of NATO will require creation of a massive reserve force. Currently, however, the military establishments of the United States, Britain, France, and Germany are shrinking, a trend not likely to be reversed. Moreover, Hungary is not even contiguous to any other NATO nation. Since Slovakia has been excluded in the first round of expansion, Hungary cannot be reinforced without a safe passage through neutral Austria.

If NATO were to expand to include the three Baltic states, the situation would be even worse. Defense of the long frontier running from Tallin to Budapest is well beyond NATO's capabilities. (That was roughly the line defended by the German *Wehrmacht* in late 1944 with five army groups; the defense of the Vistula alone involved almost 1 million men.)[11] In the Baltic region, NATO would confront Russian troops directly across the border. Without the deployment of substantial NATO forces, all three Baltic republics could easily be overrun. Even NATO officials acknowledge that including the Baltic states would feed Russian fears.[12] Russian spokesmen have said that inclusion of former Soviet republics in NATO would be grounds for abrogating the Founding Act. Recent proposals to include Slovenia and Romania, to assume the defense of those areas, which would further enlarge NATO's defense frontiers, are truly ludicrous.

In the face of current and prospective military realities, a NATO military guarantee will become a frivolous gesture. Indeed, the situation is reminiscent of the 1920s and 1930s, when France built an alliance system in Eastern Europe on the promise of French assistance to contain Germany. France then adopted a military strategy of defending itself behind the Maginot line. NATO, too, would be promising to defend its new members when, in fact, its capabilities to do so are already inadequate and declining.

Could the new members be defended by the threat to use nuclear weapons? The new NATO doctrine is that nuclear weapons have become weapons of "last resort." Moreover, the deal struck between Clinton and Yeltsin at Helsinki in March 1997 precludes stationing nuclear weapons on the territory of the new members. In their joint communiqué from Helsinki, President Clinton noted in regard to NATO's policy on nuclear weapons deployments that NATO members have "no intention, no plan and no reason to deploy nuclear weapons on the territory of states that are not now members of the alliance, nor do they foresee any future need to do so."[13] That concession was also embodied in the Founding Act. The effect is to create a second-class membership in fact if not in name.

In light of NATO's diminishing collective defense capabilities, a case can be made for including Slovenia and Romania in the alliance on the debatable grounds that the more new members, the better. The result, however, would be a logical extension of the trend toward creating an amorphous political club. That would at least be more honest than pretending that NATO remains a serious military alliance.

All of this boils down to two possibilities: either NATO membership will become only a paper promise of mutual assistance, or the alliance will have to undertake a buildup of conventional forces and return to a doctrine of first use of nuclear weapons. Obviously, in either case NATO expansion is a very hazardous and dangerous project.

The Russian Factor

NATO expansion has produced a new debate about Russia's intentions. Some observers argue that sooner or later Moscow intends to extend its influence to the republics of the former USSR and then to Central Europe. The countries applying for NATO membership clearly regard Russia as the principal threat to their security.

For over 10 years, however, relations between the United States and the Soviet and Russian state have steadily improved. Bush announced that the United States and Russia were no longer adversaries, and Clinton went even further in Moscow, proclaiming in a joint communiqué with Yeltsin on January 14, 1994, a "mature strategic partnership" with Russia. His new secretary of state, Madeleine Albright, went still further, proclaiming in Moscow that NATO has no enemy to the east and that Russia and the United States "are on the same side."[14] That mountain of conciliatory rhetoric makes the expansion of NATO even more bizarre.

Indeed, Russia will be a member of a special NATO consultative council. Ironically, the Founding Act, already subject to conflicting interpretations, further undermines NATO. That Russia will have "a voice but not a veto" is a naive incantation. Moscow will have more of an opportunity to influence every NATO decision, including decisions about military strategy, than will the new members themselves. The great irony is that the only country that could conceivably pose a threat to NATO will participate in the alliance's military planning.[15] And consultations could easily be used to delay, if not halt, further expansion.

Finally, the notion of a renewed Russian threat seems to contradict current American strategic planning. As reported in the press, a draft strategy report indicates that the American military command views the period between now and 2010 as a "strategic pause." During that time, no superpower challenge of the magnitude of the USSR's during the Cold War is likely, according to the Pentagon strategists. In other words, the countries of Eastern Europe are not likely to be threatened in a way that requires American military commitments.[16]

America's Options

Having come this far, neither the United States nor NATO can afford blithely to abandon Poland and the other East European countries. That would almost certainly cause a European crisis. The Senate is likely to approve expansion; it is even possible that it will mandate inclusion of the Baltic republics by some early date. The most likely outcome, however, is that further NATO expansion will be stalled for some years. A number of vulnerable countries will then be left in a gray area, while Russia enjoys a privileged position as a NATO consultant.

Thus, there is still a need to create a new European security system, a system that satisfies Russia, Europe, and the United States.

Notes

1. Quoted in William Drozdiak, "NATO Expansion 'On the Cheap' May Have Surcharge," *Washington Post*, March 12, 1997, p. A1.

2. U.S. Department of State, *Foreign Relations of the United States, 1948*, vol. 3, *Western Europe* (Washington: Government Printing Office, 1974), p. 32 ff. See especially the conversations between the American ambassador, Lew Douglas, and the British foreign secretary, Ernest Bevin.

3. Memorandum by John Hickerson, director of the Office of European Affairs, March 8, 1948, ibid., p. 40A. Consultations with Britain and France were approved by President Truman on March 11, and the first meeting was held in Washington on March 22; one of the British representatives was Donald Maclean, then an agent of Soviet intelligence.

4. See Secretary Marshall's message to George Bidault, March 12, 1948, ibid., p. 50. Marshall commented that "comprehensive [European] arrangements for the common defense" would appear to be an essential prerequisite to any wider arrangement that included the United States.

5. Michael R. Gordon, "The Anatomy of a Misunderstanding," *New York Times*, May 25, 1997, quotes the following exchange: "Any extension of the zone of NATO is unacceptable," Mr. Gorbachev stressed. "I agree," Mr. Baker responded (p. E30).

6. Phillip Zelikow and Condelezza Rice, *Germany Unified and Europe Transformed* (Cambridge, Mass.: Harvard University Press, 1995), p. 303 ff.

7. Quoted in ibid., pp. 316–17.

8. Warren Christopher, "U.S. Leadership after the Cold War," U.S. Department of State *Dispatch* 4, no. 25 (June 21, 1993): 448. Emphasis added.

9. Warren Christopher, "Statement before the Senate Foreign Relations Committee," November 4, 1993, text released by U.S. Department of State.

10. "Joint U.S.-Russia Statement on European Security," text in *Arms Control Today*, March 1997, p. 21.

11. John Erickson, *The Road to Berlin* (Boulder, Colo.: Westview, 1983), p. 449.

12. The acting secretary general of the North Atlantic Assembly, Simon Lunn, said that Baltic membership would "provoke the kind of security paranoia in Russia that

we are trying to put to rest." Quoted in William Drozdiak, "Baltic States Fear Being Wallflowers," *Washington Post,* October 13, 1996, p. A45.

13. White House, Office of the Press Secretary, "Joint U.S.-Russian Statement on European Security," March 21, 1997, at http://library.whitehouse.gov/cgi-bin/web.

14. Quoted in Steven Erlanger, "You vs. Us Is Over," *New York Times,* February 22, 1997.

15. Henry Kissinger, "Helsinki Fiasco," *Washington Post,* March 30, 1997.

16. William Drozdiak, "Pentagon Assesses Future Demands on a Smaller Military Force," *Washington Post,* April 2, 1997.

3. NATO Expansion: The Triumph of Policy Incoherence

Alan Tonelson

NATO expansion has already drawn a surprising amount of criticism from many mandarins and other mainstays of America's internationalist foreign policy establishment, from George F. Kennan to the *New York Times'* editorial page. Most of the critics seem primarily concerned with the possible impact of NATO expansion on Russia. They fear that bringing the alliance to the former Soviet Union's borders will speed the triumph of Russia's revanchist, reactionary forces and ultimately usher in a second cold war in Europe. Other critics center on the prospect that NATO expansion will dilute the alliance's focus. They worry about the dangers of NATO's adding to its primary defense and deterrence responsibilities "arms control and proliferation, terrorism, civil emergency, and disaster relief," to use Secretary of State Madeleine Albright's list.[1] And still others, most notably Henry Kissinger, are concerned that NATO has purchased Russia's grudging assent to expansion by agreeing to undermine the alliance's military posture on the new members' soil.

But at least as important and troubling as those potential problems is the concept of American national interest that underlies plans for NATO expansion. At best, that concept is incoherent. At worst, it is wrongheaded. As a result, despite the intentions of proponents, NATO expansion is likely to make Europe a less, not more, stable continent over the long run.

The Sales Pitch

According to its champions, NATO expansion is nothing less than an all-purpose cure for the problems ailing Europe today and looming on the horizon. For the former Warsaw Pact countries of Eastern and Central Europe, it is viewed as nothing less than a godsend. NATO expansion is expected to produce a host of global benefits as well.

41

President Clinton, for example, offers four main reasons for expanding NATO. First, "it will strengthen our alliance in meeting the security challenges of the 21st century, addressing conflicts that threaten the common peace of all." By that, the president explained, he meant that NATO expansion would facilitate carrying out future Bosnia-like peace operations.

Second, according to the president, "NATO enlargement will help to secure the historic gains of democracy in Europe. NATO can do for Europe's East what it did for Europe's West at the end of World War II—provide a secure climate where freedom, democracy, and prosperity can flourish."

Third, Clinton argues that "enlarging NATO will encourage prospective members to resolve their differences peacefully." The alliance "helped to reconcile age-old adversaries like France and Germany," the president explained, adding somewhat mysteriously, "and already has reduced tensions between Greece and Turkey over all these decades."

Finally, the president contends that enlarging NATO, along with the Partnership for Peace and other special arrangements with Russia, Ukraine, and other nonmembers, "will erase the artificial line in Europe that Stalin drew, and bring Europe together in security, not keep it apart in instability."[2]

The goals outlined by Clinton are unexceptionable. The United States would indeed be safer and more prosperous if a high degree of European stability, security, and prosperity could be ensured for decades. But making sound foreign policy involves much more than simply describing intrinsically desirable goals. Questions of cost, risk, and feasibility must be reckoned with. Policymakers must also ask whether they have chosen the right tools for achieving goals that can be secured at acceptable cost and risk—unless they want to be in the position of painting portraits with pickaxes. Policymakers must also make sure that the goals they seek are clearly defined and mutually compatible. If those criteria are not satisfied, leaders must specify which goals are indispensable and which can be abandoned. Finally, it is essential to interpret history's lessons accurately—especially if those lessons are invoked as prime policy rationales.

Unfortunately, NATO expansion flunks all of those vital tests.[3] Especially deserving of attention is the failure of proponents to identify clear, mutually compatible goals that will serve America's essential interests in Europe and to select the right tools for the job. Such factors will determine whether the United States will spend the coming decades trapped in repeated military ventures in a chronically unstable Europe or be strategically positioned to reap the benefits of Europe's successes and escape the worst consequences of its continuing troubles.

Friend or Foe?

NATO enlargement assumes that Europe can become increasingly unified and stable through the establishment of new types of security and diplomatic relationships between the Atlantic alliance and Europe's former communist countries. Most of the former Warsaw Pact countries of Central and Eastern Europe are expected eventually to become NATO members. Countries geographically close to Russia, such as Ukraine and the Baltic states, are likely to be offered unspecified "softer" security arrangements—although for public consumption the administration still insists that the door to NATO membership will remain open to them.[4] NATO will deal with Russia through a new Russia-NATO Permanent Joint Council, which will establish a Russian mission at NATO and give Moscow what Secretary Albright calls "a voice, not a veto" in NATO's affairs.[5]

The main problem with that arrangement is that it reflects NATO's inability or unwillingness to answer clearly a fundamental question: Is Russia to be viewed as a friend or an actual or potential threat? The inevitable result of the ongoing ambiguity, at least over the medium and long terms, will be to send Russia and every other country currently outside NATO a series of confusing messages likely to undermine, not strengthen, European stability.

The president, the secretary of state, and other American officials have essentially taken both positions regarding Russia. For example, in his remarks upon signing the Founding Act on Mutual Relations, Cooperation and Security between NATO and the Russian Federation, which established a new NATO-Russia link, President Clinton argued that "we are determined to create a future in which European security is not a zero-sum game—where NATO's gain is Russia's loss, and Russia's strength is our alliance's weakness. That is old thinking."[6] Yet in the final analysis, the president insisted on leaving Russia out of the new NATO.

43

That exclusionary policy has been made somewhat more puzzling by the criteria for membership laid out by Washington. As Albright has said, "We have made very clear that NATO membership is open to all democracies in Europe.... That applies to the Baltics as it does to the other countries in the region."[7] Moreover, Clinton has called Russia's 1996 presidential elections "fully democratic, open" and proclaimed that "its steadfast commitment to freedom and reform has earned the world's admiration."[8] Yet Russia's steadfastness has brought it not one inch closer to NATO membership—or even to serious consideration. Unless the administration believes that Russia is a non-European country, the U.S. position is devoid of logic.

The inability to categorize Russia clearly has produced an equally—and dangerously—ambivalent policy on NATO miliary deployments on the soil of the new members. NATO's defining feature is article 5 of the North Atlantic Treaty, which requires each member to consider an attack on one as an attack on all. But almost from its inception, the alliance faced a potentially crippling problem. Most of its military power was located in the United States—an ocean away from the likeliest theater of NATO-Soviet conflict. Whatever treaty commitments the United States made during the Cold War, NATO's European members were always worried that if hostilities broke out, America would sit out the war.

Washington ultimately assuaged those concerns—at least for the most part—by stationing in Europe hundreds of thousands of soldiers, their families, and thousands of nuclear weapons. In fact, most of those forces and personnel were stationed in Germany, directly in the probable path of Warsaw Pact invaders. Those forces served as a tripwire; since they were deployed so vulnerably, those men, women, children, and nuclear weapons inevitably would be engulfed by any fighting in Europe, thus ensuring America's participation in an East-West conflict. Although not every European member of NATO insisted on hosting tripwire forces (and in the late 1980s some countries even resisted new deployments of U.S. nuclear missiles), every member has agreed that the American defense guarantee would lose considerable credibility without some significant U.S. force located somewhere close to the likeliest theaters of combat in Europe.

NATO's newest members are unlikely to be any different. In fact, the very insecurity that has pushed them toward NATO should logically make them especially insistent on concrete signs of the alliance's commitment to their defense. Their historical experiences also teach the limits of paper treaties; after all, first-wave new NATO member Poland was abandoned by the Allies in the late 1930s—as was Czechoslovakia, the predecessor of the Czech Republic, another first-wave new member.

NATO's response has been to straddle the issue. On the one hand, the alliance is sufficiently concerned about the present and future Russian threat to offer various security guarantees to the countries of Eastern and Central Europe. On the other hand, NATO has told Moscow that it has "no intention, no plan and no reason" to deploy nuclear weapons on the territory of new members or to station "substantial" outside combat forces permanently in those countries.[9] Although NATO governments specify that those statements are not a promise of any kind, let alone a binding commitment, they raise more questions than they answer, especially in the context of the decision to enlarge the alliance.

For one thing, Russian president Boris Yeltsin has already interpreted the statements in his own way. Upon signing the Founding Act, Yeltsin declared, "There is an obligation [on NATO's part] to non-deploy on a permanent basis NATO's combat forces near Russia."[10] In addition, the alliance has been sending out some mixed signals of its own.

On January 4, 1997, German chancellor Helmut Kohl not only told Yeltsin, "We have no intention of moving our military machine to Russia's borders. I can't see anyone who would want this." He also stated, "It is absolutely clear to me that, given its geographical situation, the FRG [Federal Republic of Germany] has a special role in Russia"—thereby raising once again the specter of a Germany ultimately more determined to serve as a bridge between Russia and the West than to remain part of the West.[11] On March 23, Gen. Klaus Naumann, a German who chairs NATO's military committee, told a news conference that at a meeting with Russian generals he had "elaborated . . . with great military precision" on the meaning of NATO's nondeployment statements. Some press accounts reported that those assurances went far enough beyond NATO's official position to significantly inhibit the alliance's military flexibility.[12]

Dangerously Mixed Signals

More fundamentally, a policy of ambiguity is a recipe for profound East-West misunderstanding. After all, acknowledging no reason to station substantial forces in the new member countries and no plan or intention to do so amounts to acknowledging that no threat from Moscow is anticipated in the future, much less perceived in the present. At the same time, NATO is taking a step that Russia's leaders still "view negatively," in Yeltsin's words.[13]

The result is potentially dangerous mixed signals to Russia of strength and weakness, provocation and fear. Moscow will be facing an alliance that has reached its doorstep and rejected the possibility of Russian membership, but one that has also taken extraordinary steps to placate Russia by, in essence, agreeing to expand only on paper. That version of NATO amounts to an alliance willing to antagonize Russia but not to challenge it militarily. For now, with Russia unable even to crush ethnic rebellion in a backwater like Chechnya, the effects of such muddled messages may seem inconsequential. Yet, unless Russia indefinitely remains weak, poor, and fragmented, the long-term effects could be much more dangerous and produce a blend of mistrust and uncertainty that could easily lead to confrontation.

Washington's confused message is undoubtedly being reenforced by the military spending cuts under way throughout the alliance. The very week that Clinton and Yeltsin signed the Founding Act, the U.S. Department of Defense released its Quadrennial Defense Review, which presents the administration's view of the force levels and structures needed to support U.S. national security strategy over the next four years—as well as the funding needed to create and maintain those forces. In the view of most analysts outside the administration, the QDR has simply continued the recent, dangerous practice of pretending that an ever-smaller military can carry out an ever-expanding set of missions. From 1992 to 1997, the fighting strength of the U.S. military shrank by nearly 40 percent. Meanwhile, the Army, Navy, Air Force, and Marines were sent on more than 50 peacekeeping and humanitarian relief missions around the globe while they remained responsible for defending the American homeland plus a long list of allies in Europe, the Persian Gulf, and East Asia.

On the eve of Russian acquiescence to increasing the number of NATO members America will have to defend, the QDR announced additional cuts of 50,000 to 60,000 active-duty troops. The Russian reactionaries that NATO enlargers claim to be worried about undoubtedly have noticed that the gap continues to widen between America's professed foreign policy objectives and its willingness to adequately finance a military capable of achieving those objectives.[14]

America's European allies have been downsizing their militaries almost as fast as the United States—and from a much smaller base. According to the Defense Department's latest study of alliance burden sharing, from 1990 to 1995 U.S. military spending fell at an average annual rate of 4.4 percent. The European allies' defense budgets fell at an average annual rate of 2.3 percent during that period. Only Luxembourg, Portugal, Norway, and Greece managed real defense spending increases, and the average annual increases for the latter three were all under 1 percent. As a result, in 1995 the non-U.S. NATO members still spent an average of just 2.2 percent of their gross domestic products on defense, while the United States spent 3.9 percent. And the United States accounted for 58.7 percent of NATO's total military spending.[15] The difficulties of meeting the Maastricht European Monetary Union budgetary targets without unprecedented cuts in West European welfare states will undoubtedly lead to further downsizing of West European militaries.

To the Finland Option

The mixture of provocation and weakness, however, could have its greatest—and most tragic—effects on NATO's newest members. The countries of Central and Eastern Europe are inevitably victims of geography, and always have been. Sandwiched between Germany and Russia, they have been condemned to be battlefields when tensions between those great powers have been highest and buffers during more peaceful periods. Although, as previously discussed, various Western powers offered them security guarantees earlier in this century, those guarantees always proved worthless. The geographic position of the Central and East European countries makes them simply indefensible—at least by outsiders—at any politically acceptable or strategically sensible levels of risk and cost.

The Soviet Union's demise has given those countries a historic opportunity. For the first time, neither Russia nor Germany has the capability to conquer them (at least easily) or the desire to remake them ideologically. The nations of Central and Eastern Europe should realize that trusting in literally incredible Western guarantees and pretending that they have more and better options than are in fact available (except temporarily) do not represent their best hope for long-term security and substantial independence. Rather, they should recognize their inherent geopolitical vulnerability and focus on easing the feelings of inferiority, anxiety, and vulnerability that the Russians themselves are undoubtedly experiencing. Russia's small neighbors need to do that even at some cost to their own sovereignty.

Specifically, those countries should be exploring the option of Finlandizing their region—that is, adopting a neutral status and guaranteeing Russian forces certain military rights during crises in exchange for Russia's agreement to fully respect their independence in peacetime (and respect at least limited sovereignty at other times) and their right to maintain their own political, social, and economic systems.

Such an arrangement is admittedly not ideal. But if it worked for Finland throughout the Cold War—when messianic Leninist ideology arguably played some role in shaping Soviet foreign policy—it would seem that much more practical today. Postcommunist Russia apparently retains some expansionist impulses (although they seem directed more southward than westward), but it plainly has no interest in promulgating world revolution. Just as important, although the Finlandization option would impinge on the complete but nominal sovereignty that the countries of Central and Eastern Europe have understandably proclaimed and clung to since the end of the Cold War, it would represent by far the best deal that history has ever offered. Those countries should know that Western guarantees must be viewed skeptically. But their preoccupation with joining NATO has crowded more realistic and more innovative—if less inspiring—approaches to security off their diplomatic agendas.

Misreading History

Ambivalence and fence-sitting often seem to be hallmarks of the Clinton administration, but the ambivalence underlying current NATO enlargement plans reflects more than one individual's character flaws—or even the weaknesses of one president's foreign policy team. That ambivalence results from the secondary role that Central and Eastern Europe have always played—with good reason—in

American foreign policy and from the Clinton administration's failure to understand that the true, historical nature of America's interests in Europe is far more nuanced than administration rhetoric indicates.

Here is how the president himself recently defined those interests:

> Europe's fate and America's future are joined. Twice in half a century, Americans have given their lives to defend liberty and peace in world wars that began in Europe. And we have stayed in Europe in very large numbers for a long time throughout the Cold War. Taking wise steps now to strengthen our common security when we have the opportunity to do so will help to build a future without the mistakes and divisions of the past.[16]

For emphasis, Clinton told his audience of West Point cadets that NATO enlargement "makes it less likely that you will ever be called to fight in another war across the Atlantic."[17]

What the president is either unable or unwilling to realize is that the United States has never gone to war in Europe because Central or Eastern Europe was being threatened. Throughout the 20th century—save for Woodrow Wilson's ill-fated intervention in the Russian civil war—American leaders have always distinguished between the nation's vital interests in Western Europe and its secondary interests to the east.

Such a distinction makes eminent sense. Western Europe was plausibly, until the nuclear age, seen as a jumping-off point for an attack on the Western Hemisphere. Western Europe also had the lion's share of the Continent's economic resources, and thus it was understandably deemed essential by U.S. leaders that its wealth and know-how be kept out of the hands of would-be hegemons. Finally, Western Europe was much easier to defend or retake than Central or Eastern Europe, especially when America was faced with a nuclear-armed Soviet adversary. Thus no American president has ever used military force to defend any Central or Eastern European country under attack. And no post–World War II American president, not even Ronald Reagan, ever militarily challenged Soviet hegemony over the region.

Russia does not pose a comparable threat to the United States today. But Moscow still possesses thousands of nuclear weapons, and although its conventional forces have deteriorated significantly,

Russia can still mobilize vast armies and air forces. More important, the time horizons of a sound foreign policy must extend beyond the next year, or 5 or 10 years. Because Russia will not always be this weak, American leaders should think carefully before implementing policies based on an ultimate willingness to engage Russian military power thousands of miles away from the main locus of American military strength, and right next door to the main locus of present and future Russian strength. Thus, contrary to the president's boilerplate, extending American security guarantees to Central and Eastern Europe marks a major departure for American foreign policy. It sets a precedent that his successors are likely to regret.

The Wrong Tools

Finally, NATO expansion is clearly the wrong tool for fixing the main problems threatening the stability of either half of Europe. Washington is right to be concerned about the Continent, but NATO expansion is at best marginal to Europe's most pressing problems. Even if one accepts the argument that NATO membership will provide the security environment needed by new members to proceed vigorously and successfully with their transitions from communism to capitalism and democracy, no one pretends that membership is a sufficient condition for successful reform.

Central and Eastern Europe need both massive investment and wide-open access to new markets, both in Western Europe and around the world. An administration truly concerned about European stability would be addressing those economic problems. But the United States has so far been satisfied with small-scale, manifestly inadequate initiatives, failing even to make major efforts to promote private investment in the region.

Perhaps more important, even as the administration and other supporters of enlargement press for the admission of new NATO members, *Western* Europe has become a significantly less stable place. Again, the reasons have nothing to do with military security. Western Europe's problems are by now well-known—slow economic growth, uncompetitive industries, rigid labor markets, high unemployment, and difficulties assimilating non-European immigrants.

In particular, as shown by the latest French elections, many Europeans do not intend to go gently into that good night of a new,

Darwinian global economy. And yet, without greater economic unity, few countries in the region have the economic weight to successfully influence the terms of globalization. On their own, most would probably run into the same obstacles encountered by the late French president François Mitterrand in the early 1980s. Again, the Clinton administration barely acknowledges the problem, let alone spends significant time developing solutions.

A Hidden Agenda?

The aforementioned policy failures suggest that, despite the rhetoric, helping to find concrete, practical solutions to Europe's problems is a rather low priority of the Clinton administration. Otherwise, administration officials would be reading their American diplomatic history much more carefully. They would be defining U.S. interests on the Continent much more clearly. They would not be sending such confusing messages to friend, foe, and neutral alike. They would not be shrinking the U.S. military while making new commitments. And they would choose much better tools.

Perhaps the president has domestic image-making in mind. Perhaps he is searching frantically for a legacy—any legacy. Whatever his true purposes, let us hope that he tells Americans and Europeans alike what those purposes are before NATO enlargement becomes a fait accompli. And if he does not divulge his real agenda, let us hope that a vigilant Congress will pry it out of him.

Notes

1. Madeleine Albright, "Remarks at Inaugural Meeting of the Euro-Atlantic Partnership Council," May 30, 1997, at http://secretary.state.gov/www/statements/970530.html.

2. White House, Office of the Press Secretary, "Remarks by the President at the United States Military Academy Commencement, West Point, New York, May 31, 1997," p. 4.

3. For a more detailed discussion of thinking rigorously about the national interest, see Alan Tonelson, "What Is the National Interest?" *Atlantic Monthly*, July, 1991, pp. 35–52.

4. See, for example, Hugh Carnegy, "Baltics May Have to Take 'Second Best,'" *Financial Times*, November 22, 1996.

5. Quoted in John F. Harris, "Russia-NATO Pact Gives Moscow a Voice on European Security," *Washington Post*, May 28, 1997, p. A1.

6. Quoted in "Former Enemies Speak of Peace," *New York Times*, May 28, 1997, p. A10.

7. Madeleine Albright, Press Conference following North Atlantic Council Ministerial Meeting, May 29, 1997, p. 2, at http://secretary.state.gov/www/statements/970529a.html.

8. White House, Office of the Press Secretary, "Remarks by the President at Commemorative Event for the 50th Anniversary of the Marshall Plan, May 28, 1997," p. 3; and "Former Enemies Speak of Peace."

9. "Main Points of the Accord," *New York Times*, May 28, 1997, p. A10; and Craig R. Whitney, "Russia and West Sign Cooperation Pact," *New York Times*, May 28, 1997, p. A1.

10. Quoted in "Former Enemies Speak of Peace."

11. "Kohl Hopes for 'Sensible Solution' on NATO Expansion: Text of Report by Interfax News Agency," *BBC Summary of World Broadcasts*, January 6, 1997.

12. Quoted in Michael Dobbs, "Mixed Signals Complicate NATO-Russia Charter Talks," *Washington Post*, April 30, 1997, p. A16.

13. Quoted in "Former Enemies Speak of Peace."

14. For a good, concise discussion of the QDR, see John Hillen, "Kicking the Can Down the Road," *Washington Times*, May 29, 1997. For an analysis of defense cuts during President Clinton's first years in office, see Alan Tonelson, "Superpower without a Sword," *Foreign Affairs* 72, no. 3 (Summer 1993): 166–80.

15. U.S. Department of Defense, *Report on Allied Contributions to the Common Defense*, March 1997, pp. III–2 to III–3.

16. White House, "Remarks by the President at the United States Military Academy Commencement," p. 3.

17. Ibid., p. 4.

4. Why Die for Gdansk? NATO Enlargement and American Security Interests

Christopher Layne

NATO expansion is not a fait accompli. Before enlargement becomes fact, it must clear the final hurdle of ratification in the U.S. Senate. The ratification process will be critical because it presents one final opportunity to expose the flawed logic of NATO expansion.

Washington's efforts to enlarge NATO are evidence of U.S. policymakers' failure to understand the post–Cold War world. Instead of making national security arrangements appropriate for the new strategic environment, policymakers are using enlargement to justify the perpetuation of a Cold War alliance that has no post–Cold War rationale. It is up to the Senate, then, not only to expose the illogic of NATO expansion but also to initiate a wide-ranging and rigorous public discussion about America's future role in Europe and, indeed, the world.

U.S. Security Interests in Europe

U.S. security interests in Europe no longer require American military engagement on the Continent. The two broad strategic rationales—counterhegemony and regional stability—do not justify such engagement in the post–Cold War era. Historically, counterhegemonic concerns—the fear of a single power dominating the Continent—have shaped U.S. strategy toward Europe. Until the 20th century, America's counterhegemonic interests were secured without active U.S. involvement in European security affairs because the European balance of power prevented any single state from dominating the Continent. In 1940, however, and again after World War II, the collapse of the European balance of power impelled the United States to intervene militarily.

The emergence of regional stability concerns as a strategic justification for U.S. military engagement in Europe is a post–Cold War phenomenon. Policymakers assert that America has a vital interest in preventing regional instability because history demonstrates that the United States invariably is drawn into Europe's wars. As Sen. Richard Lugar (R-Ind.) puts it, "If history teaches us anything, it is that the United States is always drawn into such European conflicts because our vital interests are ultimately, albeit somewhat belatedly, engaged."[1]

Policymakers also argue that turmoil and instability in Europe have an adverse impact on U.S. economic interests. As then–national security adviser Anthony Lake put it, "History has taught us that when Europe is in turmoil, America suffers, and when Europe is peaceful and prosperous, America can thrive as well."[2] Consequently, the United States needs to be militarily involved on the Continent to ensure that conflict does not occur.

The U.S. military presence serves as the Continent's "pacifier" in two ways.[3] First, by extending its security umbrella over Europe, the United States promotes stability by preventing the resurfacing of the Continent's historical security rivalries. Second, the U.S. presence allows Washington to intervene on the Continent's unruly peripheries, such as the Balkans. Such interventions are important because turmoil on the outskirts of Europe could prompt America's allies to act independently to maintain order on the peripheries—again raising the specter of renationalization. Or the instability could ripple back into Europe's core and undercut America's prosperity by disrupting the economic links that bind the United States to Europe.[4]

NATO Expansion and Counterhegemony

How does NATO expansion fit into the counterhegemony and regional stability strategic frameworks? Underlying NATO expansion is fear of a resurgent Russia. Thus, NATO expansion could be viewed as a manifestation of America's traditional counterhegemonic strategy. However, neither the administration's declaratory policy (as opposed to its action policy) nor the prevailing strategic balance in Europe supports such a conclusion.

The Clinton administration has gone to great lengths to reassure Moscow that NATO is not aimed at containing Russian power. As President Clinton has stated, "NATO enlargement is not directed at anyone."[5] To be sure, there is a disingenuous aspect to the administration's rhetoric. Even while denying that enlargement threatens

Russia, Deputy Secretary of State Strobe Talbott admits that "hedging against the possibility of resurgent Russian aggression" is, in fact, one of the rationales for expanding the alliance.[6]

The extent to which U.S. support for NATO expansion is driven by latent counterhegemonic considerations is unclear. To the extent that such concerns *do* underlie U.S. policy, however, they are misplaced. In the wake of the Soviet Union's dissolution, Russia is a great power by courtesy only. Russia's economy is a shambles. The Russian army is not an offensive threat to the rest of Europe—the Russian army that fought so badly in Chechnya is not the same Russian army that pushed back Hitler's *Wehrmacht* from the gates of Moscow and planted the Red flag on the Brandenburg Gate. U.S. intelligence analysts believe it will take many years for Russia to reconstitute its conventional military capabilities and that, consequently, Europe would have ample strategic warning of a revival of Russian power.[7]

Germany is a more likely hegemon than is Russia. Germany's economy dominates Europe, and its conventional forces are more powerful and effective than Russia's. America's interest in perpetuating NATO is driven at least as much by the perceived need to "keep the Germans down" as by the need to "keep the Russians out."[8]

Neither Germany nor Russia is likely to emerge as a serious contender for European hegemony, however, because the Cold War's end has restored a stable balance of power that can be maintained by the European states. Germany's conventional military power and economic prowess are offset by Russia's (and Britain's and France's) nuclear forces. Even if Germany should someday become a nuclear power, the effect would likely be to further enhance Europe's strategic stability. A European security structure based on the national nuclear deterrent forces of Europe's major powers (including Germany) is potentially a much more stable system than a security arrangement tied to an American extended-deterrence strategy.[9]

It is difficult to visualize a process that could lead to the emergence of a European hegemon in a nuclear world. Though war is not impossible in a nuclear world, the risk of escalation makes it virtually impossible to conquer a nuclear-armed great power. That calls into question the strategic premises that historically have underlain America's counterhegemonic European strategy. Concern that a European hegemon could use the Continent's resources to threaten the United States is an artifact of the prenuclear era. As long as it maintains credible second-strike deterrence capabilities, the United States is virtually immune from external strategic threat. Simply put, in a nuclear world, America's counterhegemonic European strategy is obsolete: the prospect of a European hegemon is remote, but even if such a power emerged to dominate the Continent, the United States still would be secure.

NATO Expansion and Regional Stability

Regional stability, not counterhegemony, is the strategic rationale that best explains NATO expansion. The U.S. security guarantee to Europe through NATO is the chief expression of U.S. interest in regional security. Extending the NATO security guarantee to Central and Eastern Europe, then, would provide a concrete manifestation of U.S. interest in the region and the alleged benefits that interest entails. NATO expansion supposedly would contribute to regional stability by reassuring new members that they were secure, and it would therefore facilitate the consolidation of free-market democratic institutions in those states. Democracy and economic interdependence would in turn bolster peace and stability throughout Europe. As President Clinton has stated, NATO expansion seeks to do for East-Central Europe what it did for Western Europe after World War II: "Prevent a return to local rivalries, strengthen democracy against future threats, and create the conditions for prosperity to flourish."[10]

If regional stability is indeed the main rationale for Washington's efforts to enlarge NATO, it is important to consider several critical questions: What does preserving European stability entail, and should the United States want to assume that responsibility? Is NATO expansion a prerequisite for democracy's taking hold in East-Central Europe? Do U.S. economic interests require Washington to maintain European stability? By attempting to maintain European stability, does the United States help to deter a future European war or instead ensure that the United States would automatically be dragged into a conflict that it could otherwise avoid?

East-Central Europe historically has been a volatile region, where great powers have competed for security and dominance and where many national and ethnic rivalries remain unresolved. A partial list of potential East-Central European flashpoints includes border disputes between Poland and its neighbors (Germany, Lithuania, Belarus, and Ukraine); ethnic conflict between Hungary and its neighbors (Serbia, Slovakia, and Romania); and the Russian enclave of Kaliningrad. The argument that the United States and NATO have a vested interest in suppressing future outbreaks of national and ethnic rivalry in East-Central Europe means that the United States must, in the name of European stability, be prepared to undertake future Bosnia-type peace enforcement operations in East-Central Europe. As Talbott has argued, "The lesson of the tragedy in the former Yugoslavia is not to retire NATO in disgrace but to develop its ability to counter precisely those forces that have exploded in the Balkans."[11]

Americans should be skeptical of such arguments. It has not been demonstrated that such potential conflicts would affect U.S. security interests. Even the proponents of American intervention in the Balkans never argued that the Bosnian war directly affected the United States. They were forced instead to invoke the domino theory's discredited, shopworn clichés to make their case. The argument for U.S. involvement in Bosnia and in similar conflicts rests on hyperbolic fears of what *might* happen in the future, absent American intervention.

Moreover, Bosnia has so far been a costly and ineffective endeavor. U.S. and NATO involvement in the former Yugoslavia has accomplished very little and has certainly failed to achieve the stated goal of transforming Bosnia into a multiethnic democracy. Most experts believe that if NATO forces withdraw as scheduled in June 1998, war will resume. Barring a permanent U.S. and NATO presence, Bosnia's ultimate partition into separate Serb, Croat, and Muslim political entities is nearly inevitable. But if the purpose of NATO enlargement is to ensure Europe's stability, the United States cannot simply walk away from Bosnia (or from future Bosnia-style upheavals in Europe).[12] Bosnia thus is a preview of an expanded NATO's coming attractions.

If Bosnia is indicative of the types of missions in which an expanded NATO can expect to be involved, it is important to consider that the Clinton administration has pursued its Bosnia policy without either congressional or public endorsement. The administration has been fortunate that U.S. forces have not suffered combat losses, but it is evident that both congressional and public patience is wearing thin with a commitment that has proved expensive, has achieved little, and has no definitive end in sight. The lack of enthusiasm for the U.S. intervention in Bosnia suggests that neither Congress nor the American public is likely to support the use of U.S. forces in future East-Central European peace enforcement operations.

Furthermore, if NATO must expand to protect its members from instability originating on the periphery, enlargement is geographically open-ended. Once Poland, Hungary, and the Czech Republic have been admitted to the alliance, the argument inevitably will be made that they will be threatened by instability arising in the regions to the east of the expanded alliance. NATO enlargement thus is a prime example of how turbulent security frontier thinking results in the expansion of security commitments. It is only a matter of time before threats to an enlarged NATO impel the alliance's further expansion; indeed, there is some evidence that the United States already is contemplating eventual NATO expansion further into the peripheries, especially the Baltic region.[13]

American policymakers argue that NATO expansion is necessary to permit the consolidation of democracy in East-Central Europe. There is no necessary connection between NATO expansion and democracy's success (or failure) there, however. The impetus to democratize is internally, not externally, driven. Poland, Hungary, and the Czech Republic moved toward democracy long before NATO expansion was on the agenda. Conversely, current NATO members, such as Greece and Turkey, have had significant lapses in progress toward democracy despite alliance membership. Democracy's fate in East-Central Europe, then, has little to do with NATO enlargement.

Moreover, it is far from clear that democratization in Central and Eastern Europe (or a lack thereof) or stability in the area is of particular concern to the United States. Advocates of expansion argue that the United States has a vital interest in preserving regional stability in Europe because European turmoil would hurt America's prosperity. William Odom, former director of the National Security Agency, for example, has argued that NATO must expand to preserve regional stability for economic reasons.

> Only a strong NATO with the U.S. centrally involved can prevent Western Europe from drifting into national parochialism and eventual regression from its present level of economic and political cooperation. Failure to act effectively in

Yugoslavia will not only affect U.S. security interests but also
U.S. economic interests. Our economic interdependency with
Western Europe creates large numbers of American jobs.[14]

Contrary to the conventional wisdom, however, U.S. prosperity
does not depend on European tranquility. U.S. economic interdependence with Europe is limited. In fact, the historical record shows
that America profits from Europe's wars.[15]

That illustrates a fundamental point about the effect of geography
on grand strategy. Geostrategically, in relation to the European continent the United States (like Britain during its great power heyday)
is an offshore balancer. Offshore balancers enjoy significant strategic
advantages in comparison with continental powers. The fact that
the latter must worry constantly about possible threats from nearby
neighbors historically has worked to increase the relative power
position and prosperity of insular states. Offshore balancers can
remain aloof from continental struggles or limit the extent of their
involvement. The ability to stand on the sidelines, or fight "limited
liability wars," enables offshore balancers to gain economically at
the expense of continental powers because the latter are continually
involved in security competitions and conflict.[16] Simply stated, the
argument that America's prosperity depends on peace in Europe is
bogus. In the final analysis, the case for NATO expansion turns on
a single question: will an enlarged alliance enhance U.S. security?

The Myth of Inevitable U.S. Intervention in European Wars

Advocates of enlargement often claim that NATO should expand
to preserve European stability because America cannot expect to
stay out of Europe's wars; hence, the United States should deter
war by remaining in Europe instead of withdrawing and having to
come back later, presumably at greater risk and higher cost. Like
the argument that U.S. prosperity depends on European peace, the
claim that America inevitably is drawn into Europe's wars is a
historical canard. Since the United States achieved independence,
there have been major wars in Europe in 1792–1802, 1804–15,
1853–55, 1859–60, 1866, 1870, 1877–78, 1912–13, 1914–18, and
1939–45. The United States has been involved in three of those wars,
but it could have safely remained out of at least two of the wars in
which it fought. In 1812, hoping to conquer Canada while the British

were preoccupied with the Napoleonic Wars, the United States *initiated* war with Britain. World War I also fails as an example of a European war into which the United States inexorably was drawn. In his classic work on ideals and self-interest in U.S. foreign policy, the late Robert E. Osgood demonstrated that America's intervention in World War I was not caused by any tangible threat to U.S. security interests. American intervention in the Great War was driven by snowball and domino concerns similar to those imbedded in today's strategy of preponderance. President Woodrow Wilson feared that events in seemingly peripheral regions like the Balkans could trigger an uncontrollable chain reaction that would leave the United States isolated ideologically and confronting a hostile European hegemon that could use its military and economic power to "cut off the oxygen without which American society, and liberal institutions generally, would asphyxiate."[17]

But the consensus of military historians is that U.S. intervention did not decisively affect the outcome of the war; the American Expeditionary Force's contribution to the Allied effort was too little and too late to have a significant battlefield impact. Moreover, the argument can be made that the war would have ended in a compromise peace if the United States had not intervened. Unlike the flawed 1919 Versailles settlement, a compromise peace might not have sown the seeds of social and economic unrest that facilitated Hitler's rise to power. Had such a peace occurred, would there have been a second great war in Europe? Possibly. But, if so, it would have been a much different war than World War II. And it might have been a war the United States could have avoided.

A related argument about the U.S. stake in European stability is that American "isolationism" in the 1920s and 1930s had disastrous consequences and would have a similar effect in the future. Thus President Clinton makes the case for NATO expansion by arguing that America must not repeat the "mistakes" of the interwar period by walking away from its responsibilities. Here, two points should be made. First, recent work by diplomatic historians has debunked the notion that the United States followed an isolationist policy during the 1920s and 1930s.[18] Second, American strategy toward Europe in 1939–41 was not "isolationist" but a shrewd example of an offshore balancer's grand strategy.

In 1939–40 the United States stood on the sidelines in the reasonable expectation that Britain and France would be able to hold Germany at bay. When France was defeated stunningly in the brief May–June 1940 campaign (an outcome that surprised even many German military leaders), the United States continued following a modified offshore balancing strategy based on (1) providing military equipment and economic assistance to Britain and (after June 1941) the Soviet Union and (2) fighting a limited liability naval war against German U-boats in the Atlantic. Had Germany not declared war on the United States, the United States might have persisted in that strategy indefinitely. Such balancing is reasoned, self-interested strategy, not isolationism.

In short, the historical record does not support the claim that European wars invariably compel the United States to intervene. Only when a potential European hegemon has loomed on the horizon (1940, 1947–50) has the United States been compelled to become actively engaged in European security affairs. Wars are not a force of nature that magnetically draws states into conflict. States, that is, policymakers, have volition; they decide whether to go to war.

Risks of NATO Enlargement

Proponents of enlargement argue that NATO expansion will reduce the risk of war in Europe. But if that assumption is wrong, NATO expansion would not keep the United States out of a future major European war; it would instead ensure that the United States would be immediately drawn into such a conflict. Fundamentally, NATO enlargement is about extending solemn security guarantees to the alliance's new members. That raises the question of whether there are any vital security interests that would compel the United States to send American troops to die for Gdansk (or Warsaw, Prague, or Budapest).

Undertaking to defend another state is a solemn and portentous responsibility. The great Ohio State University football coach Woody Hayes once said that when a team uses the forward pass, only three things can happen and two of them are bad. NATO expansion shows that a similar rule applies to strategy: when a state commits itself to defending other nations, only three things can happen and two of them are bad.

61

The good outcome is that the mere guarantee successfully deters aggression. A bad outcome for an expanded NATO is that someday its commitments will be tested by an aggressor and that the United States, because its security interests in the region are minimal, will back down rather than risk the consequences of honoring its guarantee. Backing down, however, would impair the credibility of other U.S. strategic commitments. Even worse than backing down, though, would be for the United States to honor its commitments and consequently find itself engaged in a big European war in which no vital U.S. interests were at stake. In a world where an adversary may possess nuclear weapons, that is not just a bad outcome; it is a disastrous one.

It is not clear whether the single benign scenario of NATO enlargement—that the alliance will successfully deter aggression against its new members—is likely. Extended-deterrence strategies (strategies that seek to bring distant allies under the protective shelter of a guarantor's security umbrella) are hard to implement. As deterrence theorist Patrick Morgan has observed, "One of the perpetual problems of deterrence on behalf of third parties is that the costs a state is willing to bear are usually much less than if its own territory is at stake, and it is very difficult to pretend otherwise."[19] For extended deterrence to work, a potential challenger must be convinced that the defender's commitment is credible.[20]

The credibility of U.S. commitments to defend Western Europe was somewhat uncertain even during the Cold War, especially after the Soviet Union attained strategic nuclear parity with the United States, because defending Europe would have left the United States vulnerable to Soviet nuclear retaliation. There was concern on both sides of the Atlantic that the U.S. pledge to use nuclear weapons to deter a Soviet conventional attack on Western Europe was irrational and incredible (in both senses of the latter term). Indeed, extended deterrence was such a contentious issue that it repeatedly corroded NATO's unity nearly to the breaking point.

It nonetheless appears that extended deterrence "worked" in Europe during the Cold War. One should not assume, however, that an enlarged NATO's policy of extending deterrence to East-Central Europe will work equally well. If extended deterrence worked during the Cold War, it was because of a unique coincidence of circumstances that is unlikely to be replicated in the future: the intrinsic value to the defender of the protected region and the permanent forward deployment by the defender of sizable military forces in the protected region.

A crucial factor in weighing the credibility of a defender's extended-deterrence commitments is the degree of its interest in the protected area. If the Soviets had seriously contemplated attacking Western Europe during the Cold War, the risk calculus probably would have dissuaded them from doing so. In a bipolar setting, Western Europe's security was a matter of supreme importance to the United States for both strategic and reputational reasons.

Today, however, the United States has no major interests in East-Central Europe, a region that historically has been peripheral to America's security. After World War II the United States acquiesced when Moscow incorporated that part of Europe into its sphere of influence. Unlike Germany, which was strategically crucial because of its geographic location, economic resources, and manpower, East-Central Europe was not. If the Soviet Union had gained control of all of Germany, Soviet hegemony in Europe would have been possible. The same could not be said of a Soviet Union in control only of East-Central Europe. If anything, in the post–Cold War era Central and Eastern Europe's strategic importance has diminished. Thus it will be difficult to convince a potential attacker that U.S. deterrence commitments to the region are credible.

Furthermore, Moscow's stakes in the region are far more salient, by any measure, than are Washington's. It is doubtful that the United States could successfully deter a resurgent Russia from projecting its power back into East-Central Europe, or from reincorporating the Baltic republics or Ukraine. To engage in such risky actions, Moscow would have to be highly motivated; conversely, the objects of possible attack are unimportant strategically to the United States, which would probably cause Russia to discount the U.S. guarantees. NATO's declared intention to forgo deployment of tactical nuclear and conventional forces on the territory of its prospective new members further undercuts the prospects for successful deterrence.

A defender's deployment of its own forces on a protected ally's territory is one of the most powerful factors in ensuring the success of extended deterrence because that is a visible signal that the defender "means business." But to assuage Moscow's concern that an enlarged NATO will threaten Russia's security, the alliance neither plans nor intends to deploy U.S. forces in East-Central Europe. That leads to one of two conclusions: either an enlarged NATO's security guarantees will lack robustness, or U.S. policymakers do not *really* believe there is a security threat to East-Central Europe (in which case, why expand NATO?).

The Pursuit of U.S. Hegemony

But if extended deterrence in East-Central Europe will not be credible, the risk of a European war in the future will increase. That leads back to the key issue of whether the United States is, as policymakers assert, better off remaining in Europe in the hope of preventing such a war.

The Clinton administration has sought to build support for NATO expansion by invoking the heroic spirit that animated America's two great post–World War II achievements: the Marshall Plan and the Atlantic alliance, but that is a pathetic misuse of history. America's involvement in European security affairs after World War II was a manifestation of its counterhegemonic strategy. Had U.S. policymakers not believed that the Soviet Union threatened to achieve domination of the entire Continent, it is unlikely that the United States would have provided massive economic assistance to postwar Europe or that it would have reversed its long-standing policy of eschewing peacetime involvement in European security affairs. Context counts in geopolitics. Today, there are no overriding strategic concerns that compel American involvement in Europe. America's counterhegemonic concerns are not implicated in post–Cold War Europe. If one speaks at all of hegemony in today's world, it must be of *American* hegemony.

Indeed, lofty and misleading rhetoric about NATO expansion hides this crucial fact: U.S. policy in Europe aims not to counter others' bids for hegemony but to perpetuate America's own. Since the end of World War II, the United States has attempted to maintain its preponderance in the international arena to prevent the emergence of new geopolitical rivals. In the late 1940s, of course, the United States accepted the reality of Soviet power. Short of preventive war (a thought with which some American policymakers flirted), the United States could not prevent the Soviet Union's ascendance to superpower status.[21] However, from 1945 on the United States was, and was determined to remain, the sole great power in its own sphere of influence, the non-Soviet world. As historian Melvyn P. Leffler points out, American policymakers believed that "neither an integrated Europe nor a united Germany . . . must be permitted to emerge as a third force or a neutral bloc."[22]

America's postwar hegemony has been reflected in its policies. In NATO, for example, the United States has sought to remain the final arbiter of nuclear strategy, and the alliance's supreme commander always has been an American. Throughout the Cold War, Washington sought to bilateralize East-West relations to limit its allies' ability to influence the two superpowers' political-military agendas. The United States also reacted with hostility to West European attempts to assert an independent identity in international politics, especially to the policies of French president Charles de Gaulle and the *Ostpolitik* of West German chancellor Willy Brandt.[23]

In the post–Cold War world, NATO is the principal instrument by which the United States maintains primacy in European security affairs. With the Soviet Union's collapse, the threat that catalyzed the alliance's creation quite literally disappeared from the map, but Washington has refused to ask whether the alliance, and the U.S. presence in Europe, is still necessary. The explanation for the U.S. attachment to NATO is apparent: the alliance is an American-dominated instrument that Washington employs to exercise political and military influence on the Continent.

American policymakers believe that the perpetuation of American hegemony in Europe (and globally) will enhance U.S. security. That notion rests on a misreading of history and betrays a naivete about the nature of international relations. U.S. policymakers may tell Moscow that it should not perceive enlargement as a threat, but international politics continues to take place in an anarchic realm, and each state is responsible for ensuring its own security. In the competitive arena of world politics, states are concerned about the distribution of power among themselves and their rivals.

In a "unipolar" world—in which the United States is the only superpower—it should come as no surprise that Russia and other countries assign more weight to America's unchecked power than they do to Washington's assurances that U.S. power does not constitute a threat to any other state. Hegemons may claim their intentions are benign, but other states inevitably feel threatened by a hegemon's unchecked power and form alliances to balance against the preponderant state, which is why modern would-be hegemons have invariably failed.

Because other nations regard NATO expansion as a manifestation of Washington's hegemonic aspirations, they are responding as expected. Russia, the state most obviously threatened by NATO expansion, has moved to bolster its security ties with Belarus and Iran in an attempt to create counterweights to an expanded, U.S.-led alliance. More ominous in the longer term, NATO expansion has catalyzed a strategic rapprochement between Russia and China. In the spring of 1997 the Russian and Chinese governments jointly expressed their strategic unease with a world dominated by the United States and declared their intention to work together to counter American preponderance by restoring multipolarity to the international system. Today, Russia's capabilities and its options are limited. Over time, however, NATO expansion could create a self-fulfilling prophecy by provoking the very Russian threat it ostensibly seeks to deter.

Rethinking the U.S. Role in Europe

NATO expansion is a bad idea. It cannot pass the elementary test of logical coherence. If the odds of a future war in East-Central Europe are nil, an expanded NATO is unnecessary. On the other hand, if the chances of a future war are real, then for the United States, NATO expansion is an unacceptably dangerous policy. The best way for America to stay out of future European wars is not to be militarily present on the Continent when they begin.

The time has come to reassess America's continental commitment. The Clinton administration's attempt to wrap itself in the mantle of the Marshall Plan ("present at the re-creation") instead of setting out a compelling case for a renewed U.S. commitment to European security illustrates how weak the case for American military engagement in Europe really is. In 1947–49 the American effort to rebuild and defend a war-shattered Western Europe was a heroic endeavor in response to a clear and present danger—not just to Western Europe's security but to America's. Today, Europe is prosperous and peaceful and no potential European hegemon looms on the horizon (nor, from a strategic standpoint, would it matter if one did).

Moreover, the Clinton administration's present at the re-creation strategy reflects an ignorance of history. The early postwar architects of American foreign policy—Marshall; his policy planning adviser, George F. Kennan; and Dwight D. Eisenhower, who served as NATO's first supreme commander before being elected president—did not embark on the task of rebuilding and defending Western Europe for the purpose of establishing a permanent American protectorate over the Continent. Rather, they sought to use U.S. economic and military power to buy time for Europe to get back on its feet and reassume responsibility for its own affairs.

In the early 1950s Eisenhower observed that if 10 years hence U.S. troops were still in Europe, NATO and the Marshall Plan would have failed. Nearly 50 years later, the fact that U.S. policymakers are seeking to enlarge NATO illustrates the wisdom of Eisenhower's remarks: NATO expansion represents the failure of U.S. policymakers to understand the reasons for America's commitment to Europe after World War II. The time has come to complete America's historic postwar project by finally and fully devolving to a prosperous and democratic Europe the task of managing its own affairs. The task of ensuring Europe's peace, stability, prosperity, and freedom is one for the Europeans themselves, not for the United States. In the absence of a hegemonic threat, there is no reason why U.S. soldiers should be asked to die for Gdansk.

Notes

1. Richard Lugar, "Getting Back to Basics: NATO's Double Enlargement," *Congressional Record* (Senate), June 10, 1996, p. S6001. The Clinton administration shares that view. Defending the administration's NATO enlargement policy, Secretary of State Madeleine Albright has argued that "we have an interest in European security, because we wish to avoid the instability that drew 5 million Americans across the Atlantic to fight in two world wars." Madeleine Albright, Prepared statement before the Senate Foreign Relations Committee, January 8, 1997, U.S. Department of State *Dispatch* 8, no. 1 (January 1997): 8.

2. Anthony Lake, "The U.S. Faces Key Foreign Policy Challenges," U.S. Department of State *Dispatch* 7, no. 21 (June 3, 1996): 280. Making the same point, President Clinton has said, "Nowhere are our interests more engaged than in Europe. When Europe is at peace, our security is strengthened. When Europe prospers, so does America." White House, Office of the Press Secretary, "Remarks by the President to the People of Detroit, October 2, 1996," pp. 5–6.

3. See Josef Joffe, "Europe's American Pacifier," *Foreign Policy*, no. 54 (Spring 1984): 64–82.

4. Thus, in arguing that the United States had a vital interest in intervening in Bosnia, Deputy Secretary of State Strobe Talbott said, "If the fighting in Bosnia were

to spread, the political disruption, if not the military conflict, could reach out to all points of the compass, including south and east, which carries with it the peril that two of our NATO allies—Greece and Turkey—could be drawn in as well—on opposite sides." Strobe Talbott, "American Leadership and the New Europe," U.S. Department of State *Dispatch* 6, no. 25 (June 19, 1995): 510.

5. White House, "Remarks of the President to the People of Detroit," p. 8. President Clinton went on to say, "I know that some in Russia still look at NATO through a Cold War prism and, therefore, look at our proposals to expand it in a negative light. But I ask them to look again. We are building a new NATO, much as we support the Russian people in building a new Russia. By reducing rivalry and fear, by strengthening peace and cooperation, NATO will promote greater stability in Europe and Russia will be among the beneficiaries. Indeed, Russia has the best chance in history to help build that peaceful and undivided Europe, and to be an equal and respected and successful partner in that sort of future." Ibid. Further, Senator Lugar states, "Eastern Europe is where two world wars, as well as the cold war, originated in this century. . . . The best way to ensure that the United States must never fight a war again over Eastern Europe is to anchor and integrate Eastern Europe into the West once and for all. We must do for Eastern Europe what we did together for Western Europe in the early post-war period—make it secure and integrate it into a broader trans-Atlantic community." Lugar, p. S6001.

6. Strobe Talbott, "Why NATO Should Grow," *New York Review of Books* 42, no. 13 (August 10, 1995): 29.

7. On Russia's military weakness, see Anatol Lieven, "Russia's Military Nadir," *National Interest,* no. 44 (Spring 1996): 24–33; Steven M. Meyer, "The Devolution of Russian Military Power," *Current History,* October 1995, pp. 322–28; and Dale Herspringer, "The Russian Military: Three Years On," *Communist and Post-Communist Studies* 28, no. 2 (June 1995): 163–82. Russian president Boris Yeltsin intends to cut military spending to 3 to 3.5 percent of gross national product by 2000 (military spending is currently 5 percent of Russia's GNP). To secure military compliance with that cutback, Yeltsin recently replaced both the defense minister and the chief of the general staff. Michael R. Gordon, "Yeltsin Dismisses Top Defense Aides for Resisting Cuts," *New York Times,* May 23, 1997, p. A1.

8. Thus, Talbott claims that "Russia has good reason to support NATO's expanding the zone of political stability into Central Europe. After all, twice in this century Russia, in the two world wars, has suffered greatly because of that region's instability." Talbott, "Why NATO Should Grow," p. 29. To the extent the alliance facilitates U.S. containment of Germany, Russia arguably may have an interest in NATO's continuation. Indeed, Washington made that argument to Moscow in 1990 during the negotiations on German reunification, and Soviet policymakers apparently accepted it. However, reassuring Russia by "keeping Germany down" justifies NATO's existence in its current form—it is not an argument for expanding the alliance.

9. For the general argument that managed nuclear proliferation enhances strategic stability, see Kenneth N. Waltz in *The Spread of Nuclear Weapons: A Debate,* ed. Kenneth N. Waltz and Scott D. Sagan (New York: W. W. Norton, 1995), pp. V264, S233; and Kenneth N. Waltz, "The Emerging Structure of the International System," *International Security* 18, no. 2 (Fall 1993): 44–79. For arguments that the United States would be better off strategically if it withdrew from its extended-deterrence commitments to Europe and East Asia and allowed Germany and Japan to provide their own nuclear deterrence, see Christopher Layne, "The Unipolar Illusion: Why New Great Powers

Will Rise," *International Security* 17, no. 3 (Spring 1993): 1–53; and Christopher Layne, "From Preponderance to Offshore Balancing: America's Future Grand Strategy," *International Security* 22, no. 1 (Summer 1997): 86–124. For applications of Waltz's argument to Europe, see John J. Mearsheimer, "Back to the Future: Instability in Europe after the Cold War," *International Security* 15, no. 1 (Summer 1990): 64–82; and John J. Mearsheimer, "The Case for Ukrainian Nuclear Weapons," *Foreign Affairs* 12, no. 3 (Summer 1993): 50–66.

10. White House, "Remarks by the President to the People of Detroit," pp. 6–7. That, of course, is the thrust of the administration's policy of engagement and enlargement. See *A National Security Strategy of Engagement and Enlargement* (Washington: White House, February 1995). As Anthony Lake, the policy's architect, explains, "A democratic Europe is more likely to remain at peace and to be a strong partner in diplomacy, security and trade. Democratic nations are less likely to go to war against one another and more likely to join us in promoting arms control, fighting proliferation, and combating the forces of destruction. Democracy undergirds the open markets that promote prosperity." Lake, p. 283.

11. Talbott, "Why NATO Should Grow," p. 28.

12. Indeed, Secretary of State Madeleine Albright and other U.S. policymakers have said as much. Steven Erlanger, "Albright Sees an Ambitious World Mission for U.S.," *New York Times*, June 6, 1997, p. A8.

13. See Steven Erlanger, "U.S. Pushes Bigger NATO Despite Qualms on Russia," *New York Times*, October 10, 1996, p. A4. As Michael Mandelbaum has pointed out, NATO's present expansion policy is illogical because the candidates for membership are not the states that, in fact, would be most threatened by a revival of Russian power. Indeed, Poland, Hungary, and the Czech Republic are not even geographically contiguous with Russia. As he says, "Expanding [NATO's] membership to Central Europe does not take it far enough east. The countries most vulnerable to an aggressive Russia are the now-independent former Soviet republics that are Russia's western neighbors: the three Baltic states—Estonia, Latvia, and Lithuania—as well as Ukraine and Belarus." Michael Mandelbaum, *The Dawn of Peace in Europe* (New York: Twentieth Century Fund Press, 1996), p. 55.

14. William E. Odom, "Yugoslavia: Quagmire or Strategic Challenge?" Hudson Briefing Paper no. 126, Hudson Institute, Indianapolis, November 1992, p. 2.

15. The contention that the United States is economically "interdependent" with Europe is greatly exaggerated. External trade actually accounts for a relatively small component of America's gross domestic product. Merchandise exports account for only about 6 percent of America's GDP (the average for industrialized states is about 24 percent). See Helen V. Milner and Robert O. Keohane, "Internationalization and Domestic Politics: An Introduction," in *Internationalization and Domestic Politics*, ed. Helen V. Milner and Robert O. Keohane (New York: Cambridge University Press, 1996), pp. 12–13. U.S. exports to Europe constitute about 1.5 percent of U.S. GDP. Moreover, although exports to Europe account for approximately 24 percent of total U.S. exports, Europe's share of total U.S. exports has declined steadily since 1960. See Gary Clyde Hufbauer, "An Overview," in *Europe 1992: An American Perspective*, ed. Gary Clyde Hufbauer (Washington: Brookings Institution, 1990), p. 26.

16. For example, the United States gained enormously—at Europe's expense—in relative economic power and financial strength while standing on the sidelines during most of World War I. See Kathleen Burk, *Britain, America, and the Sinews of War, 1924–1918* (Boston, London: G. Allen & Unwin, 1985).

17. See Frank Ninkovich, *Modernity and Power: A History of the Domino Theory in the Twentieth Century* (Chicago: University of Chicago Press, 1994), pp. 52–53.

18. Melvyn P. Leffler, *The Elusive Quest: America's Pursuit of European Stability and French Security, 1919–1933* (Chapel Hill: University of North Carolina Press, 1979); Michael J. Hogan, *Informal Entente: The Private Structure of Cooperation in Anglo-American Economic Diplomacy, 1918–1928* (Columbia: University of Missouri Press, 1977); and Akira Iryie, *The Globalizing of America, 1913–1945,* in Warren I. Cohen, ed., *Cambridge History of American Foreign Relations* (Cambridge: Cambridge University Press, 1993).

19. Patrick Morgan, *Deterrence: A Conceptual Analysis* (Beverly Hills: Sage, 1983), p. 86.

20. Thomas C. Schelling has explained why extended deterrence raises such important concerns about credibility.

> To *fight* abroad is a military act, but to *persuade* enemies or allies that would fight abroad, under circumstances of great cost and risk, requires more than a military capability. It requires projecting intentions. It requires *having* those intentions, even deliberately acquiring them, and communicating them persuasively to make other countries behave.

Thomas C. Schelling, *Arms and Influence* (New Haven, Conn.: Yale University Press, 1966), p. 36.

21. See Russell D. Buhite and William Christopher Hamel, "War for Peace: The Question of American Preventive War against the Soviet Union, 1945–1955," *Diplomatic History* 14, no. 3 (Summer 1990): 367–85.

22. Melvyn P. Leffler, *A Preponderance of Power* (Stanford, Calif.: Stanford University Press, 1992), p. 17.

23. On America's attempt to maintain political and military control over its allies, see David Calleo, *Beyond American Hegemony: The Future of the Western Alliance* (New York: Basic Books, 1987); David Calleo, *The Atlantic Fantasy: The U.S., NATO, and Europe* (Baltimore: Johns Hopkins University Press, 1970); Ronald Steel, *The End of Alliance: America and the Future of Europe* (New York: Viking, 1964); and Ronald Steel, *Pax Americana* (New York: Viking, 1967). On Washington's distrust of Bonn's *Ostpolitik,* see Henry A. Kissinger, *White House Years* (Boston: Little, Brown, 1979), pp. 405–12. On the relation between American hegemony and U.S. international economic policy, see David Calleo, *The Imperious Economy* (Cambridge, Mass.: Harvard University Press, 1962); and Diane B. Kunz, *Butter and Guns: America's Cold War Economic Diplomacy* (New York: Free Press, 1997).

5. NATO Enlargement and the Inevitable Costs of the American Empire

Benjamin Schwarz

That NATO enlargement entails potentially enormous problems of cost and credibility will not be news to most readers of this book. But the majority of detractors—and supporters—of NATO expansion characterize it as a radical departure for American policy; hence, most opponents of expansion argue that the problems can be obviated simply by opting not to embark on that bold new course. In fact, however, NATO enlargement is entirely consistent with the underlying aims of American global strategy for the last 45 years.

Since the end of the Cold war, foreign policy commentators and officials have been trying to refashion America's global role for the post–Cold War era. But for all their talk about the need for a bold new vision, they take as a given the status quo, what former national security adviser Anthony Lake called the "imperative of continued U.S. world leadership."[1]

The Clinton administration's Quadrennial Defense Review illustrates this stasis. Supposedly, the United States spread its security umbrella worldwide to contain the Soviet threat. When the USSR disintegrated, many observers hoped that the U.S. defense budget could be reduced substantially, freeing America's energies, attention, and financial resources to meet long-neglected domestic needs. But after months of analysis, the administration's defense planners have concluded that the essential features of America's "Cold War" security strategy—U.S. leadership of NATO and the East Asian alliances and U.S. guardianship of allies' access to Persian Gulf oil—must remain inviolate.

People who call for a more modest foreign and defense policy argue that U.S. strategy seems to be extravagance born of paranoia, or of the defense establishment's anxiety to protect its budget. But, in fact, given the way the makers of U.S. foreign policy have defined

71

American interests since the late 1940s, the specific plans are quite prudent. And that is the problem.

Those who assume that the Cold War's end allows for a sweeping reinvention of America's foreign policy misunderstand the real purpose of that policy. America's "Cold War" defense posture and its globe-girdling security commitments always had a more fundamental purpose than containing the Soviet Union. As fiercely anti-communist Republican Sen. Arthur Vandenberg of Michigan said in 1947, by "scaring hell out of the American people," the U.S.-Soviet rivalry helped secure domestic support for Washington's ambition to forge an American-led world order.[2]

The Roots of America's Global Empire

Thus, at the end of both world wars and the Cold War, U.S. administrations enunciated strikingly similar conceptions of a desirable world order. For nearly 80 years, from Woodrow Wilson's "liberal capitalist internationalism" to the Clinton administration's avowed "highest priority" in foreign policy—"to strengthen the core of major market democracies"—the United States has essentially pursued the same vision: an economic and political community of the advanced capitalist states. Former secretary of state James Baker calls the creation of a global liberal economic regime America's greatest postwar achievement.[3] Whatever factors ultimately determined that vision, it has proven enormously resilient; in fact, the foreign policy community regards the maintenance of the world order that vision has inspired not as an option, not even as the best option, but as an imperative.

The architects of U.S. foreign policy realize today, no less than in 1947, that the world order they describe will not operate by itself. What Secretary of State Dean Acheson called the hard task of building a successfully functioning system has required nothing less than that the United States suspend international politics, which is in fact the purpose of American "leadership."

In 1949 John Foster Dulles described one aspect of that "hard task," which continues to dictate America's world role. The future secretary of state explained that to build what he considered a successful international economic and political community, Germany's integration with Western Europe was essential. The obstacle, he said, was that the West Europeans were "afraid to bring that strong, powerful, highly concentrated group of people into unity with them."[4] Similarly, as Dulles, Acheson, and other policymakers understood, a strong Japan was at once essential for building a prosperous and stable international order and intolerable to its neighbors.

Since the 1940s, then, the fundamental challenge facing U.S. diplomacy has been to foster a liberal political and economic order within an international system characterized—as David Hume recognized 250 years ago when bemoaning the lack of economic cooperation among states—by "the narrow malignity and envy of nations, which can never bear to see their neighbors thriving, but continually repine at any new efforts towards industry made by any other nation."[5]

A draft of NSC 48, the National Security Council's 1949 blueprint of America's "Cold War" strategy, nicely summarized the promise of and the threat to the U.S. vision of world order. Starting with the premise that "the economic life of the modern world is geared to expansion," which required "the establishment of conditions favorable to the export of technology and capital and to a liberal trade policy throughout the world" (a statement that could have been written yesterday), NSC 48's authors went on to warn, "The complexity of international trade makes it well to bear in mind that such ephemeral matters as national pride and ambition can inhibit or prevent the necessary degree of international cooperation, or the development of a favorable atmosphere and conditions to promote economic expansion."[6] Forty-six years later, the United States remains committed to the one successful, albeit tenuous, means that it has found to check the forces inimical to the integrative and interdependent character of the world order it has pursued: the system of U.S.-led military alliances.

Containing Allies

Although the continuity and fundamental goals of America's global role are obscured by focusing on the containment of its Cold War enemy, they are illuminated by examining the containment of its allies. Dulles's answer to the obstacle that inhibited European cooperation—and hence that stymied the international order believed necessary for America's, and the world's, prosperity and security—was that the American-led NATO, not an exclusively European security system, had to guard the Continent:

> The Germans would be too strong for the comfort and safety
> of our European allies; . . . the Germans can be brought into
> the West *if* the West includes the United States. They cannot
> safely be brought into the West if the West does *not* include
> the United States. The Atlantic Pact will superimpose upon
> the Brussels Pact [the post–World War II alliance of West
> European powers] another western unity that is much bigger
> and stronger, so that it does not have to fear the inclusion
> of Germany.[7]

By providing for Germany's (and Japan's) security and by enmesh-
ing their military and foreign policies in alliances that it dominated,
the United States contained its erstwhile enemies, preventing its
"partners" from embarking upon independent foreign and military
policies. That stabilized relations among the states of Western Europe
and East Asia, for by controlling Germany and Japan, the United
States "reassured" their neighbors that those potentially powerful
allies would remain pacific. The leash of America's security leadership thereby reined in the dogs of war; NATO (and the U.S.-Japanese
alliance) by, in effect, banishing power politics protected the states
of Western Europe and East Asia from themselves.

Thus the real story of American foreign policy since the start of
the Cold War is, not the thwarting of and triumph over the Soviet
"threat," but the successful effort to impose an ambitious vision on
a recalcitrant world. Freed from the fears and competitions that had
for centuries kept them nervously looking over their shoulders, the
West Europeans (and East Asians) were able to cooperate politically
and economically. As Secretary of State Dean Rusk argued in 1967,
"The presence of our forces in Europe under NATO has also contributed to the development of intra-European cooperation. . . . But
without the visible assurance of a sizeable American contingent,
old frictions may revive, and Europe could become unstable once
more."[8] Recognizing that Europe (and East Asia) could not be left
to their own devices in the postwar world, Washington pursued not
balance and diversity (George Kennan's preferred European policy
aim) but hegemony.

What the foreign policy community now calls "the danger of
renationalization" has always presented two distinct threats to
Washington's vision of a global order. The first has been the "renationalization" of regional politics. According to American logic, if

Europe were no longer "reassured" (to use a term favored in policy circles) by the United States, it would, as Rusk feared, lapse into the same old bad habits that the U.S.-led NATO has prevented—nationalist rivalries and their concomitant, economic autarky. A Continent divided into small, constricted national markets would carry dire consequences for world economic efficiency and growth and would inevitably lead (according to U.S. policymakers' favorite—in fact, it often seems, only—foreign policy guide, "the lessons of the 1930s") to war among the Europeans.

The other, almost opposite, threat has been the "renationalization" of world politics, a threat that has been, ironically, accentuated by Washington's various efforts to promote regional economic integration in Western Europe and northeast Asia. That integration, Washington has feared, could lead to the economic and security nightmare of rising regional powerhouses' forming independent regional economic blocs, thus shattering international economic interdependence and engendering a dangerous multipolar world of autonomous great powers jockeying for power and advantage.

To realize and protect its global order, Washington has had to pursue two often conflicting goals, both of which have been served by double containment's strategy of restricting U.S. allies' military and political independence. The United States must nurture economically strong and politically cohesive "partners," while constraining them—which has amounted to the imperative, in historian Melvyn Leffler's words, that "neither an integrated Europe, nor a united Germany nor an independent Japan must be permitted to emerge as a third force."[9] Thus, for instance, as Henry Kissinger succinctly noted, U.S. policy toward Europe "has always been extremely ambivalent: it has urged European unity while recoiling before its consequences."[10]

So, while there is much talk about the need to articulate a new foreign policy, a new set of interests and priorities, and a new international role for the United States in this "new era," post–Cold War policymakers do not find any really new global role possible or desirable.[11] The significance of the "debate" concerning what America's "new" foreign policy should be is that there is, in fact, no argument. There is a remarkable consensus on the maintenance of America's fundamental world role and the instruments—such as America's leadership in its European and Asian alliances and its guardianship of its allies' access to Persian Gulf oil—that sustain it (and largely account for America's spending nearly as much on national security as all the other industrialized countries of the world combined). The mantra that America cannot be "the world's policeman" may be continually enunciated, but most members of the foreign policy community would agree with Kissinger's comment about the half-hearted search for a new "global doctrine" in the mid-1970s: "The phrase that the United States cannot be the world's policeman is one of those generalities that needs some refinement. The fact of the matter is that security and progress in most parts of the world depend on some American commitment."[12]

The Pentagon's January 1993 revised Defense Planning Guidance document, for instance, describes the creation of "a prosperous, largely democratic, market-oriented zone of peace and prosperity that encompasses more than two-thirds of the world's economy"— not the victory over Moscow—as "perhaps our nation's most significant achievement since the Second World War."[13] That document identified "reassurance," "stability," and "preclud[ing] destabilizing military rivalries" as the sine qua non of global capitalist order, making the maintenance of U.S. "leadership" of its Cold War–era alliances America's "most vital" foreign policy priority. Since that requires retaining "meaningful operational capabilities," the same purposes, means, and (somewhat reduced) costs that characterized America's Cold War global strategy define its post–Cold War strategy.

The same concerns that animated U.S. officials during the Cold War fed the Bush administration's assessments of a world without American dominance. For example, Deputy Assistant Secretary of Defense for Policy Alberto Coll painted a harrowing picture in 1992 of a world in which America's international "leadership" had declined. He foresaw "a Europe breaking its Atlantic ties and plunging into unabashed mercantilism, a Middle East heading toward catastrophe, a Pacific Rim riven by resurrected political jealousies and arms races."[14] To Bush's Pentagon, America's "leadership" in ameliorating others' security problems—manifest in its Cold War alliances—thus continued to be vital despite the Soviet Union's demise.

After all, the now infamous initial draft of the Pentagon's 1992 post–Cold War Defense Planning Guidance document, which gave the public an unprecedented glimpse into the thinking that informs Washington's security strategy, merely restated in somewhat undiplomatic language the logic behind America's Cold War allied containment strategy. The United States, it argued, must continue to dominate the international system by "discouraging the advanced industrialized nations from challenging our leadership or even aspiring to a larger global or regional role."[15] To accomplish that goal, Washington must keep the former great powers of Western Europe, as well as Japan, firmly within the constraints of the U.S.-created postwar system by providing what one high-ranking Bush Pentagon official termed "adult supervision." It must, that is, protect the interests of virtually all potential great powers for them so that they need not acquire the capabilities to protect themselves, that is, so that they need not act like great powers. The very existence of truly independent actors would be intolerable, for it would challenge American hegemony, the key to a prosperous and stable international order.[16]

That understanding of America's world role and the challenges to it largely determined the content of the Bush administration's post–Cold War foreign policy. The administration squelched Franco-German initiatives designed to create more independent European defense forces.[17] The president insisted, when faced with disquieting signs of the European allies' desire for greater autonomy, that NATO could not be replaced "even in the long run." And the administration maintained a single-minded focus in its negotiations with Moscow on two interrelated objectives central to America's traditional goal of allied containment: ensuring that NATO—the primary means of U.S. preponderance and, hence, allied containment—survived in a post–Cold War Europe and ensuring that a reunified Germany would be enfolded in the alliance.[18]

Finally, the U.S. intervention in the Persian Gulf cannot be separated from America's enduring imperative of allied containment, and the concomitant requirement that the United States retain the preeminent responsibility for addressing those problems that threaten not only American interests but those of allies or clients, or which could seriously unsettle international relations. Were Washington to relinquish its "adult supervision" responsibilities and allow its partners to protect their own interests in the gulf—that is, develop naval, air, and ground forces capable of global power projection—such actions would, according to this thinking, lead to the nightmare scenario described by Coll in which, when the United States no longer keeps Europe and Japan on a tight political and military leash, the multipolar and autarkic world of power politics returns.

NATO Expansion: The Extension of Empire

The Clinton administration's argument that NATO's security umbrella must be extended to Eastern and Central Europe, then, is merely an extension of the argument that America must lead in European security affairs. In the view of the proponents of U.S. "leadership," if a U.S.-dominated NATO demonstrates that it cannot or will not address the new security problems in post–Cold War Europe (for instance, the "spillover" of ethnic fighting, refugee flows into Western Europe, and the possibility that those developments could ignite ultranationalist feelings in, for example, Germany), the alliance will be rendered impotent. If the main instrument of U.S. leadership and "reassurance" in Western Europe is thus crippled, then, it is feared, the post–Cold War Continent will lapse into the same old bad habit that the alliance was supposed to suppress— power politics—shattering economic and political cooperation in Western Europe.

According to the logic of Washington's global strategy, while the end of the superpower rivalry has reduced U.S. security risks and commitments in some respects, it has in other ways expanded the frontiers of America's insecurity. During the Cold War, stability in Europe could be ensured by the Soviets and Americans smothering their respective clients. In fact, that superpower condominium, while crushing to the Europeans, was probably the best means of ensuring America's overriding economic and political interest in the stability of the Continent, as American statesmen have often privately acknowledged. With the disappearance of the Soviet Union, however, its former charges have become unrestrained and consequently free to make trouble for each other and for Western Europe. As Deputy Assistant Secretary of Defense Zalmay Khalilizad, one of the main advocates of NATO expansion in the Bush administration, asserted, "Western and East Central European stability are becoming increasingly intertwined. For example, turmoil in East Central Europe could drive hundreds of thousands of refugees into Western

Europe—challenging political stability in key countries, especially Germany."[19]

Even more important, American strategists fear that if the newly independent states of Eastern and Central Europe are not enmeshed in multilateral security arrangements under U.S. leadership, the region could once again become a political-military tinderbox, as it was in the 1920s and 1930s, with the Baltic countries, Russia, Ukraine, Poland, the Czech and Slovak Republics, Hungary, and Romania worrying about each other and about Germany. And, as it did in the past, such a tense situation, according to a sort of post–Cold War domino theory, would threaten the stability of the entire Continent. For instance, a nuclear-armed Ukraine could provoke the nuclearization of, say, Poland, which would pressure Germany into acquiring nuclear weapons, which would ignite latent suspicions between Germany and its neighbors to the west.

So, the argument goes, since European stability is, as Sen. Richard Lugar (R-Ind.) argues, now threatened by "those areas in the east and south where the seeds of future conflict in Europe lie," the U.S.-led NATO must now stabilize both halves of the Continent.[20] The important point is that the logic of American global strategy does indeed dictate that the U.S.-led NATO move eastward. While NATO expansion is often described as a "new bargain," it is in fact only the latest investment, made necessary by changing geopolitical circumstances, in a pursuit begun long ago. For instance, although the perceptive foreign policy commentator Walter Russell Mead opposes NATO expansion as costly and provocative, his 1993 analysis of the dangers of instability in Eastern Europe pointed directly to the need for that expansion. Starting from the assumption that an economically "closed Europe is a gun pointed at America's head," Mead drew a frightening scenario of America's abjuring leadership in Eastern Europe:

> In a well-intentioned effort to stabilize Eastern Europe, Western Europe, led by Germany, could establish something like Napoleon's projected Continental System. Eastern Europe and North Africa would supply the raw materials, certain agricultural products, and low-wage industrial labor. Western Europe would provide capital and host the high-value-added and high-tech industries. . . . A Europe of this kind would inevitably put most of its capital into its own backyard, and it would close its markets to competitors from the

rest of the world. It would produce its VCRs in Poland, not China; it would buy its wheat from Ukraine, rather than the Dakotas.[21]

Since Mead is unwilling to allow America's West European partners to assume responsibility for stabilizing their neighborhood, America's responsibilities must multiply. The U.S.-led expansion of NATO is nothing more than the logical outcome of "the imperative of American leadership."

NATO expansion, then, is the manifestation of the draft Pentagon Planning Guidance's recommendation that Washington must "discourag[e] the advanced industrialized nations from challenging our leadership or even aspiring to a larger global or regional role." As Lugar explained, "American leadership on European security issues is essential. . . . If NATO does not deal with the security problems of its members, they will ultimately seek to deal with these problems either in new alliances or on their own."[22] Thus, "leadership" means not only that the United States must dominate wealthy and technologically sophisticated states in Western Europe and East Asia—our "allies"—but also that it must deal with a nuisance such as Slobodan Milosevic, so that potential great powers need not acquire the means to deal with such problems themselves.

Unlimited Obligations

The logic that dictates NATO expansion perfectly illustrates "imperial overstretch"—it ensures an exhausting proliferation of "security" commitments. After all, if the United States, through NATO, must guard against internal instability and interstate security competition not only in Western Europe but in areas that could infect Western Europe, where will NATO's responsibilities end? It is often argued, for instance, that the alliance must expand eastward because turmoil in East Central Europe could provoke massive flows of immigrants into Western Europe, threatening political stability there. Of course, turmoil in, for example, Russia or North Africa could have the same effect, as could instability in Central Asia (which could spread to Turkey, spurring a new wave of immigration to the West).

Must not NATO, then, expand even farther eastward and southward than is currently proposed? After all, Lugar argues that the U.S.-led NATO must go "out of area" because "there can be no lasting security at the center without security at the periphery."[23] Of course, if that logic is followed, the ostensible threats to American security will be nearly endless.

If America is to forestall the risks and costs that inevitably accompany expanding frontiers of insecurity, a new debate must begin. Rather than focus on the narrow issue of NATO expansion, that debate must assess the underlying assumptions that impel current policy; the debate must stop revolving around how the *pax Americana* should be administered and instead examine whether there should be a *pax Americana* at all.

Once that debate is under way, the public will realize that it has been funding an arcane endeavor. Sen. John McCain (R-Ariz.) anticipated the public's likely response to policymakers who urge NATO expansion five years ago. Upon hearing NATO secretary general Manfred Woerner's explanation that the United States should remain militarily present in Europe to stabilize security relations among the *Western* Europeans and thereby prevent "renationalized" European defense structures, McCain replied that "Americans would never accept that the maintenance of stability between Western Europeans could be a plausible rationale for continuing to deploy troops in Europe. Most Americans believe [the Europeans] can do this on their own."[24] The public is also unlikely to continue to support an imperial project that is not only costly and risky but eternal and open-ended.

Arguing for the maintenance of Washington's Cold War alliances, a high-ranking Pentagon official asked, "If we pull out, who knows what nervousness will result?"[25] The problem, of course, is that we can never know, so, according to that logic, we must always stay. And as the drive for NATO enlargement demonstrates, America's security obligations will be destined to expand, never contract.

Notes

1. Anthony Lake, "From Containment to Enlargement," Speech to the Johns Hopkins University School of Advanced International Studies, September 21, 1993, White House, Office of the Press Secretary, p. 1.

2. Quoted in William Appleman Williams, *The Tragedy of American Diplomacy* (New York: Dell, 1972), p. 240.

3. "Liberal capitalist internationalism" was coined by Gordon Levin, *Woodrow Wilson and World Politics: America's Response to War and Revolution* (New York: Oxford University Press, 1968), p. 3. On Clinton's priorities, see Lake. It was not until after World War II, however, that a domestic political and economic alignment formed—

thanks partially to the invocation of the "Soviet menace"—that permitted policymakers to reify that vision.

4. John Foster Dulles, "Statement before the Foreign Relations Committee of the United States Senate," U.S. Congress, Senate Foreign Relations Committee, *Hearings on the North Atlantic Pact*, 81st Cong., 1st sess., May 4, 1949, Committee Print, p. 346.

5. Quoted in Christopher Lasch, *The True and Only Heaven* (New York: W. W. Norton, 1991), p. 121.

6. Quoted in Bruce Cumings, *Origins of the Korean War* (Princeton, N.J.: Princeton University Press, 1990), vol. 2, p. 173.

7. Dulles. Emphasis in original.

8. Memorandum from Dean Rusk to Sen. Mike Mansfield, April 21, 1967, Lyndon B. Johnson Library, National Security File, Box 51, "The Trilateral Negotiations and NATO," Tabs 43–63, Memo 153b.

9. Melvyn Leffler, *A Preponderance of Power: National Security, the Truman Administration and the Cold War* (Stanford, Calif.: Stanford University Press, 1992), p. 17.

10. Henry Kissinger "What Kind of Atlantic Partnership?" *Atlantic Community Quarterly* 7, no. 1 (Summer 1973): 30.

11. In fact, much of the talk amounts to asserting the need to come up with new rationales to justify both specific existing commitments, such as NATO, and, generally, what is called "continuous and active international engagement," which amounts to a continuation of America's existing global role.

12. Kissinger, p. 30.

13. Dick Cheney, *The Regional Defense Strategy* (Washington: U.S. Department of Defense, January 1993). Similarly, National Security Advisor Anthony Lake explains in the Clinton administration's major foreign policy statement that "the highest priority in a strategy of enlargement must be to strengthen the core of major market democracies, the bonds among them and their sense of common interest." Lake, p. 60.

14. Alberto Coll, "Power, Principles and a Cooperative World Order," *Washington Quarterly* 16, no. 1 (Winter 1993): 8.

15. Patrick Tyler, "Excerpts from the Pentagon Plan: 'Prevent the Emergence of a New Rival,'" *New York Times*, March 8, 1992.

16. Since American prosperity hinges "on achieving and maintaining an open market for international trade and investment," former assistant secretary of the treasury and senior adviser to the National Security Council C. Fred Bergsten argues, "the containment of the risk of conflict among the economic superpowers" must be "a primary purpose of U.S. foreign policy." Bergsten maintains that, to accomplish that goal, Washington must continue to dominate the international system; it must "minimize inducements for the new economic superpowers to militarize" by "retain[-ing] an adequate military presence overseas and an adequate overall security capability to deter the new superpowers from taking action that could set the stage for frictions." C. Fred Bergsten, "The Primacy of Economics," *Foreign Policy* 87 (Summer 1992): 8–11.

17. It was rather hypocritical of the Bush administration to "welcome" European leadership in handling the crisis in the former Yugoslavia while it squelched the proposed Western European Union rapid-reaction force and the "Eurocorps," which would have made that leadership possible.

18. In 1990 Deputy Assistant Secretary of State for European Affairs James Dobbins applied the reasoning of the Defense Planning Guidance document to America's post–Cold War role in Europe. Testifying before Congress, Dobbins argued that "we

need NATO now for the same reasons NATO was created." The danger, he asserted, was that, without the "glue" of American leadership in NATO, West Europeans would revert to their bad ways, that is "renationalize" their armed forces, play the "old geopolitical game," and "shift alliances." As articulated by Dobbins, U.S. policy in Europe rests on the assumption that, acting alone, the West Europeans—particularly with Germany united—could not preserve order among themselves. Without the United States' acting as stabilizer, European squabbling would "undermine political and economic structures like the EC" and even lead to a resumption of "historic conflicts" like the two world wars. U.S. Congress, Commission on Security and Cooperation in Europe, *Implementation of the Helsinki Accords*, 101st Cong., 2d sess., April 3, 1990, pp. 8, 18; and U.S. Congress, Senate Foreign Relations Committee, *The Future of NATO*, 101st Cong., 2d sess., February 9, 1990 (Washington: Government Printing Office, 1994), p. 19.

19. Zalmay Khalilizad, "Extending the Western Alliance into East Central Europe," RAND Issue Paper, Santa Monica, Calif., May 1993.

20. Richard Lugar, "NATO: Out of Area or Out of Business: A Call for U.S. Leadership to Revive and Redefine the Alliance," Remarks Delivered to the Open Forum of the U.S. State Department, August 2, 1993, p. 3.

21. Walter Russell Mead, "An American Grand Strategy: The Quest for Order in a Disordered World," *World Policy Journal* 10 (Spring 1993): 21.

22. Lugar, p. 4.

23. Ibid., p. 1.

24. Quoted in David G. Haglund, "Can North America Remain 'Committed' to Europe? Should It?" *Cambridge Review of International Affairs* (Winter 1992–93): 18.

25. Quoted in Morton Kondracke, "The Aspin Papers," *New Republic*, April 27, 1992, p. 12.

6. New Problems for NATO: Potential Conflicts Involving the Czech Republic, Hungary, and Poland

Barbara Conry

Advocates of NATO enlargement portray it as a low-cost, low-risk initiative that will reduce tensions and promote stability throughout Europe. In fact, extending NATO to the east could embroil the alliance in an array of conflicts.

Expanding NATO to include the Czech Republic, Hungary, and Poland would create potentially dangerous security obligations for the alliance—especially for the United States—in Central and Eastern Europe. All three countries are situated in a tumultuous region, which would force the alliance as a whole to operate in a more hazardous security environment. The Czech Republic poses some risk primarily because of its proximity to potential turmoil. Hungary and Poland, however, face particular security challenges that pose significant risks for NATO.

Many advocates of enlargement contend that merely extending NATO membership to those three countries amounts to a solution to their potential problems. As Secretary of State Madeleine Albright has stated, "A larger NATO will make us safer by expanding the area in Europe where wars simply do not happen."[1] Such optimism ignores the depth of the problems in Central and Eastern Europe.

People who argue that extending NATO to countries that are potential parties to conflicts will neutralize the risk of outright hostilities often cite two examples to support their optimism: France and Germany and Greece and Turkey. Neither example, however, constitutes a precedent that indicates that expanding NATO into Central and Eastern Europe today will prevent conflicts in the area tomorrow.

It is true that France and Germany were bitter adversaries in two world wars but are today partners and allies. The two countries' membership in NATO may have been one factor—though probably not the primary factor—in that transformation. Clinton administration officials have repeatedly cited the Franco-German rapprochement as evidence that NATO membership can settle even the most antagonistic of rivalries and have called upon the alliance to work the same miracle in Central and Eastern Europe. President Clinton has predicted, "Now, enlargement can do for Europe's East what it did for the West."[2]

The conflicts in Central and Eastern Europe today bear little resemblance to the French-German relationship after World War II. Germany was a defeated power, divided into four zones of occupation, one of which was under French control. The occupation, in which the United States, Great Britain, and the Soviet Union also participated, placed severe restrictions on Germany's political and economic systems and eliminated German war-making capabilities. It would have been virtually impossible for Germany to commit any act of aggression or otherwise harass the French. Moreover, France and Germany (the Federal Republic of Germany) were both concerned about the growing Soviet threat. Once Germany joined NATO, common alliance membership may have helped to cement the bond between Paris and Bonn, but it most likely was not the decisive factor in their relationship.[3]

Proponents of enlargement have also pointed to Greece and Turkey as an example of NATO's peacemaking abilities. "Greece and Turkey can't fight. They're in the same club," Craig R. Whitney of the *New York Times* has said, voicing a sentiment that is common among advocates of NATO enlargement. The acrimonious relationship between Ankara and Athens throughout the Cold War and the deterioration in their relationship in recent years, however, are a weak testimonial to NATO's ability to stifle conflicts.

The fact that Greece and Turkey did not engage in a full-scale war during the Cold War appears to have had more to do with the Soviet threat than with NATO membership. When Turkey initially planned to intervene in Cyprus in 1964, in response to Greek Cypriot attacks on the Turkish Cypriot community, Turkish prime minster Ismet Inönü did not call off the operation because of NATO solidarity. He called it off in response to a warning from President Lyndon Johnson that NATO allies "have not had a chance to consider whether they have an obligation to protect Turkey against the Soviet

Union if Turkey takes a step which results in Soviet intervention without the full consent and understanding of its NATO allies."[4] In other words, Inönü feared being abandoned to a hostile Soviet Union.

By 1974, when Ankara went ahead with a landing on Cyprus, Turkey had developed better relations with the Soviet Union. Though Washington remained firmly opposed to the intervention, the threat to abandon Turkey to Soviet aggression had much less impact. Ankara proceeded with the intervention without regard for alliance solidarity.

Since the Soviet threat has ended, Ankara and Athens have moved ever closer to war. Despite their continued membership in NATO and a special mediation effort led by Richard Holbrooke, mastermind of the Dayton agreement that at least temporarily halted the civil war in Bosnia, Greek-Turkish relations have deteriorated to the point of nearly constant crisis.

Greek and Turkish military aircraft have had frequent confrontations over the Aegean, and those confrontations grow more dangerous as tensions between the two countries rise. In early 1996 they nearly went to war over a 10-acre Aegean islet inhabited only by goats. In October 1997 confrontations between Greek and Turkish warplanes over Cyprus prompted the Greek military to put its forces on full alert, as Greece's defense minister denounced Turkey's "cold war."[5] A major crisis—which many observers fear could be the spark that ignites armed hostilities between the two NATO members—is likely in spring or summer 1998, when the Greek Cypriot government is supposed to deploy Russian S-300 surface-to-air missiles. Ankara has repeatedly threatened to hit the missiles if they are deployed, an action that Athens has said it would regard as an act of war that would merit a response in kind.[6]

The Greek-Turkish animosity has deep historical roots and is continually stoked by actual or perceived slights, periodic crises, and other manifestations of ongoing tension. Each side points to very old grievances to justify its hostility toward the other, and any provocation has the potential to erupt into war. Unfortunately, that pattern is replicated throughout Central and Eastern Europe. Hungary, a first-round NATO invitee, has similarly long-standing problems with several of its neighbors, and prospective second- or third-round NATO candidates have even more age-old grievances. Decades of

87

NATO membership have not had a measurable impact on the Greek-Turkish relationship, and it would be foolhardy to assume that the alliance would have a greater pacifying effect on incoming NATO members.

The Hungarian Diaspora

Hungary, or, more precisely, the large Hungarian diaspora, could prove to be a major headache for NATO. Some 5 million Hungarians—one-third of all ethnic Hungarians—live outside Hungary's borders. The largest concentrations of Hungarians outside Hungary are in Romania, Slovakia, and the Vojvodina region of Serbia. Smaller groups are in Ukraine, Croatia, Slovenia, and Austria.

Budapest regards Hungarians beyond the country's borders as part of the "Hungarian cultural nation," for which it has a special responsibility. According to a 1994 government policy declaration,

> The Government attaches special importance to securing *and effectively protecting* the rights of national and ethnic minorities. True to its political and moral obligations, as spelled out in the [Hungarian] Constitution, the government intends to pay close attention to the situation of ethnic Hungarians beyond Hungary's borders. It considers assertion of their rights as a special area in Hungary's foreign policy, an important aspect of policy as such and an expression of solidarity. . . .
> . . . *Using all means at its disposal*—and acting in harmony with relevant international practice—the government will strive to bring about for the Hungarian minorities beyond Hungary's borders economic, political, and legal conditions and a societal atmosphere in which they can lead a meaningful life in the country of which they are citizens.[7]

The presence and treatment of ethnic minorities are an inherently explosive issue. As former U.S. arms control negotiator Jonathan Dean has explained,

> Actual or alleged mistreatment of minorities divided among borders has been a frequent cause of interstate wars. The typical dynamic in the latter case has been complaints by an ethnic minority that there is organized discrimination against it: decrees or laws preventing use of the minority language; the absence of schools to teach its children; suppression of publications in the minority language; or lack of equitable

political representation. The complaints often lead to local unrest and then, in response, repression by the national government, followed by friction between that government and the neighboring government dominated by the same ethnic group as the original minority next door. The first government claims outside interference in its sovereign affairs, diplomatic relations are broken, and economic sanctions applied. Armed clashes between border police or military units may take place—and sometimes culminate in war.[8]

The Hungarian case is exceptionally tense because of Budapest's clear determination to monitor and take action against any mistreatment of Hungarians outside Hungary's borders. As City University of New York expert Henry R. Huttenbach has noted, "A fear of destabilization on account of a crisis related to the several Hungarian minorities scattered in half a dozen adjacent states is never far from the surface."[9]

Moreover, Hungarian officials have already hinted that they may take advantage of NATO membership to strengthen Hungary's role as protector of Hungarians outside its borders. As one Hungarian defense ministry official has noted, "NATO membership does not mean giving up our national interests. On the contrary, it means an opportunity to assert national interests."[10] Deputy State Secretary Istvan Gyarmati of the Ministry of Defense was even more direct, commenting that "opportunities to enforce our interest will increase" and calling for an "international response . . . if Hungarian minorities in neighboring countries are threatened."[11]

Hungary and Romania

There are approximately 1.6 million to 2 million Hungarians in Romania.[12] Most of them live in Transylvania, a region that has gone from the control of Budapest to that of Bucharest and back on several occasions and has been the subject of competing territorial claims by both governments. The Hungarians in Romania were at times the target of discrimination and persecution during the Cold War. More often, however, both the Hungarian minority and the Romanian majority suffered from the economic privations and dearth of civil liberties that marked the rule of communist dictator Nicolae Ceausescu.[13]

Soon after Ceausescu's downfall in 1989, the provisional government known as the National Salvation Front promised to protect the rights of the Hungarian minority, including Hungarian-language education and local autonomy. Despite the NSF's promises, ethnic tension surged. When a new constitution was adopted in 1991, it proclaimed Romania a national state and named Romanian as the country's only official language.[14] The constitution also banned political parties founded on ethnic, religious, or language criteria and declared unconstitutional any attempts at territorial separation.[15]

Despite the questionable status and treatment of the Hungarian minority in Romania, Budapest and Bucharest concluded a bilateral Treaty of Understanding, Cooperation, and Good Neighborliness in September 1996 to normalize relations between the two countries. They agreed to refrain from using force or the threat of force to resolve disputes, respect each other's territorial integrity, work toward developing bilateral trade agreements, support one another's quest for NATO and European Union membership, and protect the rights of national minorities in accordance with the Council of Europe Framework Convention and other international documents.[16] The prospects for Hungarian-Romanian relations further improved with the November 1996 election of a new Romanian government, which has moved to bolster the rights of the Hungarian minority.[17]

At the moment, then, the "Hungarian problem" in Romania appears relatively quiet, but it is not yet clear whether the tranquility will endure. There is widespread suspicion that the Hungarian-Romanian rapprochement was driven primarily by the two countries' desires to impress NATO and therefore may be more cosmetic than substantive. U.S. officials have boasted, "The mere prospect of having NATO membership has unleashed a powerful impetus for peace," in Europe, citing Hungary and Romania as one example.[18] If that is true, Romania's exclusion from the first round of NATO enlargement may create a backlash. Such a backlash—a setback in Romanian political liberalization or the election of a more nationalist government—could easily cause a resurgence in tensions between Hungary and Romania.

Hungary and Slovakia

Prospects for the 700,000 Hungarians living in Slovakia are considerably gloomier than those for their counterparts in Romania. Immediately after the 1993 "Velvet Divorce" that separated Czechoslovakia into the Czech Republic and Slovakia, Slovakia was considered one of the more advanced new democracies and a front-runner for NATO membership. Since 1995, however, Slovakia's domestic political and economic situation has deteriorated considerably.[19]

Relations between Hungary and Slovakia have been precarious since the end of the Cold War. The two countries signed the Treaty on Good Neighborliness and Friendly Cooperation in 1996, but that agreement has failed to resolve the issue of the treatment of Hungarians in Slovakia. In fact, tensions appear to be rising. As Hungarian prime minister Gyula Horn noted in late 1997, "Slovakia's ethnic Hungarian minority has over the past few years found it increasingly difficult to enforce its rights. There are plenty of sources of tension between the two countries."[20]

Several public statements by Slovak officials suggest that Horn's assessment of the situation of Hungarians in Slovakia is accurate. At a September 1997 mass rally in Bratislava, Prime Minister Vladimir Meciar declared that the Hungarian minority interfered with the "territorial integrity of Slovakia."[21] He went on to publicly announce that he had proposed an exchange of ethnic Hungarians in Slovakia and ethnic Slovaks in Hungary at an August meeting with Horn. Because of the historical sensitivities surrounding the issue of population exchange between the two countries—a result of post–World War II population exchanges that are still a source of controversy and bitterness—Meciar's announcement appeared intentionally provocative. Hungarian opposition parties criticized Horn for failing to reveal the proposal when it was initially offered, and the tensions prompted the cancellation of a meeting between the Hungarian and Slovak foreign ministers.[22]

Jan Slota, chairman of the Slovak National Party, a minority party in the coalition government, also stirred Slovak-Hungarian animosity in September 1997, when he made a number of derogatory public statements about Hungarians during the visit of French National Front leader Jean-Marie Le Pen. Slota called Hungarians "a disaster for Europe." He also alluded to "barbarian tribes" of Huns, whom he accused of murdering children and pregnant women, that had settled in the middle of Europe.[23] Slota's statements enraged Hungarians in Slovakia, who have announced their intention to file a defamation suit against him.[24]

Statements such as those by Meciar and Slota are disturbing in themselves and raise serious questions about the fate of Hungarians in Slovakia. The statements are even more troubling against the backdrop of Slovakia's faltering progress toward democracy. Meciar is an authoritarian who has been intent on concentrating power in his own hands since Slovakia emerged as an independent nation in January 1993; he has even attempted to alter the constitution to increase his own authority.[25] He has also steadily cut back on civil liberties in Slovakia, including the rights of national minorities and of the press—which has earned him a place on the American Committee for the Protection of Journalists' list of the 10 worst enemies of the press.[26]

Meciar is also engaged in open political warfare with Slovak president Michal Kovac that is so intense that the EU has called it a threat to democracy. Kovac, once a Meciar ally, backed the removal of Meciar's government in 1994 amid charges of corruption. Since that time, enmity between the two men has paralyzed Slovakian politics and taken some bizarre and sensational twists. Kovac's son was kidnapped two years ago, for example, and some evidence suggested Slovak Intelligence Service complicity. Meciar has refused to order a thorough investigation of the incident.[27]

The parliament, too, has uncertain democratic credentials. In October 1997 Slovakia's Constitutional Court ordered parliament to reinstate a member the court said had been unlawfully stripped of his mandate. The parliament refused, prompting the EU to issue a statement condemning the parliament's defiance of the court order. The EU declared that the parliament had called into question Slovakia's commitment to democracy: "By ignoring the ruling of the Constitutional Court and thereby its authority, the Slovak parliament is creating doubts about its desire to consolidate democracy and the rule of law in Slovakia."[28]

Slovakia's drift away from democracy does not bode well for its Hungarian minority. The status and treatment of Hungarians are "closely connected with democratization, modernization, and with the emergence of a civil society," as Ivan Gyurcsik of the Bratislava Coexistence Movement and James Satterwhite of Bluffton College have noted.[29] Moreover, there could be significant implications for NATO if the situation in Slovakia continues to deteriorate. As one analysis from Dallas-based Strategic Forecasting has pointed out,

> The decision to admit Hungary into NATO because it has managed to put ethnic strife behind it misreads the situation.

Ethnic strife is solved not when Hungary decides to solve it, but when Slovakia and Romania decide to solve it. Admitting Hungary to NATO without Slovakia, it follows, does not guarantee ethnic peace, but actually increases the possibilities for tension.

The question for NATO planners: having admitted Hungary into NATO while leaving Slovakia out, how does NATO plan to stop Meciar from creating ethnic tension within NATO's structure?[30]

Hungary and Vojvodina

Vojvodina, a semiautonomous region in Serbia that borders Hungary proper, is even more worrisome than Slovakia. Unlike Romania and Slovakia—which managed to conclude at least token accords with Hungary, even if they later prove worthless—Serbia has not reached any agreement with Hungary that addresses the legal status and treatment of Serbia's Hungarian population. According to pre-1991 census figures, 350,000 to 400,000 Hungarians live in the Vojvodina and account for approximately 20 percent of the area's population. The rest of the population is predominantly Serbian, and there are small numbers of members of other ethnic groups throughout the area. Until the surge in Serbian nationalism in the late 1980s, the groups in Vojvodina coexisted reasonably well.

Since the late 1980s, however, tensions have risen dramatically. In 1989 Belgrade formally rescinded Vojvodina's autonomy. Dislocation associated with the breakup of the former Yugoslavia unsettled the region's social and ethnic balance, particularly after Serbian president Slobodan Milosevic encouraged hundreds of thousands of Bosnian Serb refugees to settle in Vojvodina. At the same time, non-Serbs in Vojvodina fell victim to the harassment that has come to be associated with virulent Serb nationalism throughout the former Yugoslavia. Human Rights Watch/Helsinki has documented numerous cases in which armed civilians and paramilitary groups inflicted beatings, expulsions, and other forms of harassment on minorities in Vojvodina.[31]

In recent years the abridgement of the social, cultural, and political rights of Hungarians has overtaken outright violence as the primary means of oppression. Serbian authorities have discouraged Hungarian-language schools in the area and have manipulated the political process to curtail Hungarian influence. In July 1996 elections, for example, Serbia redrew electoral districts to break apart Hungarian groups and link the fragmented Hungarian population with Serb-dominated areas to ensure Serb majorities.[32] The London-based Balkan Peace Team also reported that Serbian authorities played loud "Turbo-folk"—folk-influenced pop music associated with extreme Serb nationalism—at some polling stations.[33]

The Milosevic government has committed, or at least consented to, the persecution of Hungarians in Vojvodina, but a change in regime would not necessarily improve the situation. The emergence of a leader even more hostile to Serbia's Hungarians is a distinct possibility. Serbian Radical Party head Vojislav Seselj—an extreme nationalist who is a vocal proponent of a "Greater Serbia" and has a record of anti-minority rhetoric and actions—finished first in October 1997 runoff elections for the presidency of Serbia. Though the election results were invalidated because of low voter turnout, they clearly indicated considerable radical nationalist sentiment within the Serbian population.[34] Milosevic, unfortunately, may be the lesser of two evils for Hungarians in Vojvodina.

Poland and Belarus

Admitting Poland into NATO also poses serious risks to the alliance. Poland shares a border with Belarus, a Soviet successor state that "bears an eerie and increasing resemblance to Soviet society," according to the Belarus Helsinki Human Rights Watch Committee.[35] Reagan administration National Security Council official Roger Fontaine has called its political and economic prospects "among the bleakest in the region."[36] Belarus is the basket case of the former Soviet Union and the situation is worsening daily.[37]

Belarus took a stunning turn for the worse when former collective farm manager and Supreme Soviet deputy Alexander Lukashenko won the presidency in July 1994. He reversed nearly all democratic and free-market reforms in Belarus, engaging in a massive power grab that culminated in a fraudulent November 1996 referendum to adopt a new constitution. That constitution extends his term to 2001, puts key judgeships and political offices under his control, and grants him lifelong immunity from prosecution.

Claiming a mandate for virtually unlimited power, Lukashenko forcibly dissolved the elected parliament and installed a puppet assembly.[38] He has also cracked down on the media, closing down opposition newspapers, harassing foreign journalists, and otherwise consolidating a government monopoly on the press. Intimidation of nongovernmental organizations, often through questionable tax audits, exorbitant rents on state-owned buildings, and fines, is routine.[39] In addition, virtually all demonstrations, protests, and other expressions of political opposition are banned. Peaceful mass assemblies have been violently broken up by police.[40]

Such oppression has fostered an extremely tense and volatile political atmosphere. The tensions are aggravated by extreme economic instability. As one *New York Times* editorial noted, "Belarus's economy . . . is so feeble it makes Russia's economy look robust."[41] Fewer than 10 percent of Belarus's state-owned enterprises were ever privatized, and Lukashenko has renationalized most of those that were.[42] He has also restored many other elements of Soviet-style economic policies, such as subsidies and price controls. Belarus's inflation was more than 152 percent in 1996, prompting the International Monetary Fund to suspend loans to Minsk.[43] Needless to say, Belarus is in dire economic straits.

Ted Galen Carpenter and Andrew Stone have called Belarus "a political and economic volcano waiting to erupt."[44] Indeed, the combination of severe political oppression and a wrecked economy is a recipe for chaos, which could have a detrimental impact on the entire region. As the *Washington Post* has noted, Belarus "represents a potential source of instability to [its] neighbors, all of whom are seeking to find their way in a drastically changed new world: Russia, Ukraine, Poland, Lithuania, Latvia."[45] If Belarus disintegrated into civil war, there would be potentially serious implications for Poland. At the very least, refugee flows across the Polish-Belarusan border could have a destabilizing effect. More worrisome, armed conflict in Belarus could spill over into violent incidents in Poland.

That is clearly an alarming scenario that is made all the more troubling by Minsk's and Moscow's recent moves toward greater political and military integration. On April 2, 1997, Russia and Belarus signed a treaty to bring their people, economies, and militaries closer together. According to *Washington Times* reporter Martin Sieff, hard-liners in Russia touted the accord as a "first step toward reintegrating the former Soviet Union and setting up a bloc to counter the eastward expansion of NATO."[46]

The Belarusan-Russian agreement has a host of provisions dealing with various economic, monetary, and other issues outside the political and military realms. It is unclear how many of those provisions are taken seriously, particularly by Moscow. The political and, especially, the security components of the federation are apparently considered a basis for a more comprehensive program of military integration, however.[47] If that is true, any upheaval along the Belarusan-Polish border is potentially a NATO-Russian issue. It is difficult to overestimate the implications of such a development.

NATO Enlargement and Future Bosnias

Joshua Muravchik of the American Enterprise Institute has said, "The expansion of NATO can be counted on to forestall other Bosnias to come."[48] In light of the potential risks that Hungary and Poland bring to NATO, however, the opposite may be true. The only difference is that future Bosnias could explode within, rather than outside, NATO. That would guarantee nearly automatic NATO (and U.S.) entanglement in the conflict, regardless of risks—which would probably be considerable—or U.S. interests at stake—which would probably be negligible. As Jeremy Stone of the Federation of American Scientists has observed, "The country that took three years to get involved in Bosnia is mortgaging its future decision on involvement on a wide scale front in Eastern Europe without any consideration of the contingencies involved."[49]

The United States would probably have few, if any, security interests at stake in any conflict involving prospective NATO members. As Alan Tonelson of the U.S. Business and Industrial Council Educational Foundation has observed,

> NATO expansion rests on the notion that Eastern and Central
> Europe are of great significance to the security of the United
> States. In fact, that is not the case. Central and Eastern Europe
> have always played a secondary role in American foreign
> policy, and with good reason.[50]

If any of the numerous latent conflicts throughout Central and Eastern Europe were to erupt into outright hostilities involving the Czech Republic, Hungary, or Poland, the alliance—the United States, in particular—would face a serious dilemma. There would be significant pressure to uphold the article 5 guarantee to regard an attack on one member as an attack on all and therefore to respond by any means necessary—which could trigger a major conventional military operation or even a nuclear exchange.

But risking nuclear war (or even large-scale conventional war) for the sole purpose of fulfilling a treaty guarantee, absent any threat to vital national security interests, is both irrational and unconscionable. History has demonstrated on numerous occasions that great powers are not in the habit of committing suicide for the sake of minor allies. Should one of the Central or East European flashpoints explode, it is not at all clear that the United States would be able to fulfill its article 5 obligation without incurring unacceptable costs and risks. The credibility of the guarantee, then, is in question, which makes a challenge all the more likely.

Notes

1. Quoted in Thomas W. Lippman, "Senators Lukewarm on NATO Expansion," *Washington Post*, October 8, 1997, p. A24.

2. Bill Clinton, letter to Sen. Kay Bailey Hutchison, September 10, 1997, p. 3.

3. For a more thorough discussion of the evolution in French-German relations after World War II, see A. W. DePorte, *Europe between the Superpowers: The Enduring Balance* (New Haven, Conn.: Yale University Press, 1986).

4. Quoted in Andrew Mango, *Turkey: The Challenge of a New Role* (Washington: Center for Strategic and International Studies, 1994), p. 16.

5. Kerin Hope, "Greece Denounces Turkey's 'Cold War,'" *Financial Times*, October 17, 1997, p. 2; and "Turkey Retaliates for Greek Actions," *Washington Times* October 15, 1997, p. A16.

6. Paul Anast, "Greek Military Forces on Full Alert," *Washington Times*, October 13, 1997, p. A13.

7. Quoted in György Réti, "Hungary and the Problem of National Minorities," *Hungarian Quarterly* 36 (Autumn 1995): 70. Emphasis added.

8. Jonathan Dean, *Ending Europe's Wars* (New York: Twentieth Century Fund Press, 1994), p. 115.

9. Henry R. Huttenbach, "Divided Nations and the Politics of Borders," *Nationalities* 24 (September 1996): 369.

10. Quoted in Ted Galen Carpenter and Pavel Kislitsyn, "NATO Expansion Flashpoint no. 2: The Border between Hungary and Serbia," Cato Institute Foreign Policy Briefing no. 45, November 24, 1997.

11. Interview with Istvan Gyarmati, *Budapest Magyar Narancs*, November 7, 1996, Foreign Broadcast Information Service at http://wnc.fedworld.gov, November 7, 1996.

12. This range is fairly widely accepted. See, for example, Helsinki Watch Committee, *Struggling for Ethnic Identity: Hungarians in Post-Ceausescu Romania* (New York: Human Rights Watch, 1993), p. 6.

13. Andrew Bell, "The Hungarians in Romania since 1989," *Nationalities Papers* 24 (September 1996): 496–98.

14. Réti, p. 74.

15. Bell, p. 500.

16. Embassy of Romania, "Romania, Hungary Sign Historic Pact," Press release, Washington, September 17, 1996.

17. Michael Dobbs, "Lobbying for NATO Spot Intensifies," *Washington Post,* April 27, 1997, p. A26.

18. William Cohen, Remarks to the American Legion convention, Orlando, Florida, September 4, 1997, at http://hps.usis.fi/current/nato27.htm.

19. For an account of how Slovakia's faltering on the path toward liberal democracy affected its candidacy for NATO, see Jeffrey Simon, "Slovakia and NATO: The Madrid Summit and After," National Defense University Institute for National Strategic Studies Strategic Forum no. 111, April 1997.

20. Quoted in "Hungarian Prime Minister Criticizes Slovakia on Treatment of Hungarian Minority," Central Europe Online, September 23, 1997, at www.centraleurope.com/ceo/news.

21. Quoted in Jane Perlez, "Slovak Leader Fans a Region's Old Ethnic Flames," *New York Times,* October 12, 1997, p. A3.

22. "Hungarian Prime Minister Criticizes Slovakia on Treatment of Hungarian Minority."

23. Quoted in "Slovak Hungarians to Bring Suit against SNS Boss," Central Europe Online at http://www.russiatoday.com, September 24, 1997.

24. Ibid.

25. Simon, p. 2.

26. "Demonstrators Call for Freedom of Speech in Bratislava," Central Europe Online, October 16, 1997, at http://www.centraleurope.com.

27. Vincent Boland, "Meciar Undermines Slovak Ambitions," *Financial Times,* May 28, 1997, p. 2.

28. "EU Says Slovakia's Commitment to Democracy Is in Doubt," Central Europe Online at http://www.russiatoday.com, October 7, 1997.

29. Ivan Gyurcsik and James Satterwhite, "The Hungarians in Slovakia," *Nationalities Papers* 24 (September 1996): 521.

30. Strategic Forecasting, *Eastern Europe,* September 8, 1997, at http://www.stratfor.com./gintel/region/eeurope.

31. Human Rights Watch/Helsinki, "Human Rights Abuses of Non-Serbs in Kosovo, Sandzak, and Vojvodina," May 1994.

32. Balkan Peace Team Election Report, November 10, 1996, at http://www.igc.apc.org.

33. Ibid.

34. Lee Hockstader, "Radical Rival of Milosevic Nearly Wins Serbian Vote," *Washington Post,* October 7, 1997, p. A11.

35. Belarus Helsinki Human Rights Watch Committee, "Crushing Civil Society," *Belarus Chronicle,* August 18, 1997, at http://chronicle.home.by/resources.

36. Roger Fontaine, "Red Phoenix Rising? Dealing with the Communist Resurgence in Eastern Europe," Cato Institute Policy Analysis no. 255, June 13, 1996, p. 16.

37. For a comprehensive overview of economic and political instability in Belarus and the potential implications for NATO, see Ted Galen Carpenter and Andrew Stone, "NATO Expansion Flashpoint No. 1: The Border between Poland and Belarus," Cato Institute Foreign Policy Briefing no. 44, September 16, 1997.

38. Ibid., p. 4.

39. Judith Miller, "Soros Closes Foundation in Belarus," *New York Times,* September 4, 1997, p. A6.

40. Belarus Helsinki Human Rights Watch Committee, p. 1.

41. "Russia and Its Tyrant Neighbor," *New York Times,* editorial, August 25, 1997, p. A26.

42. Fontaine, p. 15.

43. Michael S. Lelyveld, "Weakening of Belarus Pact Tied to Talks," *Journal of Commerce,* April 7, 1997, p. 1A.

44. Carpenter and Stone, p. 1.

45. "Bad Neighbor," *Washington Post,* editorial, October 20, 1997, p. A22.

46. Martin Sieff, "Russia, Belarus Get Closer," *Washington Times,* April 3, 1997, p. A1.

47. Martin Sieff, "Treaty of Union with Belarus Could Divide Russia," *Washington Times,* April 3, 1997, p. A1.

48. Joshua Muravchik, "Why Die for Danzig?" *Commentary,* October 1997, p. 43.

49. Jeremy Stone, "A Dozen Key Questions Concerning NATO Expansion," *F.A.S. Public Interest Report* 50, no. 2 (March–April 1997): 4.

50. Quoted in "NATO Enlargement Risks Explored at Seminar," *Cato Policy Report* 19, no. 5 (September–October 1997): 9.

PART II

NATO ENLARGEMENT AND RUSSIA'S
RELATIONS WITH THE WEST

7. The Perils of Victory

Susan Eisenhower

Western news reports that followed the Paris summit in May 1997 proclaimed that the Founding Act on Mutual Relations, Cooperation and Security between NATO and the Russian Federation codified the end of the Cold War and represented a Russian blessing of NATO enlargement. That is a regrettable misinterpretation. In fact, Russia signed the document under duress, even if Russian president Boris Yeltsin attempted to put a good face on the event.

The agreement of then-president Mikhail Gorbachev of the USSR to the unification of Germany in 1990 had a significant impact on his eventual downfall. So the question of what effect the Founding Act will have on Yeltsin's political future, or on that of democratic forces in Russia, remains. The West has tended to take Russia's resiliency for granted, but one more serious blow from the outside to another reform-minded leader could have catastrophic consequences for Russia—at the very time that expansion itself will have drawn a new dividing line in Europe, thwarted the arms reduction process, and undermined NATO, the very alliance that has kept the peace. Those developments, alone or together, could have serious implications for U.S. national security.

Gorbachev's Lesson

NATO enlargement appears to the Russians to be motivated by a Western desire to exploit Russia's weakness under the guise of lofty intentions. To understand the feelings that NATO expansion has evoked in Russia, it is useful to consider what happened in the recent past and what is at the root of Russia's deep sense of humiliation. It is not simply loss of empire that has affected Russian attitudes; it is the way Russia has been treated by the international community, most notably by the world's so-called indispensable nation, the United States.

103

Since the collapse of the Soviet Union, U.S.-Russian relations have gone from positive, indeed downright euphoric, to tense and full of suspicion. The greatest loss has been the friendship of Russian democrats and reformers. The same people who once led the charge against the Communists no longer see the people of the United States as their spiritual soul mates but as a group intent on winning no matter what is at stake.

The erosion of trust between Russia and the West started in 1990. With the collapse of the communist East European regimes, Germany sought a fast-track road to reunification. After U.S. support was secured, it became clear that the greatest obstacle to that historic change was the Soviet Union, which feared that a strong Germany could be aligned against Moscow. After the Berlin Wall went down, however, Gorbachev and, apparently, the Politburo understood the inevitability of German reunification. The question before them was simply how it could be accomplished to provide the best outcome for the security of the Soviet Union and Europe as a whole.

In his memoirs, Anatoly Dobrynin, long-time Soviet ambassador to the United States, described the debate at the time of the Malta summit (December 2–3, 1989):

> Gorbachev responded in a general way that our policy was founded on our adherence to an all-European process and the evolutionary construction of a "common European home" in which the security interests of all countries should be respected. But he did not specify how it could or should be done, although he had with him a confidential memorandum by the Foreign Ministry outlining a concrete policy: German unification should be the final product of a gradual transformation of the climate in Europe during which both NATO and the Warsaw Pact would shift their orientation from military to political and be dissolved by mutual agreement.[1]

According to Dobrynin, that position had the broad support of the Politburo and the USSR's European and German experts. However, with the "turbulent events at home . . . there was a metamorphosis in Gorbachev's behavior . . . he began to handle all the negotiations on Germany virtually by himself or in tandem with [Foreign Minister Eduard] Shevardnadze sweeping aside our professional diplomats and scarcely informing the Politburo, who still favored an evolutionary process."[2]

Despite the views of the Soviet political and military establishments, the Soviet president was drawn into the fast-track timetable, though he favored a neutral, unified Germany. The issue was taken up at a high-level meeting in Moscow in early February 1990. A *Washington Post* article at the time told the story:

> [U.S. secretary of state James A.] Baker had tried to persuade Gorbachev at that February meeting that a neutral Germany could be more of a military threat, possibly pursuing nuclear weapons on its own, than if it were secured within the alliance. Only NATO, Baker said, could make sure that Germany would move "not one inch" eastward. Would Gorbachev rather have a powerful, prosperous Germany that was neutral and arming itself, Baker asked, or one snugly within the confines of the Western alliance? . . .
>
> [West German foreign minister Hans Dietrich] Genscher wanted to offer the Soviets a package including financial aid and food supplies, a commitment that Soviet contracts with East Germany would be honored, a revamped NATO, troop cuts, and a device to include Moscow in the new Europe. That was the CSCE, the Conference on Security and Cooperation in Europe, a 35-nation group that had no previous security role. At first the United States resisted, worrying that the CSCE would be unwieldy and threaten NATO's role as the foundation of Western security. Then, in March, Genscher and Baker met in Washington and agreed that CSCE could prove to Gorbachev that the West did not seek to take advantage of the repeated blows Soviet defense strategy suffered in the Eastern European revolutions of 1989.[3]

Genscher also promoted a "no expansion of NATO" concept, an idea that Baker, too, had advanced. It was at the February meeting that the key words were spoken, words that are still a source of debate. If a unified Germany was anchored in NATO, Secretary Baker said to Gorbachev, "NATO's jurisdiction or forces would not move eastward."[4]

Apparently, Gorbachev was receptive to that assurance and emphasized that "any extension of the zone of NATO is unacceptable." "I agree," Baker said.[5]

Heartened by Baker's comments, several months later, in May, Gorbachev gave up his idea that Germany must remain neutral or, at least, a member of both blocs. He conceded (without consulting his advisers) that the German people should be able to choose the alliance they wished to join, though it was clear that other "sweeteners" needed to be offered so that the Soviet president could sell the proposal at home.[6]

Opposition to Gorbachev's leadership, however, was growing. Many critics regarded his cavalier approach, his shoot-from-the-hip style, as disastrous, especially in the context of such major geostrategic questions. Many skeptics complained that Gorbachev was under the spell of his Western counterparts, who had used a potent mixture of intensified meetings, head-of-state diplomacy, and personal flattery, not to mention the lure of substantial financial aid to the economically beleaguered Soviet Union, to advance their interests.

On July 6, 1990, during a break in one of the sessions of the 28th Communist Party Congress, Gorbachev received word that the NATO summit under way in London appeared to be moving in what he considered "the right direction." Germany had agreed to accept troop limits after unification, and President George Bush envisioned a revamped NATO that "would provide a political rationale for keeping American forces in Europe but at a greatly reduced level."[7]

Gorbachev uttered his optimistic assessment amid damning criticism of his policies. Many speakers at the congress had risen that day to denounce the president for making too many concessions to the West. Under his leadership, they said, the country had "frittered away the Soviet Union's post-war gains." Others accused Gorbachev of "losing Eastern Europe."[8] The political and military establishments openly complained that they had had enough.

Under Gorbachev's leadership, the Soviet Union had taken an unprecedented number of unilateral steps favorable to the West. Gorbachev had argued that such measures would enable the country to emerge from its international isolation with greater prestige and economic opportunity. He had departed from the traditional Soviet script, dropping the usual intransigence and initiating a broad set of measures including opening military facilities to the West for inspection, separating the Strategic Defense Initiative from the negotiations on the Intermediate Nuclear Forces agreement, reducing Soviet conventional forces in Europe to levels set forth in the Conventional Forces in Europe Treaty, and adopting a hands-off policy with respect to the collapse of communism in Eastern Europe.

But by far the most important concession, because of its geopolitical and strategic ramifications, was the Soviet agreement to allow

Germany to reunify, along with Soviet acquiescence to Germany's membership in NATO. The Soviet Union expected the international community to validate that step by recognizing the USSR's rightful place within what Gorbachev called the "common European home." Moscow also expected to become the United States' "strategic partner," in the words of George Bush.

On September 12, 1990, the victors of World War II gathered in Moscow to sign away the Four Powers Act, thus making Germany whole and united.[9] Shevardnadze seized the sentiment of the moment, declaring that there were no winners or losers and that "the German question" would never again threaten European peace.[10]

Shevardnadze was overly optimistic in his assessment. There would indeed be some losers among Soviet progressive pro-Western policymakers: a strong conservative backlash forced Shevardnadze himself to resign as foreign minister three months later. The ministries' continued disillusionment with Gorbachev and his policies fostered a coup attempt less than a year later. Though the coup failed, Gorbachev's presidency (and the Soviet Union itself) was dissolved in December 1991.

Erosion of Trust

The dismantlement of the Soviet Union brought the promise of more reform and closer ties with the West. The new Russian president, Boris Yeltsin, continued to pursue conciliatory policies as part of a liberal-progressive agenda to bring Russia into line with other countries within the "civilized world." Hundreds of thousands of troops were withdrawn from foreign and former Soviet soil without bloodshed, and Russia refrained from attempting to militarize the Commonwealth of Independent States. Moscow also supported United Nations' sanctions against Iraq, accepted the American formula for nuclear force ceilings in the START II treaty, joined the U.S.-sponsored Missile Technology Control Regime, and worked with NATO peacekeepers in Bosnia.

Despite such gestures of Russian goodwill, however, the United States had declared itself the victor in the Cold War, brandishing all the rhetoric of a power that had successfully prevailed on the battlefield. That posture mystified most Russians, who had seen the historic events in entirely different terms. The Cold War had ended, it was true, but not in defeat. The average Russian believed that the

Cold War was over because his country had voluntarily changed its behavior. The end of the Cold War was, in the Russian view, a victory over senseless military expenditures and unnatural domination. As Dobrynin pointed out, "It is important to remember that the Soviet totalitarian regime was defeated inside our own country by our own efforts . . . so there are no victors and vanquished now."[11]

When the "evil empire" collapsed, Russian reformers were convinced that a new era had arrived in U.S.-Russian relations. They were to be sadly disappointed. Instead of entering into a "strategic partnership" with the United States, Russia was deemed "no longer a superpower" and relegated to the role of junior partner, or not acknowledged at all.

Moscow, once an integral part of the Middle East peace process, was excluded from meaningful participation in the Oslo peace accord. The United States made no effort to forewarn the Russians about the 1993 air strikes against its old ally, Libya. Pro-Western Foreign Minister Andrei Kozyrev was also marginalized throughout the Bosnian crisis and the subsequent Dayton accords. Kozyrev recalled that the United States failed more than once to alert Moscow to NATO air strikes in Bosnia:

> In February 1994, when the situation around Sarajevo once again became critical, NATO decided to bomb the positions held by the Bosnian Serbs. Russia was presented with that decision as a *fait accompli,* despite its active participation in the efforts to settle the Bosnian crisis and its traditional influence on one of the conflicting parties.[12]

Washington's dismissive attitude toward Russian foreign policy interests was made worse by other insults. Economic aid to Russia was paltry, and that which was allocated was handled badly and arrogantly. Western talk of free markets and free trade was not matched by Western policies. Almost immediately after the Soviet collapse, the United States and Western Europe set about imposing economic quotas on such things as aluminum, uranium, and aerospace and rocket-launch technology—in which Russia actually had a hope of competing internationally. Yeltsin himself worried aloud that Russia would be unable to sell its technology and know-how abroad because of protectionist walls, prompting one Russian diplomat to observe, "The Americans are frankly driving us into a corner."[13]

Throughout 1993–94, a terribly difficult period of hyperinflation in Russia, Moscow received virtually no recognition for the economic sacrifices it made to cooperate with Western policies. It is estimated, for instance, that Russian observance of the sanctions against former allies Iraq, Libya, and the former Yugoslavia cost Russia more than $30 billion in lost contracts, losses it could ill afford.[14]

Russia, an emerging democracy, did not get much credit for the peaceful (and, in Russia, politically risky) withdrawal of all of its troops from Germany and Eastern Europe, or for the removal of troops it had stationed in the Baltic region.

To the Clinton administration's credit, the construction of a NATO program called Partnership for Peace offered a temporary response to the positive moves that were occurring in Russia and within Eastern and Central Europe. PFP provided the best of all worlds: military cooperation between NATO and former Soviet bloc countries, as well as a host of other exchanges. Says John Hopkins University professor Michael Mandelbaum,

> The Partnership for Peace [made] possible military coopera-
> tion between NATO and non-members of the Alliance with-
> out alienating or excluding any of them, including Russia.
> [but] ... suddenly, without warning, on a trip to Central
> Europe at the beginning of 1994, President Clinton
> announced that the question was no longer whether, but
> rather when, NATO would expand to Central Europe.[15]

When it was clear, in 1995, that in the Clinton administration's view "the train had left the station" and NATO expansion would proceed over the objections of Russia, Alexei Pushkov, a prominent progressive Russian analyst, concluded, "Russia attempted to become part of Europe by renouncing military instruments of conducting policy and sharply curtailing its geographic presence on the continent (and also by granting independence to the Baltic countries, Belorussia, Ukraine, Moldova etc.). . . . This unprecedented attempt to become an integral part of Europe through geopolitical self-disarmament is ending in failure."[16]

Western miscalculation or overriding hubris—perhaps fueled by political expediency in American domestic politics—eventually brought Russia a sense of shame and defeat. More important, it robbed the Russians of any future incentive to cooperate with the

West or trust Western initiatives. Instead, it suggested that power, in the view of the West, is the only international currency of value.

Russian Reaction to the Founding Act

Against that background, it is not surprising that NATO expansion has been viewed with great hostility across the entire Russian political spectrum. At the heart of the issue is the sense that Russia was misled at the time of German reunification by assurances Russian officials say they received during the Two-plus-Four negotiations. Gorbachev's declaration that "any extension of the zone of NATO is unacceptable," and Baker's reply, "I agree," have become one of the most controversial exchanges. Secretary Baker admits that he said those words, and also that he never retracted that statement.

But Baker insists that the United States soon walked away from that formulation, finding wording that would enable NATO to gain access to the eastern part of a united Germany. However, it should be noted here that before German reunification there was no discussion of expanding NATO into Central or Eastern Europe. Such an idea would have seemed far-fetched at the time. The Warsaw Pact was still in place, and even Czech president Václav Havel reportedly commented that one "could not imagine a united Germany in NATO."[17] However, Baker claims now that it had always been his intention to keep the door open for Central and Eastern European countries to join NATO.[18]

Whatever the original intentions, the Two-plus-Four negotiations, which decided the fate of Germany, excluded the stationing of foreign troops and nuclear weapons carriers on the lands of the former German Democratic Republic—an assurance, in the Russian view, that NATO would not extend beyond the borders of Germany. While the agreement said nothing one way or the other about Central and Eastern Europe, its spirit excluded future expansion, especially in light of the fact that Gorbachev and Shevardnadze were repeatedly told that the West would do nothing to undermine the security of the Soviet Union.[19]

While it is tempting to nitpick the details of what was or was not said, or put in writing, the truth of the matter is that reunification was possible only because of the trust that had developed between Gorbachev and Bush. If Gorbachev had imagined there was a possibility that NATO would eventually move beyond Germany, he never would have agreed to the treaty.

Sergei Karaganov, a politically progressive Russian foreign policy analyst, has described the atmosphere surrounding the negotiations on German reunification and how the prevailing mood lulled the Soviets into complacency:

> In 1990 we were told quite clearly by the West that dissolution of the Warsaw Pact and German unification would not lead to NATO expansion. We did not demand written guarantees because in the euphoric atmosphere of that time it would have seemed almost indecent, like two girlfriends giving written promises not to seduce each other's husbands.[20]

Anatoli Adamishin, out-going Russian ambassador to Great Britain, concurs:

> After the fall of the Berlin Wall there was a feeling of euphoria in the Russian establishment. This was a new era in East-West relations and just as everything Western had been bad, overnight everything Western became good. So when we were told, during the German-reunification process, that NATO would not expand, we believed it. . . . It was extremely important for Western countries, and first of all for the United States and Germany, that the process should go smoothly, and that we should withdraw from Eastern Europe and dismantle the Warsaw Pact. So we were given repeated assurances that NATO would not expand an inch eastwards.[21]

Jack Matlock, former U.S. ambassador to the Soviet Union, who was part of those negotiations, confirms that Gorbachev had reason to believe that he had been given a "blanket promise that NATO would not expand."[22] In testimony before Congress, Matlock countered those who claimed that, even if we did give Gorbachev assurances, they were meaningless now that both Gorbachev and the Soviet Union were gone. "President Gorbachev agreed that a unified Germany could stay in NATO with the understanding that NATO would not be moved further eastward," Matlock stated. "Gorbachev, of course, is no longer in power and the Soviet Union no longer exists. Furthermore the commitment was a political one, not formalized in a treaty. Nevertheless, we expect Russia to implement agreements made by its predecessor and it does not question its obligation to do so."[23]

The Russians have also indicated that they received assurances from the former members of the Warsaw Pact at the time of that alliance's collapse in July of 1991. "At the time of the disbandment of the Warsaw Pact," says retired general and popular presidential hopeful Alexander Lebed, "almost all of the leaders of the socialist bloc countries of Europe gave sworn assurances to their people and the Soviet leaders that they were not leaving the Warsaw Pact in order to join NATO." On whether or not those assurances should still count, Lebed added, "These promises were given on behalf of the states concerned and they do not change with the arrival to power of a new party."[24]

By the time Madeleine Albright became secretary of state and declared that NATO would accelerate its process for bringing in new members, it was clear how much the trust Gorbachev had had in Bush was worth. The Russians now deeply regret that they did not get the specifics in writing. "The current collision between Russia and NATO could have been avoided," Pushkov has said, "if the Soviet leadership had at the time taken the Americans and Germans at their word and codified their intentions not to expand NATO. The Russian leadership is now saying that they will not be fooled again."[25]

Reliving 1990

"They will not be fooled again." Those words were written in March 1997, two months before the details of the Founding Act were revealed. Pushkov and many others were shocked to discover that yet again their president had caved in to Western pressure. This time, even though each country knew the history of the agreement of 1990 and the potential for disaster inherent in ambiguous security agreements, Russia was still unable to negotiate a legally binding treaty with the United States and NATO. Not only did Moscow fail to get ironclad assurances in a number of key areas; there are, apparently, glaring differences in interpretation between the signing parties—specifically, on how much influence Russia will have on NATO actions and on the fate of former Soviet republics' candidacies for NATO membership.

The most important Russian political figures have roundly denounced the agreement in statements reminiscent of those made by the members of the Communist Party who attacked Gorbachev at the fateful 28th Party Congress.

On May 29, 1997, Radio Rossii Network reported that Gennady Zyuganov, leader of the Communist Party and former presidential candidate, called the signing of the Founding Act a "complete and unconditional surrender." Another member of his party, Oleg Shebkaryov, responded along the same lines: "Russians cannot understand why our unilateral decision to abandon the Warsaw Pact should be answered by the aggressive advance of Western armies."[26]

Lebed, who was once rather nonchalant about expansion, blasted both the West and his government for the sell-out in Paris.

> The Russian-NATO deal [gives] rise to political, legal, and military risks. Russia received from the Soviet Union the role of guarantor of the post-war order in Europe. Any partial revision of that order places in doubt all the other components, including the inviolability of national boundaries and the rights to displaced cultural artifacts. . . .
>
> The deal on expanding NATO to the east is the second Yalta, but a Yalta without Russia. It sets the spheres of influence of the victors of the Cold War—NATO and the United States. Russia is a defeated party signing its act of capitulation. . . . Even after the agreement, national-patriotic forces should deny completely the legitimacy of the expansion of NATO.
>
> Russia has every reason to do so, since the Soviet Union's agreement to German unification and entry into NATO was qualified by clear undertakings not to expand the bloc's activities to the east. Soviet leaders received assurances to that effect from the leaders of the United States, Britain, France and the former West Germany.[27]

Leading democratic reformers were no more charitable in their assessment. Grigory Yavlinsky, leader of the moderate Yabloko Party, said, "It is absurd to believe in NATO's peaceful intentions . . . many centuries of history teach us that Russia's weakness should not be exploited."[28] And further: "NATO's eastward expansion is evidence that the West does not believe in Russia's becoming a democracy in the near future."[29]

Optimism in Western circles regarding the alleged indifference of the Russian people to enlargement is also wishful thinking. Far from being without opinion on the subject, the Russian people have consistently polled "unreservedly negative," according to the Russian Center for Public Opinion. In a poll conducted by *Moskovskiye*

Novosti before the signing, 51 percent of Russians viewed NATO expansion as a "serious threat," and only 14 percent disagreed with a negative premise.

"Indeed," commented *U.S. News & World Report*, which published the polling figures, "many Russians express amazement that the alliance is expanding at a time when Russia is so weak that the only security threat it poses is to itself, and see a conspiracy of carefully orchestrated humiliations by the West beginning with the collapse of the Soviet Union."[30]

Pavel Felgenhauer, a military analyst for the progressive newspaper *Segodnva*, sees the Russian attitude hardening on the issue. "Public opinion is changing," he warns. "NATO expansion will turn a whole generation of Russians anti-American."[31]

Fallout

Russia has already begun to step up its efforts to find new allies. Lebed, among many others, is a proponent of widening those contacts.

> If NATO expansion contributes to Russia's exclusion from Europe (and that is what we are talking about) and if Russia is turned into a buffer between the Atlantic world and Asia, then Russia should side with China and India. These two powerful Asian powers are becoming Russia's main strategic partners.[32]

Pressure on Russia's near abroad is also likely to increase, as efforts to deepen integration of CIS countries may be pursued. Recent integration with Belarus is an example. If a second round of candidates is invited to become NATO members, that pressure will likely increase, and many people worry that that move will dramatically increase tensions between possible future NATO members, such as the Baltic republics or Ukraine, and their Russian minorities.

Another logical result of the expansion of NATO, and one that could have far-reaching implications for the United States, is that the arms reduction process will grind to a halt. The Duma, despite Yeltsin's undertakings at the Helsinki summit, has already delayed the ratification of the START II treaty. Many analysts are concerned that with the new configuration of forces on the NATO side, the Russian military, now in steep decline, will be forced to rely increasingly on nuclear weapons to counter those forces.

John Steinbruner of the Brookings Institution recently wrote,

> The NATO question is not about immediate political senti-
> ment or feelings of cultural affinity. Ultimately it is about
> the disposition of military forces and in particular about the
> management of nuclear weapons . . . the operational safety
> of nuclear weapons is a much more urgent matter than exten-
> sion of traditional deterrent protection. Constructive engage-
> ment with Russia is a far more urgent matter than expansion
> of NATO, even for the favored few of Central Europe.[33]

But perhaps the most worrying result of NATO expansion is the
role it has had and will continue to have in undermining Yeltsin
and other democrats in Russia. As was the case in 1990 and 1991, the
country's economic condition is in sharp decline, morale in critical
institutions of power is low, and the Russian president has delivered
more for the West than he has for his own country.

Karaganov and other progressives have already attacked the Yeltsin government for mismanagement of the NATO expansion issue.
Like Gorbachev in 1990, Yeltsin and his foreign minister acted essentially alone in reaching their decision, against the better judgment
of their political and military establishments. Also like Gorbachev
in 1990, Yeltsin relied on his "friend Bill" more than many thought
appropriate or even wise. Karaganov said,

> We should have been tougher. . . . We committed a serious
> error because we have been much too timid for several
> years. . . . As long as three years ago we should have said
> no [to NATO expansion], and under no circumstances what-
> soever! Now we have said no but did not exactly come right
> out and say so. We should have been more direct about the
> issue. Then enlargement would probably never have taken
> place at all.[34]

Lebed, disgusted with Yeltsin's performance, made the same observation on the eve of the signing ceremony in Paris.

> One can only ask whether Yeltsin has a clear understanding
> of what he is signing. Does he realize what is going on?
> Either he is deliberately deceived or he is himself deceiving
> Russian society. However you look at it, the presidential
> formulation "not against NATO but with NATO" boils down
> to "under NATO."

115

So what could the president have done? The only honorable alternative, since we could not get a binding declaration, would have been not to sign any agreement at all. We should leave the question of our attitude to NATO expansion hanging, making of it an example of unilateral Western action.[35]

Yeltsin and his foreign minister, Yevgeny Primakov, did not take that course. They understood that they had few, if any, options in their negotiations with NATO. And once the Clinton administration said that NATO would expand, with or without them, they chose to get what they could, which in the Russian view was virtually nothing.

A Dangerous Game

NATO enlargement has done a great deal of damage to U.S.-Russian relations. Given the rhetoric of late, constructive engagement will be increasingly hard to maintain, especially if the domestic situation in Russia does not improve.

Yeltsin, whose hold on power is increasingly tenuous, knows that he took a huge gamble, just as Gorbachev and Shevardnadze did in 1990. His predecessors lost. What will happen now if Yeltsin loses, especially as there are no other popular reformers waiting in the wings? In light of Yeltsin's poor health, a continuing power struggle among his lieutenants, Russia's faltering economy, growing hardship for the population, and the deterioration of Russian institutions, the discrediting of the democratic forces and a severe domestic crisis are distinct possibilities. The West has now given some future Russian demagogue the platform he may need to evoke the image of an external enemy, a threat that could unify the country as it did during other periods of national crisis. Adamishin underscored that recently when he said, "[Russia] is going through a painful transition. . . . The worst feeling in the world is the sensation of being powerless, of being unable to do anything to alter events. I don't understand why the West is playing such a dangerous game, edging Russia into this position."[36]

After World War II we understood just what those dangers were. In considering the "German question," we knew that we could not afford to make the same mistakes an earlier generation had made after the end of the Great War. The post–World War II leadership advanced some principles that became the basis of our successful handling of a defeated, and later an allied, Germany.

During the Two-plus-Four negotiations, George Bush explained to Mikhail Gorbachev why the United States supported Germany's bid for reunification and why the Soviet president had to see that step in the framework of enlightened self-interest.

> It appears to me that our approach to Germany, i.e. seeing it as a close friend, is more pragmatic and constructive, although I will say frankly that many people in the West do not share this view. Like you, there are some West Europeans who neither trust the Federal Republic of Germany nor Germans in general. However, all of us in the West agree that the main danger lies in excluding Germany from the community of democratic nations and forcing some special status and humiliating conditions upon the Germans. Such a development could lead precisely to a revival of the German militarism and revanchism you fear.[37]

If you were to replace "Germany" with "Russia," that statement would have the same force and would express a vision, a grasp of history, that is badly needed today. The West would do well to employ similar principles in its relations with Russia. To fail to do so runs the risk of spending much of the 21st century relearning the lessons of the 20th.

Notes

1. Anatoly Dobrynin, *In Confidence: Moscow's Ambassador to America's Six Cold War Presidents (1962–1986)* (New York: Times Books, 1995), p. 630.

2. Ibid.

3. Marc Fisher and David Hoffman, "Behind German Unity Pact: Personal Diplomacy from Maine to Moscow," *Washington Post*, July 22, 1990.

4. Quoted in Philip Zelikow and Condelezza Rice, *Germany Unified and Europe Transformed: A Study in Statecraft* (Cambridge, Mass.: Harvard University Press, 1995), p. 180.

5. Michael Gordon, "The Anatomy of a Misunderstanding," *New York Times*, May 25, 1997, p. 3.

6. Advocates of NATO expansion use the principle that Germany should be able to choose, which is outlined in the Helsinki Final Act, to promote NATO expansion.

7. Quoted in Jim Hoagland, "Bush's NATO Success Advances U.S. Goals," *Washington Post*, July 7, 1990, p. A18.

8. For an account of that, see Michael Dobbs, "Gorbachev Hails Summit," *Washington Post*, July 7, 1990.

9. The declaration became effective on October 3, 1990.

10. Quoted in Zelikow and Rice, p. 363.

11. Dobrynin, p. 639.

12. Andrei Kozyrev, "Partnership or Cold Peace?" *Foreign Policy* 99 (Summer 1995): 10.

13. Quoted in Susan Eisenhower, "A Troubling Chill in U.S.-Russian Relations: How U.S. Actions Look in the Russian Press," *Perspectives on Change*, July 16, 1993, p. 14. Russia was never without options and eventually entered, for example, into a deal to sell nuclear reactors to Iran, much to the displeasure of the United States. Since the expansion of NATO has been declared a "done deal," Russia has pursued other such deals.

14. Hannes Adomeit, "Russia as a 'Great Power,'" *International Affairs* 71, no. 1 (January 1995): 57.

15. Michael Mandelbaum, "NATO: A Bridge to the Nineteenth Century," Occasional Paper, Center for Political and Strategic Studies, Washington, June 1997.

16. Alexei Pushkov, "NATO Begins Its 'Eastern Set,'" *Moskovskiye Novosti*, no. 67 (October 1–8, 1995): 11; also in *Current Digest of Russian Press*, no. 47 (November 3, 1995): 9.

17. Zelikow and Rice, p. 177.

18. Baker further stated that when the United States insisted that the territory of the German Democratic Republic be fully included in NATO, "[we were] thereby moving NATO eastward." Gordon, p. 3. The assumption that including that territory constituted a precedent for "NATO expansion" was not clarified with the Soviets, which it should have been. The whole notion of "precedent" is a Western legal notion that was not particularly well understood in Soviet culture. Furthermore, the Two-plus-Four treaty itself opened the way for possible deployments within GDR territory, but such a decision would be made by Germany in a "reasonable and responsible way, taking into account the security interests of each contracting party" (Zelikow and Rice, p. 362), of which the Soviet Union was one, and Russia its successor.

19. Many statements to that effect were made on the record, for example, this one made to Gorbachev: "'I want you to know,' Baker reassured me, 'that neither the President nor I intend to derive any advantage from the developments.'" Mikhail Gorbachev, *Memoirs* (New York: Doubleday, 1996), p. 528.

20. Quoted in Anatol Lieven, "Russian Opposition to NATO Expansion," *The World Today*, October 1995; also quoted in Adam Garfinkle, "NATO Enlargement, What's the Rush?" *National Interest* 46 (Winter 1996–97): 106.

21. Quoted in Carey Schofield, "Russian 'Betrayed' over Expansion of NATO," *Electronic Telegraph* (UK), May 20, 1997.

22. Quoted in Gordon, pp. 2–3.

23. Jack F. Matlock Jr., Testimony on NATO expansion before the Senate Foreign Relations Committee, May 3, 1995, pp. 1–2.

24. Alexander Lebed, "Old Enemies, New Problems," *St. Petersburg Times*, June 2–8, 1997.

25. Quoted in Alan Philips, "Russians Find 'Proof' That the West Misled Them," *Electronic Telegraph*, March 21, 1997.

26. Quoted by Fred Weir, *Hindustan Times*, April 18, 1997.

27. Lebed.

28. Quoted by Fred Weir, *Hindustan Times*, April 4, 1997.

29. Anna Varshavskaya, wire services ITAR-TASS, May 6, 1997.

30. Christian Caryl, "Remember Napoleon," *U.S. News & World Report*, March 24, 1997.

31. Quoted by Fred Weir, *Hindustan Times*, April 16, 1997.

32. Lebed.

33. John Steinbruner, "Russia Faces an Unsafe Reliance on Nukes," *Los Angeles Times*, March 3, 1997.

34. Quoted in Bjarne Nitovuori, "Karaganov Admits 'Error' in Policy toward NATO," *Helsinki Hufvudstadsbladet*, March 22, 1997.

35. Lebed.

36. Quoted in Schofield.

37. Gorbachev, p. 533.

8. NATO Enlargement: Coping with Act II

Jonathan Dean

The Founding Act on Mutual Relations, Cooperation and Security between NATO and the Russian Federation, the document of understanding signed by NATO and Russia in Paris in May 1997, is a good idea on its own merits. Even though conflicting U.S. and Russian interpretations of its content undermine the act's value, it is nonetheless worthwhile to establish a systematic means of communication between NATO and Russia and to attach Russian military officers to many NATO staffs. But NATO enlargement—whose negative impact the Founding Act was intended to cushion—remains a bad idea.

If NATO enlargement were to stop with the admission of the three Central European candidate countries—Poland, the Czech Republic, and Hungary—that were invited to apply for membership in July at Madrid, the Founding Act might be helpful in persuading Russia to come to terms with that development. Then, whether NATO enlargement was a good idea or a bad one, we could all get back to business.

Prospects for Further Rounds of Expansion

But the question of NATO enlargement will not end with the admission of three new members. The Clinton administration has made clear that it plans to push for further expansion. Two days after the signing of the Founding Act, Secretary of State Madeleine Albright said at the NATO ministerial meeting in Sintra, Portugal, "We must pledge that the first new members will not be the last and that no European democracy will be excluded because of where it sits on the map. . . . That is why it is essential that NATO begin a new phase of dialogues with the aspiring countries after Madrid."[1] NATO had already pledged itself in December 1996 to remain open to the accession of additional members once the first group of candidates had been accepted. At the Madrid summit, alliance leaders actually specified five more candidates—Romania, Slovenia, and the three Baltic states—that will probably be invited to negotiate accession agreements in April 1999, when the Madrid candidates will be admitted to full NATO membership.[2]

Today, there are nine candidates for NATO membership in addition to the three Madrid entrants: Albania, Bulgaria, Estonia, Macedonia, Latvia, Lithuania, Romania, Slovakia, and Slovenia. Austria, Finland, and Sweden are also considering applying. The day after the Madrid summit meeting, the ambassadors of the three Baltic republics—Estonia, Latvia, and Lithuania—were on NATO's doorstep, clamoring for admission in the next round. The prospect of NATO membership for those three small states, which would bring the alliance directly to the borders of Russia, will confirm Russia's worst fears and renew active controversy over the entire enlargement issue.

The three Baltic governments are unlikely to stop pressing their candidacy—visibly and noisily—until they are admitted. The three governments have already indignantly rejected a "charter" like the one developed for Russia; they want only full NATO membership, and they will not stop agitating for it until they get it. Senate Republicans have introduced a bill endorsing the candidacy of the Baltic states, and Majority Leader Trent Lott has pledged his support.[3] The risk that the Republicans could accuse the Clinton administration of yielding to Russian pressure and dragging its feet over this question in the 1998 and 2000 election campaigns will ensure visible and energetic administration support for the candidacy of those three countries. Baltic candidacy is also being pushed by the Scandinavian countries—even Finland and Sweden, who are not now members of NATO—in the interests of Baltic solidarity and of bolstering their own security situations.

The motives of the three Baltic governments are wholly understandable: they are seeking at any cost to ensure their own security in the face of Russian political opinion that barely concedes their independent existence. Unfortunately, their geographic situation means that NATO could not defend them militarily against Russian pressures except by threatening to use nuclear weapons. Given that the issue of NATO membership for the Baltic republics will certainly elicit a hostile reaction from Russia, the situation that will be created is not one that a farsighted American government should get itself into unless the stakes are the life or death of the United States. In this case, those are not the stakes. Instead, they are the historically understandable desire of three small countries for reassurance, which can be provided in ways other than this potentially suicidal one.

Ukraine will be satisfied—for a time—with the charter it received at the Madrid summit. However, if the Baltic states get into NATO or seem to be succeeding in their quest, Ukraine will likely become a candidate, too. None of the other candidates for NATO membership is a former Soviet republic or adjoins Russian territory. Thus, the candidacies of the other states will not cause so much reaction from the Russian political elite—although their candidacies should cause Americans to ask many questions about whether the United States should extend a security guarantee to so many countries.

All of this means that the negative aspects of NATO enlargement will not end with the accession to NATO of Poland, Hungary, and the Czech Republic. Instead, the NATO enlargement issue will cause continuing friction with Russia. It has already held up Duma ratification of START II, and it will seriously impede Russian cooperation on other valuable arms control projects. East European states will be caught up in a political maelstrom of rival candidacies. The needless and destabilizing remilitarization of Eastern Europe will continue, at a cost that will greatly exceed the $30 billion the Clinton administration has estimated for the Madrid candidates. With at least five more probable members, those costs will at least double. And if all 16 countries named here should become members of NATO, the costs would be from three to five times the administration's estimate.

In the minds of its leading proponents, the NATO enlargement project is designed to prevent a repetition of the situation that led to two world wars—the existence of a belt of small, weak East European states caught between competing major powers. But the enlargement project may well create the very situation it is intended to prevent: quarrels between two power blocs over weak buffer states. In particular, the hostile reaction of the Russian political elite on this issue will long mold the views of the average Russian on foreign affairs. The NATO enlargement controversy will revive paranoid theories of hostile encirclement, which have played such a negative role in Russian history, and dispose Russians to a dangerous revisionist attitude toward the post–Cold War settlement in Central and Eastern Europe. The situation will be handcrafted for an unscrupulous political demagogue.

Alternatives to NATO Enlargement

There are better alternatives to NATO enlargement. They include strengthening the Organization for Security and Cooperation in Europe, already a pan-European organization, to become more effective. They also include building the Partnership for Peace into a more serious program. Above all, they include pressing the European Union—to which Russia does not have the same built-in, automatic hostility as it has to NATO—to move more rapidly toward its own enlargement in Eastern Europe. Negotiations on that subject are scheduled to begin in 1998. The European Commission has already specified the Czech Republic, Poland, and Hungary, as well as Slovenia and Estonia, as the first group of enlargement candidates, and if all goes well, the first three countries will be admitted to the EU by 2003 or so, only a few years after their possible admission to NATO.[4]

From the outset, the real interest of the East European countries has been in membership in the EU and in the long-term economic support such membership promises. For many East European states, NATO membership is only an interim surrogate for the real goal. Opinion polls in the main candidate countries show higher public interest in EU membership than in membership in NATO.[5] Negotiations for membership in the EU are slow paced and may take several years. However, there is no crisis in Eastern Europe that requires haste or rapid solution. If membership in the EU for some East European states takes several years to work out, then so be it. One of the most questionable justifications for the NATO enlargement project is the argument that a pending crisis in Eastern Europe makes immediate expansion of a military alliance—NATO—a necessity. There is plenty of time to develop a more productive answer to East European concerns. But in the present rush to enlarge NATO, Western legislators and populations—who will have to assume the costs and risks of enlargement—are being stampeded into unwise decisions.

Logically, the serious problems associated with NATO enlargement should occasion serious debate over the entire project when the amendment of the North Atlantic Treaty to include Poland, Hungary, and the Czech Republic is presented for ratification to the U.S. Senate and other NATO legislatures. It is to be hoped that the Senate will conclude that the entire project should be kept on hold while other alternatives are more thoroughly studied. But, whatever the Senate's decision on the candidacy of Poland, Hungary, and the Czech Republic, part of its decision should be a firm requirement for a moratorium on further NATO enlargement.

The administration should use that moratorium to consult with other NATO governments to develop a special program for the Baltic states that takes into account their sensitivities, those of the Russians, and the Baltic states' exposed geographic position and offers them reassurance outside the NATO framework. Specifically, the administration should work with the EU to develop for the Baltic states a special, intensified form of EU association with most of the benefits of EU membership—an approach that can go into effect rapidly. It would be in the political interest of all EU countries to avoid the acute friction with Russia that would result from the active NATO candidacy of the Baltic republics by making available to them a more constructive alternative, such as close EU association.

Toward Comprehensive Enlargement

If, in fact, despite the risks, the legislatures of all present NATO members do approve the membership of the Madrid candidates, the extended moratorium on further candidacies does not prove feasible, and the administration and the EU fail to develop a special program for the Baltic states, only one effective possibility of limiting the damage from NATO enlargement will remain open. The basic problem of NATO enlargement is that by including some countries and excluding others, especially Russia, it establishes a new dividing line in Europe. What is clearly missing is a comprehensive all-European solution. The Germans have an expression that would apply in such circumstances: *Wenn schon, denn schon*—"If you are going to do something that may be questioned, then do it right and go all the way."

In these circumstances, the Clinton administration should draw the logical conclusion from its project to enlarge NATO. Acceptance of the first group of candidates, if it comes, will mean that the United States and other NATO members are committed to NATO as the prime security organization of Europe. No serious alternative—including the OSCE and the EU with its military arm, the Western European Union—will then remain for that role. Both the logic and the politics of the situation will then require that the United States go the next step and open NATO membership to all democratic European states.

Specifically, the administration should prepare a 20-year plan for the comprehensive enlargement of NATO, a plan that would provide for NATO membership for all of the candidates, including the Baltic states (and Ukraine if it so desires), and also, at the end of the 20-year period, of Russia itself. The plan should be detailed and credible.

Russia has shown interest in membership in NATO on several occasions. Soviet president Mikhail Gorbachev suggested it; Russian president Boris Yeltsin suggested it. Early this year Prime Minister Viktor Chernomyrdin suggested at the Davos economic conference that Russia become a member of the NATO council. Perhaps Russian membership could be ultimately achieved by amalgamating the new Founding Act's permanent joint council with NATO. Regardless of the method, if Russia can be genuinely convinced there is a solid plan and a solid prospect for its own ultimate NATO membership, it is less likely to object in the interim to membership even for the Baltic states and Ukraine, much less the other candidates.

There are some problems with such a solution, although none of them is as large as those caused by the NATO enlargement project itself. At present, one function of NATO is to ensure against a resurgent Russia—a not unreasonable mission, given Russia's unstable polity. That is why this proposal for comprehensive enlargement suggests a 20-year period for Russia to settle down. Russia will either do so in that time period or will at some point during that period take such a negative course as to make its entry into NATO impractical.

Russia is also characterized by some Europeans, for example, by President Václav Havel of the Czech Republic, as a vast Eurasian country—too large and too alien to be absorbed into NATO without changing NATO's own nature.[6] But Russia is a European country, and if it becomes a functioning democracy, its other characteristics will not be so important. True, the addition of 10 more members, including Russia, would probably change the nature of NATO. However, over time, as Havel himself has suggested, NATO should change from a military alliance directed against a specific enemy to a collective security organization with the capability of mounting military missions supported by coalitions of willing members.[7]

There is another practical concern. The primary reason many members of the Senate today favor NATO enlargement is suspicion of Russia—Russians are right when they conclude that many of those legislators intend the enlargement of NATO as an anti-Russian measure. If a plan to make NATO membership genuinely comprehensive were publicly advanced now, such legislators would probably reject it. They might even vote against the first tranche of NATO enlargement if it were seen as part of a comprehensive plan of enlargement that would include Russia at a later date.

But we are now only at the beginning of the wide public debate the NATO enlargement project calls for; the potential long-term costs of the project are becoming more evident, and the need for remedial action will also become more clear. Moreover, it is the administration's obligation, having conjured up the NATO enlargement project, to cope with those factors and to reach a decision on the timing of a proposal for comprehensive enlargement of NATO.

The task of devising a new security architecture for Europe that the administration has spoken of so frequently will not be completed until there is an enduring, effective place in that architecture for all European states, including Russia. That is what is missing from the NATO enlargement project in its present divisive and exclusionary form. If the administration fails to carry out this task properly, we will all pay the costs.

Notes

1. Madeleine K. Albright, "Statement at North Atlantic Council Ministerial Meeting, Sintra, Portugal, May 29, 1997," Office of the Spokesman, U.S. Department of State.

2. Statement of the Secretary General, NATO Press Office, July 8, 1997.

3. Trent Lott, "The Senate's Role in NATO Enlargement," *Washington Post*, March 21, 1997.

4. Lionel Barber, "No Turning Back from Brave New Europe," *Financial Times*, July 17, 1997.

5. George Cunningham, "EU and NATO Enlargement; How Public Opinion Is Shaping Up in Some Candidate Countries," *NATO Review*, May–June, 1997.

6. Václav Havel, "NATO's Quality of Life," *New York Times*, May 13, 1997; and Jim Hoagland, "At Center Stage for Havel: NATO," *Washington Post*, May 9, 1996.

7. Ibid.

9. Russia's Search for Identity

Stanley Kober

Any discussion of NATO expansion should begin with the acknowledgment that its purpose is noble: to bring an end to the trauma of war that has been the scourge of Europe for too long. Given the absence of attacks on the NATO member countries since the inception of the alliance, it is tempting to build on that record of success and thereby spread the benefits of peace. And, certainly, one can understand the desire of those countries that are not members to seek the security that membership has signified in the past. Indeed, if that were all it took to guarantee their security, it would be difficult to reject their overtures. Yet if the establishment of peace were that simple, the problem of war would have disappeared long ago. Since war has not disappeared, we must conclude that its causes are more complex, and its prevention more complicated.

Ultimately, alliances (and collective security arrangements) protect peace by the deterrence of war. "If it had been known that this war was coming on, [America's] moral judgment would have concurred with that of the other Governments of the world, with that of the other people of the world; and if Germany had known that there was a possibility of that sort of concurrence, she never would have dared to do what she did," President Woodrow Wilson told the Senate Foreign Relations Committee in explaining the rationale for the League of Nations. "Without such notice served on the powers that may wish to repeat the folly that Germany commenced, there is no assurance to the world that there will be peace even for a generation, whereas if they know beforehand that there will be that concert of judgment there is the most tremendous guaranty."[1]

1914: A Spectacular Deterrence Failure

Germany was aware of the possibility of war, however, when it issued its famous "blank check" to Austria-Hungary. Russia's ties

129

to Serbia were well-known, as were its ties to France and France's to Britain. Indeed, in the blunt words of a German White Paper, "We were perfectly aware that a possible warlike attitude of Austria-Hungary against Serbia might bring Russia into the field, and that it might therefore involve us in a war, in accordance with our duty as allies."[2] Germany's miscalculation was in assuming that Russia would not come to Serbia's aid, in part because it doubted the strength of the Russian-Serbian bond, but more important, because it felt that Russia was in no condition to go to war. As the German chancellor, Prince Bernhard von Bulow, put it in a confidential memorandum in June 1908, "Russia, as a result of the war with Japan, will for some time be incapable of much action."[3]

Deterrence failed in 1914, not because the two sides were unaware of the alliances arrayed against them, but because each thought the other would yield. Ironically, the Germans were right in their military assessment. Russia was not ready for war, and its disastrous military performance led to the Russian Revolution and the execution of the czar and his family. But Russia went to war because it felt betrayed. Russians "are convinced that Austria has been acting in bad faith," the German military plenipotentiary in St. Petersburg reported to Berlin on July 29, 1914. "All this has turned opinion very much in Serbia's favor, which country Russia considers it her duty to protect without regard to the serious consequences which will result."[4]

Russia's New Sense of Betrayal

Russians are now experiencing that same sense of betrayal, because they apparently were promised when Germany was reunited that there would be no further expansion of NATO. In the words of Russian foreign minister Yevgeny Primakov,

> In conversations with Mikhail Gorbachev, Eduard Shevardnadze and Dmitri Yazov, held in 1990–1991, i.e., when the West was vitally interested in the Soviet troop withdrawal from the German Democratic Republic and wanted us "to swallow the bitter pill"—the disintegration of the Warsaw Treaty Organization (OVD)—François Mitterand, John Major and [James] Baker, all of them said one and the same thing: NATO will not move to the east by a single inch and not a single Warsaw Pact country will be admitted to NATO.

This was exactly what they said. These conversations were not codified in the form of official documents at that time.[5]

Recently, declassified Russian documents on this subject were made available to Alexei Pushkov, a prominent Russian writer on foreign affairs and member of the independent Council on Foreign and Defense Policy. According to an account in the *Times* (London),

> After talks with Mr. Major on March 6, 1991, Marshal Dmitry Yazov wrote: "The British Prime Minister declared that he 'does not foresee conditions under which at the present time or in the future the east European countries could enter Nato.' "
>
> Mr. Hurd made a similar point to the then Soviet foreign minister, Alexander Bessmertnykh, on March 26, 1991, who recorded: "D. Hurd asserted the absence of Nato plans to include the countries of eastern and central Europe in the North Atlantic Treaty in one form or another."
>
> It was alliance policy at the time that Nato was not planning to expand, and similar assurances were made by Chancellor Kohl of Germany and James Baker, the former U.S. secretary of state. In February 1990, Mr. Kohl told the then Soviet president, Mikhail Gorbachev: "We consider that Nato should not expand its sphere of action. We need to find a reasonable settlement."[6]

In fact, when Gorbachev was in Washington in the fall of 1996 to promote his new book, in which he mentions those assurances, the subject came up during a meeting at the *Washington Post.* Columnist Jim Hoagland asked Gorbachev "about a suggestion in his memoirs that the United States was reneging on promises to him about NATO expansion." Gorbachev replied that "he had reached a 'gentlemen's agreement' with the Bush administration in February 1990 that NATO would not expand eastward beyond Germany. He acknowledged that since no one could imagine then that the Warsaw Pact would shortly disappear, he had not pressed for formal commitments about other countries, and the Americans had therefore not given them."[7]

Hoagland goes on to express his admiration of Gorbachev's "candor" in admitting "this major strategic error."[8] But what was the error? Instead of being grateful for a peaceful end to the Cold War, are we now to mock Gorbachev for erring in trusting us too much?

Is this the basis on which to build the post–Cold War world? If so, what reaction can we expect from the Russians other than a feeling of betrayal and suspicion? "The current collision between Russia and NATO could have been avoided if the Soviet leadership had at that time taken the Americans and Germans at their word and codified their intentions not to expand Nato," comments Pushkov. "The Russian leadership is now saying that it will not be fooled again."[9]

Conflicting Interpretations of the Founding Act

The result of that distrust was the adoption of the Founding Act on Mutual Relations, Cooperation and Security between NATO and the Russian Federation, a written document defining the future relationship between the two parties. Hailed as the end of the Cold War, the Founding Act seems instead to be the foundation of a new confrontation. No sooner had it been announced than the two sides began disagreeing about its meaning. For example, NATO has said that the Founding Act gives Russia a voice but not a veto concerning NATO's actions, but that is not the way it is being interpreted in Russia. According to Sergei Rogov, the head of the Institute of the USA and Canada,

> Russia and NATO retain their rights in the sphere of defense and cannot veto each other's moves there. The decision-making on the matters of European security, including the use of force in peace-making operations, is to be done in the new joint standing council where Russia's vote equals that of the sixteen, so far, NATO members. The council is to work on the basis of consensus; moreover, its decisions on peace-making are to be endorsed by the UN Security Council, where Russia has the right of veto, or the OSCE [Organization for Security and Cooperation in Europe], of which Russia is a member.
>
> Since aggression against NATO is very unlikely, all other power actions of the alliance in excess of lawful defense will have to be agreed with Russia first through the council, and then in the UN [Security Council] and the OSCE. Hence, the west has no free hand to make unilateral steps the likes of the air strikes at the Bosnian Serbs in 1995.[10]

That interpretation, with its reference to Bosnia, is especially note-worthy in light of recent indications that the United States is becoming increasingly impatient with the situation in that country and might seek to play a more forceful role.

Another point of disagreement is the admission of future members. According to Yeltsin's press secretary, Sergei Yastreshembsky, the admission of states that were formerly part of the Soviet Union is "absolutely unacceptable" to Russia, and if it occurs Russia will announce "its withdrawal from the Founding Act" and review all its relations with the alliance.[11] But according to NATO secretary general Javier Solana, "The decision about the opening of NATO will be taken by the 16 countries of NATO. Nobody else. We can consult with Russia on some issues, but not on others. We shouldn't on this."[12]

To resolve that dilemma, the Clinton administration has once again begun to hold out the possibility of eventual Russian membership in NATO. "Where are the geographical limits to NATO expansion?" Deputy Secretary of State Strobe Talbott recently asked. "The right answer is, Let's see—and let's not be in a rush to proclaim new limits. . . . To draw a new line on the map would be a betrayal of the alliance's shared vision of an undivided, increasingly integrated Europe."[13]

Excluding Russia from Europe

If the sentiments expressed by Talbott were shared by all who favored NATO expansion, its negative consequences might not be so profound. (Although one does wonder at what point NATO would begin to resemble the United Nations, or more particularly, what would distinguish its membership from that of the UN Security Council.) Yet it is clear that many, if not most, proponents of NATO enlargement see it as an effort to protect the new members from Russia and are vigorously opposed to the idea of Russian membership. "A responsible Russian role in the building of international order does not need to be based on Russian de facto participation in the Western defense alliance," writes Henry Kissinger, objecting to the provisions of the Founding Act. "If there is no distinction between members and non-members, what remains of the alliance?" The new members, he insists with evident approval, "are seeking to participate in NATO for reasons quite the opposite of what the

133

Founding Act describes—not to erase dividing lines but to position themselves inside a guaranteed territory by shifting the existing NATO boundaries some 300 miles to the east."[14]

Talbott and Kissinger cannot both be right about the purpose of NATO expansion, and it would appear that Kissinger is closer to the mark. In the blunt words of Estonian foreign minister Toomas Ilves, "If Russia didn't threaten us, we'd have better things to do."[15] Or as Martin Palous, a member of the faculty of Prague's Charles University and one of the signatories of Charter 77, a 1976 proclamation that called for the communist Czechoslovak government to fulfill its human rights obligations, explains, "We have spent so much time on the wrong side of the barricade that if new barricades are to be drawn, we definitely would like to be on the right side."[16]

In short, NATO expansion, far from overcoming the division of Europe, is simply drawing new lines designed to ensure that Russia will always remain outside. "Enlarging NATO means enlarging the zone of stability in Europe and in the world," President Václav Havel of the Czech Republic said, reciting the approved mantra, during his recent visit to the United States. But for him, enlarging NATO means excluding Russia. "I can hardly imagine the North Atlantic Alliance that would work with the Russian Federation as a full member," he added. Russia and NATO "should share a good and profound relationship, but it does not mean that these two entities should become one."[17]

Havel's position is disturbing for two reasons. First, it represents such a change in his views from the days when the Cold War was ending. In a speech to the Polish Sejm in January 1990, he recommended that "both military alliances [NATO and the Warsaw Pact] could be dissolved, and the process of Pan-European integration could be finally set in motion."[18] Now that the Warsaw Pact has been dissolved, he has decided that NATO should remain, not to promote all-European integration, but to prevent it. Russia, according to his view, is not part of Europe. Even more important, it never can be. "The Alliance," he declared in June 1996, "should unequivocally restate that it is open to all Euro-Atlantic countries that share its values and are ready and willing to defend them with NATO's structures." But Russia, he insisted, falls outside that framework because it is not Euro-Atlantic but Euro-Asian.

> The Russian Federation is and will always remain a power with great gravitational potential and with security partners

of its own. World peace is hardly conceivable without good cooperation between the Euro-Atlantic region and this large and influential Euro-Asian entity.

Yet, these two entities can cooperate creatively and build a deepening partnership only if both are clearly defined, have distinct boundaries and fully respect each other's identity.

I think this is what the Alliance should tell Russia clearly in the near future. NATO should affirm its desire to strive for the best conceivable partnership, but it should also stress that such a partnership can be built only when each of the parties knows its true identity and when neither attempts to dictate how the other should define itself, or whom the other may or may not accept as allies.[19]

That distinction between two fundamentally incompatible identities represents an apparent repudiation of Havel's earlier views. Indeed, he seems to be adopting views he previously condemned. "A person who was accustomed for many years to living under rigorous rules that prevented him from making his own decisions suffers from a kind of shock," he once explained. "They find themselves in a state of uncertainty, in which they tend to look for pseudo-certainties. One of those might be submerging themselves in a crowd, a community, and defining themselves in contrast to other communities."[20] Even worse, by insisting on a distinction between Euro-Atlantic and Euro-Asian, Havel appears to be turning on its head the advice he gave several years ago. "The greatness of the idea of European integration on democratic foundations consists in its capacity to overcome the old Herderian idea of the nation state as the highest expression of national life," he argued in 1993. "The greatness of this idea lies in its power to smother the demons of nationalism, the instigators of modern war."[21]

Advocates of NATO expansion have praised it as a means of overcoming ethnic rivalries that have undermined the peace of Europe. But if it causes someone like Havel to talk about incompatible Euro-Atlantic and Euro-Asian identities, we have to wonder if NATO expansion will not inflame rather than smother the demons of nationalism. "NATO is a symbol of Western civilization," his brother Ivan Havel has explained. "Therefore if we are left out of it, then we are not considered Western enough."[22] Precisely. But that holds for the Russians also. "How come that the new Russia, which has discarded its former ideology, remembered of God, sworn loyalty to the new ideals of democracy and fallen into the embrace of its recent 'probable adversaries,' is not accepted to Western civilization?" a Russian scholar has asked plaintively. "What else must it do?"[23]

The second danger with Havel's approach is that, if we tell the Russians they are really Asians and that they must seek their allies elsewhere, just whom do we expect those allies to be? We already have our answer. "We shall do everything to minimize the consequences of NATO expansion for Russia's security," President Yeltsin has stressed. "We shall continue to deepen integration within the Commonwealth of Independent States, especially with Belarus. We shall strengthen cooperation with neighboring countries, first of all with China."[24]

The Emerging Moscow-Beijing Axis

The rapprochement between Russia and China is usually dismissed by Western observers, but some in Asia appear to take it more seriously. "The insistence by Secretary of State Madeleine Albright that enlargement of NATO will 'vanquish old hatreds, promote integration and create a secure environment' takes on a hollow ring at this point," Hong Kong's *South China Morning Post* said in an editorial during the April 1997 Jiang-Yeltsin summit. "The Sino-Russian accord is more likely to achieve that goal for the East. In the light of this new alliance, Western powers may need to reassess their policy, and show more understanding of Russian sensitivities. The China-Russia card is too important for them to ignore."[25]

Despite protests to the contrary, the Russia-China rapprochement seems to be inspired in large part by the resentment both countries bear toward the United States. "Both oppose the re-emergence of group politics and the resurgence of the Cold War thinking," said an article in *Beijing Review* reporting on the summit. "Russia supports China on the issues of Taiwan and Tibet, refusing to back the United States and other Western states to place pressure on China on human rights. China, for its part ... sympathizes with Russian concerns that NATO's enlargement will endanger its security interest and destabilize Europe.... Now is the best period in the history of Sino-Russian relations."[26] For their part, the Russians seem unconcerned that their growing military cooperation with China could represent a threat to them in the future. "In selling arms to China Moscow lays emphasis on such systems the effective use of which on land theaters of military operations to the north of China's borders is very problematic," *Pravda* has reported. "On the other hand, these systems may be useful in case of China's conflict with the pro-American regime in Taiwan."[27]

To be sure, *Pravda* is not the authoritative source it once was, but it is not alone in its explanation of why the Chinese are interested in a strategic partnership with Russia. "The advantages which China will get from this [border] agreement are obvious," explains *Nezavisimiya gazeta*. "The military contacts between the USA, Japan and South Korea, which grow stronger with every passing year, and their growing military presence in the region are bound to worry China, which does not plan to give up the status of the leading power in the Asia-Pacific region. Now that the border [troop] reductions agreement was signed, Beijing will be able to focus its attention on the problems on its eastern borders."[28] Similarly, an article by the InterPress Service in December 1996 reported that "there are many in Moscow who believe that Beijing's only interest in forging military ties with Moscow after 40 years of strained relations, is so that China can withdraw its troops from the long Sino-Russian border and redeploy them in its bid to reunify with Taiwan, if necessary, by force. . . . Any alliance between Russia and China may actually increase tension by giving Beijing the confidence to actively pursue its territorial claims."[29]

In this regard, we should note that the Chinese have insistently refused to renounce what they regard as their right to use force to prevent Taiwanese independence. And although most observers believe any sort of confrontation is many years down the road, some recent reports suggest a crisis could come much earlier. "The reunification of Taiwan with the mainland has become a more urgent mission for the whole Chinese people," Foreign Minister Qian Qichen declared after the death of Deng Xiaoping.[30] An extraordinary report in February 1997 in the *South China Morning Post* may reveal what the Chinese foreign minister has in mind.

> The past two months have witnessed a series of high-level meetings on Taiwan. . . .
> Sources close to Beijing's Taiwan policy establishment, however, have indicated that the top echelon of the CCP

[Chinese Communist Party] has decided to take on Taiwan aggressively immediately after leadership changes have been completed at the First Session of the Ninth National People's Congress (NPC) in March 1998. . . .

Military preparations for possible "liberation warfare" continue. The generals' warlike rhetoric, which had disappeared for several months, has again dominated many an internal meeting in Beijing.

For example, Defense Minister Chi Haotian pointed out recently: "It looks like we have to beat them [Taiwanese] up before reunification can be expedited."[31]

The question, of course, is what the United States would do in that eventuality. The common assumption is that China would not dare to use military force against Taiwan if it knew its action would lead to a military confrontation with the United States, but that assumption may be unsound. "The recent [1996] Taiwan Strait crisis indicated that whether this issue can be handled appropriately or not has become a matter of war or peace," Chen Qimao, president emeritus of the Shanghai Institute for International Studies, wrote in an American foreign affairs journal in the fall of 1996. "If Taiwan becomes independent under the support of some foreign powers, China will use every means possible to reverse this, including the decisive use of military force, even at the risk of a military conflict with the United States."[32] When I recently asked the Chinese ambassador to the United States whether U.S. arms sales to Taiwan amount to support of Taiwanese independence under this definition, he replied bluntly, "Yes."

We have here the outlines of a potential disaster. "Taiwan is the single most important and most sensitive issue in China-U.S. relations," Foreign Minister Qian told the Council on Foreign Relations in April 1997. "U.S. arms sales to Taiwan . . . undermine China's sovereignty and pose a security threat to China's mainland."[33] In early June 1997, the *South China Morning Post* reported that a senior Chinese general had "hinted that should the administration of President Lee-Teng Hui 'go further ahead in the road to independence,' the PLA [People's Liberation Army] might consider limited military action against Taiwan."[34]

The emerging Moscow-Beijing axis is perhaps the most important reason why NATO expansion is so dangerous. No one can object to the improvement in relations between two countries, but if NATO expansion drives Russia and China together and thereby emboldens China to use military force against Taiwan, the United States will be faced with an awful choice: either abandoning Taiwan or risking a conflict with China and possibly Russia as well. In such a conflict, it is not clear that other NATO members could remain aloof. "The expansion of the North Atlantic Alliance with a simultaneous movement of the geographical frame of its possible actions can draw the members of the block into armed conflict outside of Europe," Ambassador Yurii Rakhmaninov wrote last year. "This raises suspicions in other parts of the world, especially in Asia."[35]

Repeating the Errors of 1914

Those who dismiss that scenario as too irrational should be wary of repeating the overconfidence of the Germans and Austrians before World War I. "By making up their minds in favor of NATO's eastward expansion as an unconditional foreign policy priority, the leading Western countries have embarked on a truly slippery course in relations with Russia," warns Dmitry Trenin of Russia's Academy of Sciences. "At a certain stage, Russia's politics can trespass the line which divides rational and irrational behavior, and the West can notice this line too late."[36]

NATO has been regarded as such a success that the idea that it could possibly outlive its usefulness—might even become counterproductive—appears unthinkable to most foreign policy specialists. Indeed, in her confirmation hearings, Secretary of State Madeleine Albright affirmed that NATO "is a permanent alliance."[37] By using that language, she repudiated, presumably unwittingly, the legacy of George Washington. "'Tis our true policy to steer clear of permanent Alliances, with any portion of the foreign world," he told the American people in his Farewell Address. "Taking care always to keep ourselves, by suitable establishments, on a respectably defensive posture, we may safely trust to temporary alliances for extraordinary emergencies."[38]

By portraying NATO as a permanent alliance, the administration claims to be learning from the history of European wars. It would appear, however, that President Washington's assessment was more accurate, for a blind reliance on deterrence through a "permanent" alliance has not been a source of peace and stability for Europe.

"European history has seldom, if ever, seen an alliance of such strength and durability as the Triple Alliance," Prince von Bulow proclaimed in *Imperial Germany*. "The founders of the Triple Alliance intentionally created a guarantee of peace. They have not been disappointed in their hopes, for the steadfastness of the Triple Alliance has more than once in the course of the last thirty years warded off the rising danger of war."[39]

Imperial Germany was published in 1914. Let us hope that history does not repeat itself.

Notes

1. Quoted in Henry Cabot Lodge, *The Senate and the League of Nations* (New York: Charles Scribner's Sons, 1925), p. 354.

2. Quoted in Sir Horace Rumbold, *The War Crisis in Berlin: July–August 1914* (London: Constable, 1940), p. 339.

3. Bernhard von Bulow, *Memoirs: 1903–1909* (New York: Putnam, 1930), p. 318.

4. Telegram from Military Plenipotentiary von Chelius to the German Foreign Office, in *Outbreak of the World War: German Documents Collected by Karl Kautsky*, ed. Max Montgelas and Walther Schuking (New York: Oxford University Press, 1924), p. 304.

5. "A Minister Who Is Not under Opposition's Fire," *Obshchaya gazeta* (Moscow), September 19, 1996.

6. Alan Philps, "Russians Find 'Proof' That West Misled Them," *Times* (London), March 21, 1997.

7. Jim Hoagland, "Gorbachev on Tour," *Washington Post*, October 31, 1996. Gorbachev is not the only one to describe those assurances as a gentlemen's agreement. I first heard the term applied in this context by Jack Matlock, former U.S. ambassador to the Soviet Union.

8. Ibid.

9. Quoted in Philps.

10. Sergei Rogov, "No Free Hand for the West," *Izvestia*, May 27, 1997. An English transcript of the article may be found at novosti.russianet.ru/products/dr, May 27, 1997.

11. Quoted in Marianna Shatikhina, "Raising the Question of Any State Which Has Emerged in the Post-Soviet Space Joining NATO 'Is Absolutely Unacceptable' to Russia, Says Sergei Yastreshembsky," *RIA Novosti*, May 26, 1997, at ria-novosti.russianet.ru/products/hotline.

12. Quoted in "NATO Not Open to Vetoes," *USA Today*, May 23, 1997.

13. Strobe Talbott, "The Case for Expanding NATO," *Time*, July 14, 1997, p. 6.

14. Henry Kissinger, "The Dilution of NATO," *Washington Post*, June 8, 1997.

15. Quoted in James Morrison, "Embassy Row: Estonia's New Minister," *Washington Times*, December 3, 1996.

16. Quoted in Shikha Dalmia, "Judging Costs of Reunifying East Europe into the West," *Detroit News*, May 4, 1997.

17. Quoted in Judy Aita, "NATO, Russia Should Have Special Relationship, Havel Says," U.S. Information Agency, May 14, 1997, at www.fas.org/MHonArc/NATO-L_archive/msg00098.html, May 15, 1997.

18. Václav Havel, *Toward a Civil Society*, trans. Paul Wilson (Prague: Lidove Noviny, n.d.), p. 28, and *New York Review of Books*, March 29, 1990.

19. Václav Havel, "NATO—The Safeguard of Stability and Peace in the Euro-Atlantic Region," at www.csdr.org/Havel.htm.

20. Quoted in Henry Kamm, "Havel Calls the Gypsies 'Litmus Test,'" *New York Times*, December 10, 1993.

21. Václav Havel, "How Europe Could Fail," *New York Review of Books*, November 18, 1993, p. 3.

22. Quoted in Dalmia.

23. Irina Zhinkina, "How Much Russia Should Pay to Become a U.S. Partner," *Krasnaya zvezda*, April 22, 1997, at ria-novosti.russianet.ru/products/dr, April 23, 1997.

24. Quoted in a report by Sergei Shargorodsky, Associated Press, May 6, 1997.

25. "The Moscow Connection," *South China Morning Post* (Hong Kong), April 25, 1997.

26. Xia Yishan, "Sino-Russian Partnership Marching into 21st Century," *Beijing Review*, May 5, 1997, p. 10.

27. Anton Surikov, "War against Russian Arms," *Pravda*, January 16, 1997. An abridged English text is available at ria-novosti.russianet.ru/products/dr, January 16, 1997.

28. Natalia Pulina and Alexander Reutov, "An Agreement Conceived in Soviet Period Was Signed with China Yesterday," *Nezavisimiya gazeta*, April 25, 1997, at ria-novosti.russianet.ru/products/dr, April 25, 1997.

29. Yojana Sharma, "China-Russia: Military Alliance Appears Unlikely at the Moment," InterPress Service, December 18, 1996.

30. Agence France Presse, "China to Step Up Drive for Reunification with Taiwan," AsiaOne, February 28, 1997, at www.asia1.com.

31. Willy Wo-lap Lam, "Biding Time on Taiwan," *South China Morning Post* (Hong Kong), February 5, 1997.

32. Chen Qimao, "The Taiwan Strait Crisis," *Asian Survey* 36, no. 11 (November 1996): 1066.

33. Qian Qichen, "Toward a China-U.S. Relationship for the 21st Century," April 29, 1997, at www.china-embassy.org/Cgi-Bin/Press.pl?405.

34. "PLA Could Erase Taiwan Air Force,'" *South China Morning Post* (Hong Kong), June 11, 1997.

35. Yurii Rakhmaninov, "The Reasons for and Possible Consequences of NATO Expansion," *International Affairs* (Moscow) 42, no. 4 (1996): 14.

36. Dmitry Trenin, "Transformation of Russia's Foreign Policy," *Nezavisimaya gazeta*, February 5, 1997, at ria-novosti.russianet.ru/prodcuts/dr, February 13, 1997.

37. Madeleine Albright, Confirmation hearing, at www.state.gov, January 8, 1997.

38. George Washington, "Farewell Address," in *Writings* (New York: Library of America, 1997), p. 975.

39. Bernhard von Bulow, *Imperial Germany* (New York: Dodd, Mead, 1914), pp. 66–67.

10. The NATO-Russia Accord: An Illusory Solution

Anatol Lieven

The widespread impression in the West now seems to be that, with the signing of the Founding Act on Mutual Relations, Cooperation and Security between NATO and the Russian Federation, the question of relations with Russia has been solved and Russia's objections to NATO expansion dealt with. Nothing of the sort is the case. Although it is understandable that Western governments wish to give that impression, it is worrisome that so many Western journalists, and even Western diplomats, seem genuinely convinced that relations have somehow been raised to a new and better level. The celebration of the accord is another sign of a disturbing trend in contemporary Western diplomacy: the obscuring of real and dangerous issues by the empty rhetoric of goodwill and, still worse, by the apparently genuine self-deception that such talk really can substitute for agreements on substantive issues.

It is true that intelligent Russians realized that they had no choice but to sign the accord. In particular, the Yeltsin administration had to accept it to save some shreds of face in the matter and to avoid revealing the bankruptcy of its NATO policy. However, that does not mean that both the government and Russian patriotic opinion are not extremely bitter about NATO's action, or that enlargement has not dealt another blow to even pro-Western Russians' confidence in Western promises and intentions.

The question of the West's promises to the Soviet Union and Russia in 1989–91 remains a matter of contention. Even if nothing was signed, NATO went out of its way to give Moscow the impression that it would not expand eastward. I was in the Baltic states in those years, and I remember very well that the leaders of the national movements in all three states stressed repeatedly in public that, when their countries achieved independence, they would be neutral, nonaligned states. The phrase "bridges between the West and Russia" was often used. In Latvia especially, that intention was accompanied by official promises that the local Russians, irrespective of when they entered Latvia, would automatically receive full civic rights. It was partly on the basis of those promises that the Balts received critically important support from Boris Yeltsin and the Russian democratic movement. We may all understand and sympathize with the reasons that led the Balts subsequently to change their positions. In all fairness, however, we must also recognize that the Russians have some reason to feel aggrieved, by both the Balts and their Western backers.

Linked to but even more important than the question of Russian trust in Western intentions is the fact that on the most critical issue dividing Russia and NATO—the question of NATO's future expansion to take in the Baltic states, and perhaps other countries in the territory of the former Soviet Union—nothing whatsoever has been settled. NATO has stated that the doors remain open for future members, and clearly the Balts have as good a moral claim to membership as do the Central Europeans. Some Clinton administration officials appear to have assured them informally that they will be admitted in the foreseeable future. On the other hand, Yeltsin has stated explicitly that if NATO expands into former Soviet territory, the Founding Act will be abrogated, and there will be a risk of a complete breakdown of Russia's relations with the West. In that, Yeltsin undoubtedly has the support of the overwhelming majority of Russian public opinion, whether liberal, communist-conservative, or nationalist. I cannot see at present how NATO can square that particular circle. Since many West Europeans are also strongly opposed—though so far, in private—to seeking confrontation with Russia over the issue, expansion to the Baltic states also risks dividing, not strengthening, NATO. In the words of one European diplomat, "Of course, like everyone else, we assumed that PFP [Partnership for Peace] would last for a decade at least, and Clinton took us by surprise in 1994 with NATO expansion. We couldn't afford another split with the USA, after what happened in Bosnia, so we went along with it. Next time, we'll be better prepared."[1]

Russia's Legitimate Concerns

While we may not agree with all of Russia's concerns about or positions on the question of NATO expansion, we should admit in all honesty that most of those concerns are legitimate and normal by international standards. Such concerns are expressed by liberal, pro-Western Russians and are similar to the kinds of concerns addressed by all major powers in the world, including those of the West. It is necessary to emphasize that point because, in a malignant piece of hypocrisy, former national security adviser Zbigniew Brzezinski and others have tried to portray Russian worries about NATO expansion as an additional reason to fear and distrust Russia—as if you were to slap a man in the face and then tell him that he should kiss your hand and that your judgment of him will depend on his response.[2]

Apart from the feeling of moral insult, Russian concerns do not, it must be stressed, have to do with the countries of Central Europe, nor with Romania as long as the question of unification with Moldova does not reemerge. Except for Poland, which borders on the Russian enclave of Kaliningrad, none of those countries shares a border with Russia, nor do any of them have Russian minorities. Moreover, there is no hope of drawing them into either a new union or a Russian sphere of influence—hopes that do exist, albeit in a fading form, with regard to Ukraine.

Russian fears concerning the Baltic states are threefold. First, NATO membership for the Balts will imply Western endorsement of their often very anti-Russian positions in international affairs. That development will be seen by Russian public opinion as a deep humiliation and will weaken accordingly any Russian government that is in power at the time, especially if that government is or can be portrayed as pro-Western. Those who think that such a move by NATO would not gravely weaken the position of men like Deputy Prime Ministers Anatoly Chubais and Boris Nemtsov have not listened to what those leaders have been saying.

Second, there is the fear that NATO membership would act as a shield for more radical exclusionary policies toward the Russian immigrant populations in Latvia and Estonia. The West may assure the Russians that, on the contrary, NATO would ensure that the Balts respected international norms in that matter. But the Russians have some reason to worry that, once Latvia and Estonia are safely in NATO and the European Union, the incentives for the Latvians and Estonians to follow Western advice on the issue will greatly diminish. NATO and the EU have not, after all, proved very successful at moderating the nationalist passions of either the Greeks or

145

the Turks. If I were a Russian, I would not place much confidence in NATO and the EU being able to modify Estonian or Latvian nationalism, if it were to take a turn for the worse. Those Russian fears are exaggerated, but they are also genuinely felt.

Finally, there is the question of Kaliningrad. NATO membership for the Baltic states would isolate Kaliningrad and give the Lithuanians the military backing, if necessary, to blockade the enclave. Now one might well ask why NATO would possibly want to do something so crazily provocative, but Russians have heard the repeated calls from Baltic and some sections of Scandinavian opinion for the demilitarization of Kaliningrad and from some Lithuanian nationalists for its internationalization or even partition.[3] To start tampering with the borders of 1945 risks a return to the cataclysms of the past. Moreover, although I have heard a few liberal Russians say that they would be perfectly happy to see Kaliningrad become a demilitarized free city and European free-trade zone, I don't think you'll find a single Russian who would want to see that occur under what would inevitably be seen as NATO military pressure. That point also applies to the other Russian military and military-civilian enclaves (or exclaves) left outside Russia's western borders: Transdniestria and the military port of Sevastopol.

There could be no more serious or dangerous issue in international affairs than an attempt to bring pressure to bear on a sovereign state to withdraw troops from part of its own territory. The question of Sevastopol has been suspended for 20 years by the leasing arrangement included in the May 1997 treaty between Russia and Ukraine; and perhaps at the end of that time the Russians will peacefully withdraw, as Ukrainian officials insist privately must be the case; or on the other hand, perhaps the Ukrainians will peacefully sign another 20-year lease, to allow time and change in both countries and the wider world to solve the issue. Perhaps. But it should be easy to see why, from a Russian point of view, the closer NATO gets to Russia's borders, the more danger there will be that issues like Sevastopol will be solved by Western dictate, and in a manner unfavorable to Russia. Once again, those are legitimate concerns by international standards.

American Hostility toward Russia

But why, it may be asked, should Russians assume that on any given issue the West will take an anti-Russian line? Is that not in itself evidence of inveterate, irrational Russian suspicion of the West?

146

Unfortunately, even the most pro-Western Russians keep finding solid evidence to justify their fear. Anti-Russian opinions are reflected every day in some portion of the American media.[4] There exists in the West generally, but especially in the United States, a strain of opinion that is full of implacable hostility, which amounts in some cases to irrational hatred, not toward the Soviet legacy or even Russia as a state, but toward the Russian nation and Russians as a people. At times, that view of an unchanging Russian drive for aggression and conquest finds explicitly racist forms, as in George Will's statement that "expansion is in the Russians' DNA." Or Peter Rodman's comment: "The only potential great-power security problem in Central Europe is the lengthening shadow of Russian strength, and NATO has the job of counter-balancing it. Russia is a force of nature; all this is inevitable."[5] When related to NATO expansion, such attitudes produce statements like those of Henry Kissinger, that Russia today is a "weakened adversary" who should not be conciliated. Explicitly or implicitly, that is the view of a good many extreme russophobes in the West. It is connected to the regret one sometimes hears that it was not possible in Russia to impose decommunization along the lines of the political purification carried out in Germany and Japan after World War II. To such attitudes, there is a very simple reply: if the West had crushed the Soviet Union in war, the world today would indeed be a very different place— blackened, flattened, and with a very much smaller population.

The astonishingly peaceful dissolution of the Soviet empire was largely due to the fact that, during the critical period, the Reagan and Bush administrations succeeded in persuading the Soviet and Russian leadership (and the Russian people) that they would not be treated as defeated enemies, but rather, having freed themselves of communist tyranny, would be welcomed as honored partners of the West. That promise was also crucial in allowing the Yeltsin administration to begin free-market reforms in Russia.

As seen from Moscow, the positions of many American politicians—though not the Clinton administration—on NATO expansion, the Conventional Forces in Europe (CFE) Treaty, START II, and the Anti-Ballistic Missile Treaty, when taken together and if put into practice by a future U.S. administration, would constitute a formal breach of international good faith. And good faith, as well as democracy, security, free trade, and so on, is after all one of the pillars of a stable international order. What good faith could there be in simultaneously expanding and strengthening NATO and insisting that Russia abide strictly by the CFE? What moral consistency is there in insisting that the United States be allowed to tear up the ABM Treaty but that Russia ratify START II? What sort of lesson do such actions give the Russians about how international affairs will be conducted in the New World Order?

The implacable hostility of some Western opinion shapers toward Russia is shown by the fact that Russian withdrawal from former Soviet (and even czarist) territory has not led to the slightest modification of their view of innate Russian imperialism. Even stranger, the overwhelming evidence of Russian weakness has not led those people to stop exaggerating Russian strength. Hence we are treated to the strange sight of Kissinger frantically flogging the half-dead Russian bear—which if present trends continue will in three years or so have only twice the gross domestic product of Poland—while in the background the Chinese dragon inexorably gains strength and in a generation or so will have the world's largest economy. Under those circumstances, to mistake the lesser danger for the greater and structure one's whole international posture accordingly is precisely the error that Kissinger himself dissected and mocked Louis Napoleon III of France for committing in the 1850s and 1860s.[6] Not only did Napoleon III err disastrously in concentrating on defeating Austria while ignoring the rising power of Prussia, but he also dedicated himself to making alliances with or expressing emotional support for small nations that could not help France in a crisis and that France had no real intention of helping in case of war. In advocating such a policy regarding NATO expansion, Kissinger is breaking the rules of his own book.

In some cases, the hatred of Russia is implacable because it is rooted not in the present, nor even in the Soviet experience, but in ethnic memories of Russian aggression and oppression dating back hundreds of years. On those memories has been erected a historicist and deeply bigoted portrayal of the Russian people and Russian culture as permanently devoted to conquest and expansion.[7] The unique crimes of Soviet communism—very often not committed by Russians and very often committed against Russians—are mixed up indiscriminately with the policies of the czars and of the Yeltsin administration. No attempt is made to compare Russia's experience with that of other European colonial empires, either in their bloody rise or their often even bloodier disintegration. Nor is any attempt made to compare Russia's attempts to preserve a sphere of influence with those of other major powers.

In this context, Russians often compare themselves with France and ask why behavior that in the case of France draws from Americans no more than an irritated shrug provokes in the case of Russia torrents of hysterical rhetoric. Are Moscow's various clients in the former Soviet republics really worse than Mobutu Sese Seko or some of Paris's other clients in Africa? And has Russia since the fall of communism committed worse crimes than have some of the West's honored allies in the past?

To this may be made the objection that Russia's behavior clashes with U.S. interests, for example in the field of energy, in a way that France's or Turkey's does not. That is entirely true—but I am not suggesting for a moment that there are not real differences of interest between Russia and the West, and that the West will not have on occasion to defend its interests very strongly. For example, the West will need to respond to Russian sales of arms to the West's enemies. Such situations should, however, be handled on a case-by-case basis, not incorporated into an architecture of prejudice and hostility.

The other reason why the Russians are right to fear both that NATO expansion will continue and that it will be directed against them is the nature of U.S. domestic politics. Russia has no political lobby in the United States, whether ethnic, as in the case of the East Europeans, or business, as in the case of China. Since U.S. foreign policy is increasingly dictated by short-term electoral considerations, and since many U.S. leaders lack any clear conception of what the interests of the United States as a whole—as opposed to those of particular American or pseudo-American groups—actually are, the cards are permanently stacked against Russia. Any move seen as anti-Russian will always earn a certain measure of domestic political credit in the United States. Moves seen as pro-Russian will attract at best indifference and at worst hostility.

The mass of the American people, of course, has no interest in such a strategy, but that is the point. They are uninterested in the whole issue, whereas the enemies of Russia are passionately interested in pushing the United States in an anti-Russian direction. Whatever sympathy there is for Russia is limited to sections of the political and foreign policy elites, which are themselves deeply unpopular with many Americans.

Moreover, those groups' sympathy for Russia, being based on reason and a sense of U.S. and Western interests, is contingent. That is to say, it is affected by Russia's behavior and Russian attitudes. In my own case, my respect for Boris Yeltsin was destroyed by the Chechen War, and if the Russian people had shown enthusiasm for that war, my sympathy for them would also have been very badly damaged. Consequently, if the Russian government were to commit military aggression against the Baltic states or Ukraine, or if Russia as a whole were to swing in an extreme ethnic chauvinist direction, I and most other currently sympathetic members of Western opinion-shaping communities would become determined opponents.

The russophobes have an advantage because their task is much simpler. Since their approach is based neither on evidence nor in many cases even on an attachment to American, as opposed to other, national interests, they need not adapt it to changing circumstances. In response to every new development, their self-set task is the same: to put the most anti-Russian gloss possible on whatever happens and to find the most anti-Russian policy that is compatible with short-term Western safety.

Even the sympathy of the Clinton administration is directed not toward Russia but toward the Yeltsin administration; and the desire for accommodation with Yeltsin is dictated, not by a perception of Russia as a long-term partner, but by the fact that the administration has invested so much of its own credit in Yeltsin that it simply cannot afford to see him fall. That inevitably makes Russians fear that a change either in the U.S. administration or in their own could bring a complete end to any residual American attempts at cooperation with Russia. It also increases their sense that any nonbinding agreements with the United States are worthless in the longer term.

The Nature of Russian Nationalism

The attribution to ordinary Russians of an eternal desire for conquest and expansion is very strange, historically speaking. Of all the major European imperial peoples, the Russians were the least consulted by their governments. At one time or another, British, French, Germans, and even Americans all provided enthusiastic electoral support for imperial programs and wars. Whether the Russians would or would not have done so cannot be established—because they were never asked.

However, Russians have had another way of showing their indifference to imperial ideology: the myth of Russian soldiers as enthusiastic fighters in this century for imperial or ideological programs is disproved by all the evidence. No more than any other European population have the Russians shown enthusiasm for sacrifices for imperial, as opposed to national, goals. In fact, whenever the Russians have fought outside ethnic Russian territory, they have been beaten, above all because of their poor morale and their lack of interest in the cause at issue. They were beaten by the Japanese in 1905, the Germans in 1914–17 (when as far as ordinary Russian troops were concerned, the battle lines ran through not Russia but Poland), the Finns in 1939, the Afghans in 1979–89, and the Chechens in 1994—even though the latter were technically in Russia.[8] The Soviet counterattack of 1941–45 began only when the Germans had penetrated deep into Russian territory, and the "Great Patriotic War" was certainly not seen by ordinary Russians as a war of conquest or expansion. If the Russians had attacked the Germans, they would no doubt have been beaten again, as they were in 1914.

It should be apparent from the events of recent years that a great majority of Russians have a complicated and rather weak sense of national identity and are thoroughly doubtful about the need for Russia to play an imperial role—especially if that means paying major costs in money or lives. Had it been otherwise, had the Russian people been as attached to imperial dreams as the russophobes say they are, the collapse of the Soviet Union would have been a much grimmer affair, and Boris Yeltsin could not conceivably have lasted long in power. A people with a strong sense of military pride would have swept from power the government responsible for the multiple defeats and humiliations in Chechnya.

Even more important, the Russian diaspora, so often portrayed as a potential source of fifth columns, has in general shown an extremely weak capacity for mobilizing along Russian national lines; and a key reason is that the diaspora's identity is not in fact nationally Russian, let alone that of imperial colonists. Instead, it remains that of Russian-speaking people who, in the case of Ukraine, for example, have very little to distinguish them from most of their Ukrainian neighbors.

Until now, it is important to remember, the Russian state was never a Russian national state as such, and Russian loyalties were focused on institutions that, although they embodied large elements of "Russianness," were not purely Russian: the Orthodox religion, the czar, Marxism, the Communist Party, the Soviet Union. That has left a legacy in which ethnic nationalism in Russia is rather weak compared with that of its neighbors—a very good thing for us all, and something we should be careful not to change.

None of the major Russian parties today (with the partial exception of Vladimir Zhirinovsky's, now fortunately in eclipse) espouses a narrowly ethnic version of Russian nationalism. Instead, the image, derived from Soviet culture, is that of the Russians' "leading" a voluntary alliance of other peoples. Gen. Alexander Lebed and other Russian politicians dubbed "nationalist" (or even "ultranationalist") in the West have spoken repeatedly of the Russian Federation as a "multinational" state. Lebed (and indeed the Russian government) has also spoken of Islam and Buddhism, along with Orthodox Christianity, as Russia's "traditional" religions, which the state should foster and support.[9] (Such an attitude does not, however, necessarily imply democracy; it is quite compatible with a more or less benevolent dictatorship.)

Russians' image of their society is to a great extent a myth, and often a hypocritical one, when it comes to the real history of Russia, but it has been of great importance in moderating Russian political attitudes toward Russia's ethnic minorities like the Tatars and Yakuts (the Caucasians are a somewhat different case, for the specific reason of a pervasive Russian dislike of their highly visible commercial and criminal activity).

Equally important—and of critical importance when it comes to Western policy toward Russia—has been Russia's ambitions for leadership or hegemony within the former Soviet Union, a hegemony that cannot today or for the foreseeable future be based mainly on coercion; it has to have a genuine element of consent and mutual interest. It would be manifestly impossible for a Russian government to have such a program and yet adopt a narrowly chauvinist position at home.

The risk is that if the program of Brzezinski and Kissinger were to be adopted—and the West were to be successful in depriving Russia of any significant role beyond her borders, excluding her

from all meaningful Western and European institutions and surrounding her by Western-backed, ethnic nationalist and anti-Russian
neighbors—the Russian elites and, much more important, the Russian people might swing in what could be called a "Kemalist" direction, after Gen. Kemal Ataturk, the founder of modern Turkey. Some
well-meaning Western observers have even suggested that that is
the model Russia ought to follow.

Those people have not thought through the implications of their
arguments, or what a true Ataturk, and a determined Kemalist Russian nationalism with a real capacity for mobilizing and inspiring
the Russian army and people, would mean for Europe today. Exclusion from Western institutions would virtually dictate that, unlike
Kemalism, Russian nationalism would develop in an anti-Western
direction and Russia would seek anti-Western allies. Much more
important, just as it would in part be a reaction against the ethnic
nationalism of neighboring states, so it would in turn produce further
chauvinist reactions among Russia's neighbors (and of course her
own minorities). That would risk a downward spiral of hatred,
oppression, unrest, and ultimately war. Such Russian nationalism
might lose all ambitions as regards Tajiks, Georgians, and Uzbeks,
but it would certainly not lose interest in the ethnic Russians beyond
Russia's borders. On the contrary, it would generate an ideology
capable of mobilizing them to fight for Russia against the states in
which they live.

In this context, the Turkish example is apposite but of course the
very opposite of encouraging. After the Ottoman Empire's final
defeat and dismemberment in World War I, which led to attempts
to break off large pieces of what Turks considered their own ethnic
territory, a military-nationalist movement led by Kemal, and based
on younger and more radical elements of the Turkish elites, especially the military, decided to rebuild and strengthen the Turkish
state on the basis of Turkish ethnic nationalism. Kemalist Turkish
nationalism also involved very strong authoritarian, military, and
chauvinist elements and absolutist claims to cultural control over the
entire population within Turkey's new and much reduced borders—
something that had been wholly lacking in the governing philosophy
of the Ottoman Empire.

The result was a relatively successful experiment in modern state
building and development, but one that has been a disaster for

Turkey's ethnic minorities. Armenians, Greeks, and Kurds were respectively subjected to genocide, massacre, and expulsion, and an attempt was made to completely suppress their languages and cultural identities. Later, of course, the Kemalist state philosophy also threatened intervention in neighboring states harboring ethnic Turkish minorities, most notably Cyprus. For Russia to swing from her present mild and highly constricted "imperialism" to such a form of nationalism would be no gain for Russia, her neighbors, the rest of Europe, or indeed humanity. Yet it is that risk that we run if we adopt a policy of trying to wholly suppress Russia's influence outside her present borders.

The Danger of Crowding a Great Power in Distress

It is not the post-Soviet Russian state that ought to worry us in our dealings with Russia. Russians tend to despise their own state, and it is in any case far too weak for the foreseeable future even to threaten its immediate western neighbors, let alone the West. What we should beware of creating is a new and dangerous spirit in the Russian people. Inflicting humiliations on the Russian state in Central Europe, or even in the Transcaucasus, is unlikely to stir up any really strong public reaction in Russia, since Russians themselves have a rather distanced relationship with those areas. The expansion of NATO into Central Europe, which is certainly felt as a humiliation by Russian political elites, may irritate ordinary Russians, but it does not fill them with a strong desire to fight back. The farther NATO expands eastward, however, the greater the risk that, sooner or later, the Euroatlantic countries will stumble into a conflict that affects not just the Russian state and the elites but is felt—truly felt—as a matter of vital national interest by the mass of the Russian people. At that point, the consequences will be unpredictable and horribly dangerous.

Perhaps I could end on two personal notes. The first is drawn from my experience as a war correspondent in Afghanistan, the Transcaucasus, and most recently Chechnya—usually, be it noted, on the anti-Soviet or anti-Russian side. We are being bombarded at the moment with a flood of self-congratulatory, comforting media material to the effect that the new revolution in computer technology will give an unassailable military advantage to the United States.[10] That is particularly comforting to a society that does not wish to think about the possibility of heavy casualties, or indeed about the ugly realities of combat, but prefers a sanitized version of war presented by people who most often have never seen a battlefield.

But all my experience, and most historical evidence, suggests that while military technology is obviously of great importance, what is always critical is morale, and that means not just a willingness to kill but a willingness to die. It does not matter if you can kill 10,000 enemy for every 1,000 combatants you lose, if even that thousand is unacceptable to your own public opinion. How many Americans are prepared to die for a Ukrainian Sevastopol, if the Russians prove willing to die on the other side? That issue has admittedly now been shelved for 20 years—but what are 20 years in the life of a nation? What will be NATO's policy when the issue comes up for review 20 years from now, if Kissinger has his way?

And why should we be so anxious to turn Ukraine into an anti-Russian buffer state, when in fact Russia has not threatened Ukraine, has not supported Russian separatists in Crimea, and is not trying to turn the Russians of other areas into a fifth column? On the contrary, the integration of Russians into the new Ukrainian state is proceeding very well. The threat to that benign process comes not from Moscow but from the failure of Ukraine to reform and develop economically, and from more radical, ethnic Ukrainian nationalism that will end by alienating the Russians and Russian speakers. The potential threat to Ukraine comes from within, and it is precisely that exclusivist nationalism that might draw strength from Western encouragement of Ukraine as an anti-Russian buffer state. If that coincided with a sense of ethnic nationalism among Russians in Russia and, still more important, in Ukraine, the results could be very ugly.

A final note: In the late 1970s I was a teenager growing up in England, another former imperial power fallen on hard times, and I vividly remember the malaise of that period. Of course, the pit into which Britain had sunk was not nearly as deep as the one in which Russia now finds herself, but it was still pretty deep compared with Britain's previous status, and the sense of decline was undoubtedly exacerbated by an underlying feeling of national loss and humiliation. Britain did not look like a country that would be willing to fight, and fight hard, for a very distant and utterly unimportant former imperial outpost like the Falklands. That at least was what the Argentine government calculated in 1982, and a very bad miscalculation it was. I would not wish us to imitate it in our relations with Russia.

Notes

1. Confidential interview with author.

2. For a recent exposition of Brzezinski's views, see his article, "The Germ of a More Secure Europe," *Financial Times*, May 27, 1997.

3. A personal note: I come on my father's side from a Baltic German family. I don't at all like what the Russians have done to the former East Prussia. A British author recently described Kaliningrad today, thanks to Soviet rule, as "the armpit of the Baltic," which just about sums it up. But a great many of us Europeans, and all of us from Eastern Europe, if we are honest, will admit, privately, that there are quite a few contemporary borders that—if we had a completely free hand in a perfect world—we might wish to see redrawn. But as every sane, responsible European knows, we must keep those thoughts to ourselves.

4. See, for example, John Laughland, "Don't Let Russia Neutralize NATO," *Wall Street Journal*, April 3, 1997; and George Will, "Eastward-Ho—And Soon," *Washington Post*, June 6, 1996.

5. Ibid.; and Peter Rodman, "Four More for NATO," *Washington Post*, December 13, 1994. See also William Safire, "If Russia Reneges on CFE, Speed NATO Expansion," *Washington Post*, March 3, 1997; and "More Caucasus Meddling," editorial, *Wall Street Journal*, April 10, 1997.

6. For Kissinger's critique of Louis Napoleon's foreign policy, see Henry Kissinger, *Diplomacy* (New York: Simon & Schuster, 1994), especially pp. 103–37.

7. For a recent discussion of such allegedly continuing trends in Russian culture by the foremost academic proponent of that view, see Richard Pipes, "Russia's Past, Russia's Future," *Commentary*, June 1996, pp. 30–38. Pipes, it should be noted, has opposed NATO expansion, in part precisely because it will tend to diminish whatever chances he thinks there are of Russia's developing in a democratic and pro-Western direction.

8. On the demoralization of Soviet soldiers during the Finnish war, see Roger R. Reese, *Stalin's Reluctant Soldiers: A Social History of the Red Army, 1925–41* (Lawrence: University Press of Kansas, 1996). The nature of contemporary Russian nationalism, in the context of the defeat in Chechnya, is analyzed in my forthcoming book, *Flaying the Bear: Chechnya and the Collapse of Russian State Power* (New Haven, Conn.: Yale University Press, forthcoming March 1998).

9. Alexander Lebed, Press conference, Moscow, June 24, 1996, attended by the author.

10. See, for example, John Keegan, "Tales of Combat to Come," *Washington Post*, December 1, 1996.

PART III

INS AND OUTS: CREATING A NEW
DIVISION OF EUROPE

11. NATO's Manifest Destiny: The Risks of Expansion

Hugh De Santis

The Clinton administration has stumbled into its policy of NATO enlargement. In its desire to placate the new democracies in Europe and burnish the president's historical legacy, it has unwisely pressed its less-than-enthusiastic security partners to open the alliance's doors to the post-Soviet states. If the Madrid meeting at which the alliance invited Poland, Hungary, and the Czech Republic to apply for membership had ended a period of muddled policymaking, both proponents and critics of enlargement might breathe a sigh of relief. Unfortunately, the situation is worse than it appears. Most worrisome are the underlying attitudes that give impetus to the policy of NATO enlargement: the image of unipolarity and the underlying narcissistic belief that the post–Cold War world is a reflection of American values. By refusing to see the world as it really is, the United States is blinding itself to the potentially destabilizing consequences of NATO enlargement and their adverse effects on American interests.

If nothing else, the Madrid summit made good on President Clinton's pledge to the former Warsaw Pact states to extend the alliance's security umbrella eastward. Vaguely informed by strategic logic, that landmark event represents the president's instinctive accommodation of the political appeals of the newly independent states of Europe. In response to the entreaties of the East European states for closer security cooperation, which intensified as a result of the Bosnian crisis, the resurgence of the Russian authoritarian right wing, and the niggardly refusal of the European Union to enlarge its franchise, the United States unveiled its Partnership for Peace

The views expressed here are solely those of the author and do not necessarily reflect the views of the U.S. Department of Defense or any other agency of the U.S. government.

initiative in 1994. A kind of halfway house that circumvented automatic military guarantees to avoid arousing renewed Russian fears of encirclement, the PFP laid out a set of criteria that the emerging democracies would have to satisfy to ensure their political, economic, and military compatibility with the West.

For the United States and the European allies, the PFP was a holding action. For the Central and East European states, however, it was a step toward eventual NATO membership. Buoyed by Clinton's encouraging "when, not if" rhetoric, many of the new democracies met their PFP obligations with alacrity and, not surprisingly, insisted that the West honor its commitment. The caboose, as it were, began to push the train. Propelled by the U.S. presidential election of 1996, the train quickly picked up steam. In an effort to woo American voters with ties to Eastern Europe and to blunt the (equally ill-considered) Republican foreign policy offensive on NATO enlargement, Clinton declared that 1997 would mark the beginning of the alliance's enlargement. And so it did.

NATO has thus far offered membership only to Hungary, Poland, and the Czech Republic. Other suitors will have to bide their time and, of course, preserve their virtue until Brussels calls. While the new inductees await the outcome of the post-Madrid deliberations that will presumably confirm their NATO-worthiness, and parliaments in the East as well as the West prepare for the anticipated ratification of enlargement in 1999, the Clinton administration is betting that those left behind will sedulously continue to enact political and civil-military reforms and resolve lingering territorial disputes in the hope that they will be next.

But the East European states that were passed over in Madrid may harbor resentment toward the West. Countries that have worked diligently to meet the criteria for membership may conclude that they have been abandoned by NATO and consequently reevaluate not only the wisdom of integration with the West but also the value of democratic reform. The first phase of NATO expansion may further alienate Russia. Differences between Moscow and Western officials over the intent of the Founding Act on Mutual Relations, Cooperation and Security between NATO and the Russian Federation already threaten to scupper joint security arrangements.

Such concerns may prove to be much ado about nothing. Still, they cannot be ignored or glibly dismissed, as they have been by too many proponents of enlargement in and out of the Clinton administration, with the complacent conviction that the tide of history is now irreversibly running toward liberal democracy. Before we plunge into a morass from which we may not easily extricate ourselves, we ought to assess the risks that may lie ahead in the interest of limiting the political, military, and ecomonic costs of enlargement. The following four scenarios, which traverse the optimism-pessimism spectrum over the short and long term, might form the basis for such an analysis.

Scenario no. 1: NATO-ville

Let us assume that naysayers, heretics, and traditional NATO-phobes grossly misread post–Cold War security trends and that the first wave of alliance expansion proceeds smoothly, neither insulting the bevy of maids in waiting nor, thanks to the face-saving Founding Act, offending Russia. In this scenario, the governments in all three invited countries mount a successful public relations campaign and win parliamentary ratification. Powerless to prevent NATO's enlargement, Russia offers no meaningful opposition. The U.S. Senate, persuaded by the administration that refusal to ratify would irreparably damage NATO and destroy the credibility of the world's last remaining superpower, acquiesces. So do West European parliaments, which are more preoccupied with the European Monetary Union.

To reassure the former Soviet bloc states outside NATO that they have not been forgotten, and to reinforce the process of democratic reform and the resolution of territorial and ethnic disputes, the allies intensify their political-military dialogue through a network of new and existing institutions, including the PFP and the 27-member Atlantic Partnership Council. Bilateral discussions between the allies (and Russia) and NATO aspirants, or what is being called the "extended dialogue," subtly reaffirm the West's nuptial intentions without setting the date for the wedding by announcing NATO's desire to begin accession talks with Slovenia and Romania by the end of 1998. Having relaxed the criteria for monetary union to maintain political support for the euro and stabilize stock and bond markets, the EU announces the first tranche of single-currency states, including an economically chastened France that has abandoned its reinflationary course and acceded to the need for austerity.

Encouraged by NATO's dialogue and especially by the resumption of progress toward European economic integration, the "outs"—including a democratically rejuvenated Slovakia that has thrown off the yoke of Vladimir Meciar—accelerate their reform agendas. Although Moscow remains a vocal critic of further NATO enlargement, particularly in the former Soviet republics of the "near abroad," it is economically and militarily bereft of levers with which to arrest Western expansion. More to the point, it knows that compliant behavior is a prerequisite for gaining access to the bustling markets of the world's industrial democracies. Reformers such as Anatoly Chubais, Boris Nemtsov, and Gregoriy Yavlinsky join forces to relaunch perestroika and redouble their commitment to liberal-democratic reform, and Russia ratifies START II and the Chemical Weapons Convention and negotiates further reductions of conventional arms in Europe.

However improbable, that is the scenario on which the Clinton administration is banking, partly because of its propensity to define international behavior, especially in the post–Cold War period, in rational-actor terms. Naively, policymakers seem to expect that other states will make the same choices that the United States would make if it were faced with the same set of circumstances. Indeed, U.S. policymakers seem congenitally predisposed to view the revolutionary events of 1989–90 and beyond as replications of the American experience, that is, to see the emerging democracies in Eastern Europe, no matter how different their cultures and traditions are from our own, through the prism of our own exceptionalist values, beliefs, and ideals.

Scenario no. 2: NATO-sclerosis

It is altogether reasonable to expect that the United States and NATO will be able to manage developments in Eastern Europe and Russia in the interval between the Madrid summit and the investiture of the new members in the alliance in 1999. What happens after 1999 is another matter.

In all likelihood, the road from Madrid to Brussels will not be smooth. Both the Czech and Hungarian publics have become less inclined toward NATO membership over the past year, especially if it entails increased military spending at the expense of social programs.[1] Given the equally intransigent domestic opposition to budgetary cuts required by the Maastricht guidelines for entry into the EMU, West European governments are also unlikely to foot the bill. And, given its support for a balanced budget, the Clinton administration will likely find it difficult to persuade taxpayers to pay Europe's bills. Regardless of how the burden-sharing issue is resolved, the cost of enlargement is bound to provoke sniping between Washington and allied capitals. And when all is said and done, neither the United States nor Western Europe will be eager to proceed with the next round of enlargement.

Furthermore, differences of interpretation of provisions of the Founding Act, not unlike differences over the deployment of allied forces in eastern Germany following reunification, will almost certainly create new disputes that will keep Russia and NATO at loggerheads over expansion of the alliance for the next two years. NATO expansion will further impede progress on new and existing arms control treaties. The Duma may well obstruct efforts to amend the Conventional Forces in Europe treaty. In such unsettling circumstances, alliance cohesion is also likely to suffer, with the old guard loath to do anything that might destroy the foundation of the consultative council and antagonize Russia and new members worried that they and their eastern neighbors may yet be abandoned by the West, military guarantees notwithstanding.[2]

Finally, the end of the first phase of NATO enlargement will coincide with the run-up to the U.S. presidential election in 2000. Even if the candidates were to support further enlargement of the alliance, the exigencies of domestic politics and the foreign policy immobility that naturally follows changes of administration make it unlikely that serious preparations for the next round would take place before late 2001 or early 2002. Given those considerations, we are probably heading for a more uncertain near-term environment in which the United States and its NATO partners will have to muddle through what is bound to be a period of political instability in Europe.

In this scenario, the adroit use of political and diplomatic tools of statecraft will be required to sustain support for NATO enlargement. In the absence of concrete steps toward the next phase of enlargement, the Atlantic Partnership Council would be expected to assume a greater management role in the alliance's efforts to buttress sagging spirits in the East and to maintain alliance cohesion. Bilateral talks between the allies and the NATO supplicants will be equally important. In both cases, NATO will have to walk a fine line between keeping hope alive and avoiding the appearance of beginning accession talks.

That will be no easy chore. On the one hand, the allies will be inclined to proceed deliberately to ensure that Russia consents to the next phase of enlargement. On the other hand, they will face criticism from both new and aspiring alliance members about giving Russia a veto over NATO's security decisionmaking and thus creating another Yalta. As NATO prepares to celebrate the parliamentary blessings of enlargement, the new inductees will begin to clamor for inclusion in the EU after 2000. That effort will be closely watched by the countries still seeking admission to NATO and the EU and by Russia. It will also be closely followed by the U.S. Congress, which would prefer the EU to assume greater responsibility for the safety and welfare of the emerging democracies and thus reduce the economic burden on NATO, which is to say, the United States.

Scenario no. 3: An Informal Russian Sphere of Influence

As time goes by, the task of NATO expansion will become more arduous. Even the most ardent suitor will tire of promises of betrothal absent the long-awaited proposal. Disaffection is inevitable. Clearly, such a political and diplomatic stalemate is not sustainable indefinitely. Indeed, it may not last beyond the next two years. The politically predictable course of events encouraged by the rational-actor model may be immediately tested by the post-Madrid debate in both the petitioning states and the allied countries.

Although favorably disposed toward NATO membership, the public in the Czech Republic and Hungary is emphatically unwilling to be saddled with increased defense outlays, even though defense spending in both countries, particularly Hungary, is much lower than the NATO average. Not only have the governments in Prague and Budapest poorly laid the groundwork for the debate over the cost of NATO membership that lies ahead, they have toadied to their respective publics. Czech prime minister Václav Klaus announced yet another military downsizing in April, in response to the slumping Czech economy and the challenge of Milos Zeman's Social Democrats, who support NATO membership with reservations. Faced with powerful opposition to increased military spending and calls for a referendum on NATO, Hungarian prime minister Gyula Horn is no less reluctant to press for higher defense bills. Consequently, Czechs and Hungarians are likely to become "free riders" in NATO, which will place greater economic burdens on the United States and the West European allies. That is bound to raise the hackles of the public in NATO member countries and, no matter who ends up subsidizing the new members, reduce the prospect of a second round of enlargement any time soon.[3]

Except in Slovakia, where Prime Minister Meciar engineered a referendum to encourage opposition to NATO in the expectation that his country would be excluded at Madrid, the angry reaction of Western publics will not be lost on the "outs." The failure to be included in the first tranche of invitees will more than disappoint Romanian supporters of NATO—elites as well as the public, which has increasingly warmed to the idea since 1994. Indeed, that failure may be viewed by many Romanians as a defeat for the political stewardship of President Emil Constantinescu and Prime Minister Victor Ciorbea. The exclusion of Slovenia, which does not meet NATO military standards but parallels the Czech Republic in economic performance and the institutionalization of democracy, would reinforce feelings of rejection in Romania and elsewhere. If Slovenia, which boasts about its former ties to the West as part of the Hapsburg Empire, is not eligible for membership, what chance would Bulgaria, Romania, or Ukraine have in the foreseeable future?[4]

Except in a few countries—Slovenia, Estonia, perhaps Slovakia—perceptions that the NATO window may be closing to new members will exacerbate economic anxieties throughout the former Soviet empire and threaten stability. To be sure, the recent ascendancy of democratic reformers in Bulgaria and Romania has contributed to wishful thinking in some quarters in the United States that real economic reforms cannot be far behind. But the economies of the East European states are in a hapless state. Continued stagnation and ebbing hopes of being bailed out by the West, particularly if the launch of the euro is delayed, can only increase social tensions and unravel what support there is for market reforms.

The damage done by the neocommunist governments in Romania and Bulgaria has left both countries with shoddy infrastructures and obsolete industrial plants, shaky banks, and minuscule capital markets. The currency board in Bulgaria, which the International

Monetary Fund has advocated to curb hyperinflation, will be bitter medicine for employees of state-owned firms who lose their jobs and for exporters whose goods may be priced out of foreign markets. IMF-mandated cuts in consumer and industrial subsidies will probably also raise the threshold of pain above tolerable limits in Romania, further shrinking a contracting economy and causing workers to take to the streets. Conditions are even worse in corruption-plagued Ukraine, despite substantial American aid, and in Belarus, where a Soviet-style economy operates with such inefficiency that Russian reformers diluted Yeltsin's proposed union treaty to avoid being saddled with Belarus's financial mess, not to mention the autocratic style of President Alexander Lukashenko.[5]

Even worse, economic despair will feed nationalistic nostrums in the region. All of the former client states of the Soviet empire harbor feelings of resentment toward the West for its perceived betrayal of Eastern Europe during the interwar years and at Yalta. Exclusion from NATO—read, exclusion from Europe—would reinforce perceptions of Western betrayal, as an editorial in the Romanian daily *Ziua* observed.[6] It would also help to discredit democratic parties and thus redound to the advantage of ultranationalist politicians who lurk in the shadows in all those countries except Slovakia— where Meciar has brazenly manipulated public opinion to strengthen his hold on power—no matter the outcome in Madrid.

With little prospect of financial or security assistance from the West, and none at all if economic and political reforms are suspended or abolished, what alternative would the East European states have but to establish closer ties with Moscow, especially if Russian nationalists were to gain power? Although the East European states would not want to fall under Russia's sway again, the perceived abandonment by the West and the reemergence of a more nationalistic Russia that may begin to reassert its security prerogatives in Europe will ineluctably cause them to reorient themselves eastward. Indeed, some states are already hedging their bets.

Belarus, which is pushing for reunification with Russia, and Ukraine, which depends on Russia to buy its goods and supply its energy and thus has little room for maneuver, are the most obvious examples. But Bulgaria has also begun to establish more extensive trade ties with Moscow. In April 1997, as part of a larger agreement to liberalize trade, the head of the Union of Democratic Forces–led caretaker Bulgarian government, Stefan Sofiyanski, and Russian prime minister Viktor Chernomyrdin signed an accord to develop a pipeline that will transport Russian natural gas to the Balkans and also ensure deliveries to Bulgaria. Russia has also begun to help modernize the Kozlodui nuclear power plant in Bulgaria. And although Sofia has not yet decided whether to purchase 14 MiG-29 aircraft, the Russian proposal to invest in the Bulgarian aircraft repair plant in Plovdiv, which would create badly needed jobs, is a powerful inducement. Partly because of Bulgaria's historic and cultural ties, partly because of its parlous economic condition, reform-minded President Petur Stoyanov has made it clear that NATO membership cannot hinder the development of Bulgaria's relations with Russia.[7]

To be sure, other would-be suitors have not hedged their bets to the same degree as Bulgaria. Its impressive economic growth notwithstanding, Slovakia comes the closest. Exclusion from the first tranche of enlargement can be expected to elicit feelings of rejection among Slovaks and an increased interest in neutrality, which Meciar has encouraged in an effort to force NATO's hand. If, as expected, Bratislava continues to receive the cold shoulder from the West and is denied admission to other Western institutions such as the Organization for Economic Cooperation and Development, Meciar could make good on his threat. Slovakia has already signed several agreements with Russia on the supply of gas, oil, and nuclear fuel. It has also purchased six attack helicopters and accelerated cooperation on defense technology as part of a recently concluded military accord.[8]

Although Romania and the Baltic countries have reoriented their economies to the West, uncertainty about NATO membership and a protracted delay in European economic integration would necessarily prompt reconsideration of that policy. Without technical and financial aid from the West, Prime Minister Ciorbea is not likely to maintain public support for reforms. Like Slovakia, Romania would be forced to look to Russia, even if a nationalist government came to power in Moscow. Despite assurances from NATO capitals, the Baltic states would also probably refocus their economic policies, especially if Moscow took steps to manipulate the flow of freight and to find alternative routes for the transit of its exports.

Admittedly, Moscow will have to use carrot-and-stick tactics on the failed suitors more cleverly than it has in the past. In March 1997 the Russian ambassador in Prague clumsily threatened to revoke agreements to deliver Russian gas and nuclear energy, among other commodities, if the Czech Republic proceeded with its plans to join NATO. Prague responded by signing a gas deal with Norway. Coming on the heels of similar agreements with Germany and the United States, it reinforced the Klaus government's commitment to free itself from dependence on Russian raw materials. Russia's threats to reconsider the status of the Crimea and its continued military presence on Ukrainian territory similarly spurred President Leonid Kuchma's consultative agreement with NATO.

Yeltsin appears to have gotten the message. The Russian government has begun to cultivate the economic interests of NATO-bound states such as Hungary and to apply political and diplomatic pressure more deftly to exploit opportunities created by their inability to satisfy the financial obligations of alliance membership. As illustrated by the May 31, 1997, friendship treaty with Ukraine, which, in establishing a legal basis for berthing Russian ships at Sevastopol, acknowledged Ukrainian sovereignty, the Russian government has also begun to reduce the incentive of NATO aspirants to become part of the alliance.[9]

Scenario no. 4: Redivided Europe

The blow to Russian prestige inflicted by NATO enlargement may be greater than it appears, however, in which case Moscow's behavior may not be as restrained as the United States anticipates. The anti-NATO alarms sounded by the Russian right may be little more than a ruse to blame the country's socioeconomic crisis on the West, and for reformers such as Andrei Kozyrev, Sergei Kovalev, and Konstantin Borovoy, harping on NATO expansion is so much waffle. The real threat to Russian security is internal, specifically, widening social and economic inequities, the lack of a civil society, and the failure of an infirm president to devise a practicable strategy to address the domestic disarray.

Alas, the public may not be counting on the Kozyrevs or such new reform guardians as Chubais and Nemtsov to solve their problems. Nominally, the March 27, 1997, demonstrations in Red Square in Moscow and in more than 1,200 other cities reflected the public's frustration over delays in the payment of an estimated $10 billion in wages and pensions. But they also conveyed latent popular rage over the effects of reform. According to opinion polls conducted by the All-Union Center for Public Research in March 1997, two-thirds of the Russian public, especially the middle-aged and the elderly, are disillusioned with reform. If presidential elections were held today, Communist leader Gennady Zyuganov and former general Alexander Lebed would muster the greatest support.[10]

Significantly, Zyuganov and Lebed also present themselves as defenders of Russian interests, and they appeal to nationalists who interpret NATO expansion as a calculated plan—not unlike the Versailles settlement imposed on Germany after World War I—on the part of the United States to transform the European geopolitical situation in order to contain a potentially remilitarized Russia. There is a growing perception that the United States is trying to isolate Russia, weaken it militarily, and reduce it to the status of a colonial outpost of the industrialized West. Even Westernizing liberal reformers may have a hard time with NATO enlargement because it de facto raises barriers between Russia and the West.

The extension of a protective Western security glacis to the Baltic states—which Vice President Al Gore has virtually guaranteed to Lithuanian parliamentary chairman Vytautas Landsbergis—and to Ukraine would exacerbate Russian feelings of alienation from Europe all the more and magnify Versailles-like images of humiliation. Reminiscent of the disingenuous American offer to let the USSR join the Marshall Plan a half century ago, the Founding Act that Yeltsin brandished before the Duma is likely to be reviled as a condescending take-it-or-leave-it gesture that a proud Russia must reject or succumb to "quiet conquest." As former Soviet president Mikhail Gorbachev told Congress in April 1997, it is ill-advised for NATO to treat Russia the way the allies treated Germany after World War I because "you cannot humiliate a people without consequences."[11]

The Clinton administration is anticipating that an increasingly liberal-democratic Russia will eventually become inured to, if not wholly approving of, NATO enlargement. But the next American president could confront an authoritarian-nationalist Russia after 2000, led by Lebed or someone like him, that would seek not only to reimpose the authority of the state over the public—what Kovalev refers to as *derzhavnost*—but also to restore a balance of power in Europe and challenge the West. The elements of an anti-Western strategy would plausibly include a diplomatic offensive throughout Europe, military modernization, and possibly the formation of a new framework of alliances. Foreign Minister Yevgeny Primakov has already urged the anti-NATO faction in the Duma to press its misgivings on European parliamentarians, and Yeltsin's sacking of Defense Minister Igor Rodionov in May 1997 may give impetus to military reform. Unless NATO unequivocally renounces the deployment of nuclear weapons in Eastern Europe and allows a Russian veto on alliance security issues, the Duma will probably oppose a revised CFE mandate and refuse to ratify START II.[12]

Moreover, despite the West's oft-stated peaceful intentions, Russia may decide to counteract NATO's military capabilities. Rather than reduce the number of long-range nuclear weapons to 3,500, as START II would do, Moscow may choose to restock its nuclear arsenal. It may be more than coincidental that Rodionov's replacement as defense minister, Gen. Igor Sergeyev, is the former head of the strategic rocket forces. Funds to finance military reform, including the payment of back wages and nuclear modernization, will probably be siphoned from domestic programs and justified in the time-honored tradition of defending the security of the Motherland. Just as Stalin rallied a war-battered Russian people to the colors in 1946 on grounds that the fascist menace had not disappeared, a nationalist firebrand like Lebed might argue that the Cold War has not ended.

As for the creation of new alliances, Russia can be expected to establish closer links to countries in the "far abroad," notably China and Iran, that also oppose a U.S.-directed unipolar world. Russia and China have entered into a new friendship pact that, in addition to scaling back troops along their long border, calls for closer trade relations and continued transfers of Russian arms (Su-27 fighter jets, anti-missile systems, rocket technology, and diesel submarines) and military technology to China. Contacts with Iran also have increased in response to the imminent expansion of NATO's eastern extremities and the concentration of American military assets in the Persian Gulf. There is also a growing concern in Moscow that the United States, under the perceived NATO pretext of providing peacekeeping forces, is intent on gaining a foothold in the Caspian Sea and its vast oil resources. American transport of oil from Central Asia to the Turkish port of Ceyhan would deprive Russia of markets in the Transcaucasus and the Near East. In addition to increasing contacts between their oil, gas, and petrochemical industries, the two states have entered into discussions to increase bilateral trade in machine building, transportation, and agriculture as well. Like China, Iran is eager to expand military-technical cooperation with Russia.[13]

Realistically, an Eastern bloc is not likely to emerge in the near future. The Sino-Russian agreement certainly does not constitute a full-blown alliance. China is hardly likely to sacrifice its access to Western capital and technology for the sake of arresting NATO expansion. Moreover, despite the growing arms trade between the two countries, Moscow remains suspicious of Beijing. Given China's increasing energy needs, the two countries are rivals in Central Asia and the Middle East. Some Russian experts also fear that the military modernization of the Peoples Liberation Army, which Yeltsin is aiding, represents a direct threat to Russia in the future, particularly if China were to take steps to reclaim lands in Siberia and the Far East seized by the czars. Partly to counter a potentially aggressive China, Russia has intensified its ties with India, which is not only a major arms buyer but a huge market for Russian goods.

Pitfalls also litter the path of Russian-Iranian relations. Russia and Iran are competitors in the Caspian region, not to mention in Central Asia and the Transcaucasus. The clash of cultures in Central Asia also poses obstacles to cooperation. Indeed, the two countries remain at loggerheads over resolution of the conflict in Tajikistan.[14]

Although Western governments cannot dismiss the possibility that further enlargement of NATO may lead to a new set of alignments between Russia and its eastern neighbors, such cooperation will be a tortuous process until Russia's economic health revives and its military once again becomes a cohesive force. Even then, the emergence of an Eastern bloc would not pose a strategic threat to the West before 2010. The more palpable and proximate consequence of NATO enlargement is likely to be Russia's political-military encroachment on the states along its borders and what that portends: the redivision of Europe.

The absence of Romania from Madrid's nuptial rites and the draconian effects of economic reform are likely to provoke political instability in the years ahead, and they could lead to the rise of a nationalist-authoritarian government, say, a coalition of Gheorghe Funar's Party of Romanian National Unity, along with other rightist groups, and Ion Iliescu's Party of Social Democracy. Appeals for the restoration of Bessarabia and Northern Bukovina would surely follow. Since Petru Lucinschi replaced the pro-Romanian Mircea Snegur as president of Moldova, Chisinau's relations with Russia and the breakaway Transdniestrian republic have undeniably improved. Nevertheless, if right-wing, pro-union firebrands in both countries were to force the issue in the wake of Romania's perceived rejection by the West, Russia could militarily intervene in Moldova, ostensibly to defend the interests of the Dniester Republic, and begin to circumscribe Bucharest's ability to maneuver in foreign affairs.[15]

Ukraine also has equities in the Transdniester region. To complicate matters, the border treaty signed by Romania and Ukraine to remove obstacles to NATO enlargement has left the issue of sovereignty over Bukovina and Zmiynyy Island unsettled. Romania's demand for the restoration of historic territory would fan the flames of nationalism in Ukraine and exacerbate the persisting lord-vassal relationship between Moscow and Kiev, their friendship treaty notwithstanding. Indeed, the participation of Ukraine in PFP exercises such as Sea Breeze-97 may be seen in Moscow as a thinly veiled attempt to prevent the reunification of Crimea with Russia. Although Kiev has emphasized the humanitarian character of Sea Breeze-97, such exercises in the future could serve as a convenient pretext for Moscow to try to reassert its authority over Ukraine. The gravitation of the Baltic states into NATO's orbit can be expected to prompt a similarly hostile reaction from Russia because of the perceived threat posed by NATO forces on its borders and the encirclement of Kaliningrad.[16]

Russia's formal reabsorption of the near abroad into its sphere would be accompanied by the forced reintegration of the Commonwealth of Independent States. Until now, Yeltsin's overtures to the newly independent states for closer political and economic cooperation have largely fallen on deaf ears. Having rediscovered their national roots, Russia's former appendages have been understandably reluctant to share in a condominium that Moscow would dominate. The CIS has certainly not ensured Azerbaijan's territorial integrity, and it has sanctioned the presence of Russian troops in Georgia's breakaway region of Abkhazia. Wary of Russian exploitation, oil-rich states like Azerbaijan and Turkmenistan have exercised increasing independence, as evidenced by the former's decision to support the U.S.-backed pipeline route to Turkey that bypasses Russian territory.

Questions of political autonomy would be moot, however, if ethnonationalist instability on Russia's western borders, an expansion of NATO's peacekeeping presence in the Balkans, or the export of fundamentalism from Iran or the Taliban movement in Afghanistan caused

Moscow to circle the wagons. In his March 1997 speech to the CIS commemorating five years of post-Soviet cooperation, Yeltsin conveyed unmistakable concern about "the increasing attempts [of foreign interests] to establish power centers in the post-Soviet space" and admonished the members to draw closer together to protect their common security.[17]

In this pessimistic scenario, NATO enlargement could lead to the formal redivision of Europe in the first decade of the next century: in the West, a NATO-EU-centered group of states extending into Central Europe; in the East, the establishment of Russian military control over the near abroad, suzerainty over Romania and Bulgaria, and the Finlandization of Slovakia. Even without the formation of a Sino-Indo-Russian bloc as a counterforce to NATO and the West, closer relations between Moscow and Delhi could complicate American efforts to prevent a military clash in South Asia. Likewise, Sino-Russian rapprochement could complicate U.S. strategic planning in East Asia, particularly if Beijing believes it has removed, or at least neutralized, the threat to its northern borders and is emboldened to challenge the preeminence of the United States in the western Pacific.

The German Wild Card

It would be simpleminded to imply that a renewed U.S.-Russian face-off, much less the repolarization of the international system, could be attributable solely to NATO enlargement. For the next two years, the probability of a redivided Europe as a consequence of enlargement is relatively low. Over the longer term, however, we are likely to see new divisions in Europe before we see further NATO enlargement in the Balkans and in the Russian near abroad.

Whether enlargement sets in motion a process that redivides Europe will depend not only on the actions of the United States, Russia, and the ex-Soviet republics and satellites; it will also depend on what the West Europeans do. Concerns about renewed instability on the Continent and about the continuation of the American military presence may shake the European allies, particularly Germany, from their post–Cold War torpor.

Although the Kohl government has supported NATO enlargement, it has little interest in expanding NATO beyond the confines of Mitteleuropa, which is becoming increasingly Germanized. Above all, it seeks to preserve stability in the Balkan and Baltic regions.

According to reports circulating in Europe, Kohl has privately assured Yeltsin that he would resist NATO enlargement to Ukraine and the Baltic countries. German defense minister Volker Ruehe purportedly told Russian journalists in May that the alliance should also refrain from stationing foreign troops in Eastern Europe.[18]

Precisely to avoid sending the wrong signal to Russia and thereby renewing political and possibly armed confrontation, Bonn-Berlin may secretly establish some modus vivendi with Moscow—somewhat like the Rapallo arrangement after World War I—in an effort to stem the course of NATO enlargement and resurrect the notion of a "common European home." In exchange, Yeltsin or whoever follows might pledge to end the corruption that has eroded public confidence in reform and to foster greater harmonization of interests in the CIS.

Germany's *ostpolitik* gambit would surely entail the assumption of new financial burdens. It would be politically costly as well. It would strain relations with Washington and concomitantly weaken the U.S. defense commitment to Europe. It would also obligate Germany—in concert with France—to assume greater responsibility in a more Europeanized European security system. With or without the threat of Russia, a Eurocentric security policy is likely to emerge at some point anyway as a consequence of friction between the allies and Washington over extended peacekeeping in Bosnia, the eventual resumption of EU political and economic integration, and the inevitable assertion of German political-security leadership in Europe.[19]

NATO Expansion and Unintended Consequences

Whether this skein of events unravels in exactly this manner, or at all, it is incontrovertible that in a complex, increasingly interdependent world that cannot be easily compartmentalized along subregional or regional lines, efforts to shape the international system will have manifold repercussions, not all of which are predictable or controllable. In the case of NATO enlargement, the actions the United States and its allies took in Madrid will have potentially far-reaching consequences in Europe and beyond.

In thrall to our cultural legacy, American policymakers may narcissistically fantasize that we have entered some Elysian state of posthistory and that NATO, in the spirit of manifest destiny, is replicating the American national experience of democratic expansion. But the truth is that the world remains in flux and the newly independent post-Soviet states are not irrevocably committed either to liberal democracy or to the United States. Considering the risks that we face, prudence dictates that we seriously weigh the consequences of our actions while there is still time to do so. Like the failed suitors for NATO membership, we too might want to hedge our bets.

Notes

1. "NATO Enlargement: Views from the European Continent," U.S. Information Agency, February 1997, pp. 4, 6; and "Hungarian Public Widely Opposed to Military Spending Increase," U.S. Information Agency, April 21, 1997, pp. 1–4.

2. See "West Europeans Now More Uncertain about NATO Enlargement," U.S. Information Agency, February 7, 1997, pp. 1–2.

3. See "NATO Enlargement," p. 4. Author's confidential interviews of personnel from the Department of State and the Central Intelligence Agency, April 1 and 30, 1997; Robert Frank, "Czech's Economic Success Loses Edge," *Wall Street Journal*, May 28, 1997, p. A12; and "Bohemia's Fading Rhapsody," *The Economist*, May 31, 1997, pp. 65–66.

4. Author's confidential interview of personnel from the Department of State, April 1, 1997; and Chris Hedges, "Slovenia Discards the Yoke That Was Yugoslavia," *New York Times*, May 31, 1997, p. A3.

5. See, for example, Therese Raphael, "Reform Finally Comes to Romania," *Wall Street Journal*, May 12, 1997, p. A14; "Those South-eastern Laggards," *The Economist*, October 19, 1996, pp, 54–56; "Hope at Last," *The Economist*, April 26, 1997, pp. 48–49; "Romania Starts to Build," *The Economist*, May 3, 1997, pp. 39–40; Raymond Bonner, "Ukraine Staggers on Path to the Free Market," *New York Times*, April 9, 1997, p. A8; and Lee Hockstader, "Belarus, Russia Move toward a New Union," *Washington Post*, April 3, 1997, p. A23.

6. "Romania, Braving the Odds, Knocks on NATO's Door," *New York Times*, March 28, 1997, p. A10; and author's confidential interviews.

7. "Russia Modernizing Nuclear Plant in Bulgaria," ITAR-TASS, February 21, 1997; "Aide Speaks of Arms Sales to Bulgaria, India," *Nezavisimaya Gazeta*, April 4, 1997; "Chernomyrdin, Bulgaria's Sofiyanski Sign Agreements," RIA Novosti, April 15, 1997; and "Stoyanov Views Economic Crisis, Prospects for NATO," interview in the Hungarian *Nepszabadsag*, February 26, 1997, Foreign Broadcast Information Service at http.//fbis.fedworld.gov (hereafter FBIS), February 21, April 10, April 16, and February 28, 1997, respectively.

8. "Energy Dependence Seen as Key Factor in NATO Debate," Bratislava SME, February 24, 1997; "Chernomyrdin Visits Bratislava," *Nezavisimaya Gazeta*, April 30, 1997; and "Slovakia Acquires 6 Ka-50 Attack Helicopters," *Krasnaya Zvezda*, November 29, 1996, FBIS, February 24, May 1, and February 7, 1997, respectively.

9. "Progress Seen on Affecting Economic Ties with Czechs," *Segodnya*, April 17, 1997; Hungarian Foreign Minister Kovac's interview in *Rzeczpospolita*, February 21, 1997; "Kremlin in 'Sheep's Clothing'? How Long Can It Wear It?" *Vseukrainskiye Vedomosti*, April 22, 1997; and "The Shadow of NATO Hangs over Russia," *Nezavisimaya Gazeta*, April 17, 1997, FBIS, April 18, February 28, April 29, 1997, respectively; Sergei Khrushchev, "Russia Can Turn NATO Expansion into an Economic Opportunity," *Asia Times*, May 30, 1997, in Johnson's Russia List at djohnson@cdi.org, May 30,

1997; and David Hoffman, "For Yeltsin, Business Prospects Outweighed NATO Threat," *Washington Post*, May 27, 1997, pp. A1, A11.

10. Stanislav Kondrashov, "We Are More of a Threat to Ourselves Than Any NATO," *Izvestiya*, February 19, 1997, FBIS, February 20, 1997; "Two-thirds of Russia Is Gloomy over Future," March 20, 1997, in Johnson's List, March 30, 1997; and Michael Specter, "Protesting Privation, Millions of Russian Workers Strike," *New York Times*, March 25, 1997, p. A3.

11. "Landsbergis Gets U.S. Assurances over NATO Candidacy," Tallinn BNS, April 12, 1997; Irina Zhinkina, "What Russia Will Have to Pay to Become United States's Partner," *Krasnaya Zvezda*, April 22, 1997; and "Source of Threat to Russia's National Security," *Rabochaya Tribuna*, April 1, 1997, FBIS, April 8, 18, and 28, 1997; Ronald Steel, "Playing Loose with History," *New York Times*, May 26, 1997, p. A17; "Saying 'No' to NATO No Breeze for Liberals," *St. Petersburg Times*, March 31, 1997; and Harry Dunphy, "Gorbachev Cautions U.S. on NATO," Associated Press, April 15, 1997, Johnson's List, April 31 and April 15, 1997.

12. "Primakov, Duma Anti-NATO Group to Discuss 'Concerted Action,'" Moscow Interfax, April 17, 1997, FBIS, April 18, 1997; see also Sergei Kovalev, "On the New Russia," *New York Review of Books*, April 18, 1996, pp. 10, 12; and Michael R. Gordon, "Yeltsin Dismisses Two Military Chiefs for Resisting Cuts," *New York Times*, May 23, 1997, pp. A1, A10.

13. "All Duma Groups Support Cooperation in Iran," Moscow Interfax, April 10, 1997; and "China as Partner, Potential Threat Eyed," *Segodnya*, April 7, 1997, FBIS, April 11 and 17, 1997; Lee Hockstader, "Russia, China Sign New Friendship Pact," *Washington Post*, April 24, 1997, pp. A27, A29; and "Can a Bear Love a Dragon?" *The Economist*, April 26, 1997, pp. 19–21.

14. "RF-Iranian Ties: Energy Policy Surveyed," *Nezavisimaya Gazeta*, March 20, 1997, FBIS, April 8, 1997; and Michael R. Gordon, "Russia Is True to West, in Its Fashion," *New York Times*, May 1, 1997, p. A3.

15. "PFD Heads Oppose Joining CIS, View Dniester Peacekeeping," Chisinau Infotag, April 3, 1997; "Dniester Status Viewed in Light of Moldova's NATO Games," *Rossiyskaya Gazeta*, March 29, 1997; and "Lucinschi Counting on Bucharest's Help with West," *Bucharest Azi*, February 11, 1997, FBIS, April 4, April 7, and May 1, 1997.

16. Aleksandr Mineyev, "Romanians Ready for 'Sacrifices,'" *Trud-Ukraina*, February 8, 1997; Oleksandr Borysenko, "'Sea Breeze-97' and Its Opponents," *Sevastopol Flot Ukrayiny*, March 29, 1997; "Academic Interviewed on NATO Enlargement," *Komsomolskaya Pravda*, April 4, 1997, FBIS, April 9 and 15, 1997; and Matthew Brzezinski, "Ukraine May Find Itself in Shadow of Mother Russia," *Wall Street Journal*, May 30, 1997, p. A14.

17. Text of Yeltsin's speech to the CIS in ITAR-TASS, March 28, 1997; and Marina Kuchinskaya, "Baltic Countries Waiting in Line to Get into NATO," *Nezavisimoye Voyennoye Obozreniye*, March 29, 1997, FBIS, April 1, 1997; Hugh Pope, "Azerbaijan Leader Favors Pipeline Backed by U.S., in Rebuff to Russia," *Wall Street Journal*, May 9, 1997, pp. 1, 4; John F. Burns, "In Afghanistan, a Triumph of Fundamentalism," *New York Times*, May 26, 1997, p. A3; and "Russia's Old Imperial Map Is Still Shrivelling," *The Economist*, May 24, 1997, pp. 47–48.

18. "Germany's Lostpolitik," *The Economist*, December 7, 1996, p. 46.

19. Aleksandr Fomenko, "Prospects for 'Moscow-Berlin Axis' Eyed," *Nezavisimaya Gazeta*, April 8, 1997, FBIS, April 18, 1997.

12. A Strategy to Unite Rather Than Divide Europe

James Chace

The commonest error in politics is sticking to the carcasses of dead policies.

—Lord Salisbury

The Western alliance is dead. Suggested originally by British foreign secretary Ernest Bevin to counter Soviet expansionist aims against Western Europe, NATO effectively came to an end in 1990 with the collapse of the Soviet bloc and the reunification of Germany.

That is what alliances are meant to do. Absent the threat against which they were founded, alliances have no reason for being. That was true after 1818 of the Quadruple Alliance formed by Russia, Prussia, England, and Austria against Napoleonic France. It was true in 1946 when the Grand Alliance of America, Britain, and Russia against Nazi Germany fell apart.

The North Atlantic Treaty Organization was formed in 1949 to keep the Soviet Union from expanding westward beyond a line that stretched from the Baltic in the north to the Adriatic in the south. The alliance was made into an integrated military organization not only to be a more effective fighting machine but also to keep Germany down; or more diplomatically, to make sure Germany would be integrated into a Western political, economic, and military system.

And it worked. Germany is no threat to anyone. The Soviet Union was contained from further expansion westward, if indeed Moscow ever seriously intended such an expansion by military means. Now that the Cold War is over, such an alliance would normally dissolve. The Europeans could then form a security organization of their own, if they wished, as a military adjunct to the European Union. In time, the United States would likely become the guarantor of last resort of a European balance of power.

NATO and the New European Order

But NATO is not fading away. On the contrary, it has embarked on a quest for new missions and new members. The alliance's actions in Bosnia may be the lineaments of a new Western order. NATO military forces have been working to enforce a peace settlement. Moreover, they have been doing so with the help of non-NATO forces from Central Europe and elsewhere. Most striking of all, Russian troops have been serving in the Yugoslav theater under an American commander (a diplomatic nicety that allows the Russians, for domestic political reasons, to claim that they are not serving under a NATO commander).

The Yugoslav war indicated that the main threat to peace in post–Cold War Europe was likely to come from small conflicts within the European continent rather than from the overweening demands of an expanding or unsatisfied great power—which, for the past century, has been either Russia or Germany. NATO has not been disbanded because many champions of the alliance believe it could be useful for dealing with such regional conflagrations. There is, after all, a military organization in place, and constructing an efficient military organization can be an arduous task. Moreover, the United States is the only power that possesses the logistical capacity to move large numbers of troops and munitions to a war zone, and NATO is the only organization that ties U.S. military resources to Europe.

Yet no one seems willing to reorganize NATO into the pan-European security organization that is its logical future. Instead, the Clinton administration, abetted by the Republicans in both the Senate and the House, urged the expansion of NATO to include just Poland, Hungary, and the Czech Republic. That leaves the other Central and East European countries—including Russia—that were once part of the Soviet bloc waiting outside a door that may be closed to them indefinitely. In the interim, Washington has created the Partnership for Peace as a program under NATO auspices that offers military cooperation—from help in setting up proper procurement systems to joint training for peacekeeping missions—to the countries of the former Soviet bloc.

The problem with that scheme is that excluding a major power such as Russia violates a cardinal principle of the European system, which is to include even former enemies in the system. The victors over France after the Napoleonic wars recognized that principle at the Congress of Vienna. The France of His Most Christian Majesty Louis XVIII was not the enemy, as his foreign minister, Talleyrand, pointed out at a delicate moment in the deliberations of the victor powers; thereafter, France became part of the Congress system, a member of the Concert of Europe. And it never again became the aggressor power that it had been for almost 200 years.

Unfortunately, the principle of inclusion was forgotten by the victors after World War I. Not only were the Germans denied any say in the peace settlement, but both Germany and the newly Bolshevik Soviet Union were excluded from the League of Nations. (The United States, as we know, refused to join the league.) That is not to say that Russian and German membership, or even American membership, in the largely toothless world organization would have prevented World War II; but certainly the exclusion of the Soviet Union in the 1930s from any alliance with Britain and France contributed to Hitler's belief that he could expand at will and encouraged Stalin to finally break with the West and sign the Nazi-Soviet nonaggression pact in 1939.

If history is any guide, what would seem to be needed at this moment is an all-European security organization in which both Russia and the United States would participate. Not NATO dismantled, or NATO expanded, but NATO transformed. To exclude Russia until some auspicious moment when it will have proved itself solidly democratic—as NATO now plans to do—is to encourage the very elements in that angry and impoverished country that threaten democracy. To exclude Russia is to redivide Europe.

Moreover, although NATO has pointedly excluded the Baltic states, Romania, Slovakia, and other aspirants from the first round of expansion, the alliance insists that those countries may hope for membership someday. In short, not only is a fresh dividing line being drawn across Europe; it is a line that will almost surely result in uncertainty and resentment on the part of those on the wrong side.[1]

NATO and Democracy

To those who object to NATO expansion, the Clinton administration portrays the Western alliance as a means of ensuring that countries within the alliance remain free-market democracies. Yet that was certainly not the primary aim of the old NATO. On the contrary,

NATO during the Cold War was a military alliance that sometimes took in members with less than sterling democratic credentials because of their strategic value. Portugal, for example, had long been a dictatorship when it joined NATO in 1949 and remained so until the mid-1970s. Neither Greece nor Turkey was a model of democracy at the time of accession, but they were strategically valuable real estate. (Spain would likely have been a founding member of the alliance had it not been for Franco's open support of Hitler during World War II; Washington was, however, eager to sign a bilateral military agreement with Madrid in order to obtain basing rights.)

Moreover, there is no evidence that NATO has a decisive influence on its members' progress toward democracy. NATO membership did not prevent the rise of the junta in Greece in the 1970s—a significant lapse from even the shaky democratic system it had enjoyed when Athens was admitted to NATO. Nor has NATO had any apparent impact on Turkey's erratic democratic progress. There is little reason to believe the alliance will fare better with its new members than it has with long-standing NATO countries.

One reason NATO has had little success in bolstering the democratic standing of its member states is because, as a military alliance, it has at its disposal no means of influencing the internal politics of its members. Should one of the countries now being admitted—to say nothing of those already in NATO—choose a nondemocratic form of government, there is no provision for expelling it. The alliance took no action against Greece or Turkey in response to those countries' detours from the path toward democracy. Nor is it likely to take action against the transgressions of future members.

To ensure democratic progress in Europe, the European Union should offer the countries of the former Soviet bloc associate and, eventually, full membership. Standards of democratic behavior are conditions of membership in the EU, and sanctions can be employed against authoritarian behavior through the Council of Europe. The EU, however, has been reluctant to open its doors to the poorer nations to the east. In some ways, NATO membership appears to be a surrogate for admission to the EU. But the two organizations are entirely different, and to the extent that the West's objective is to foster democracy in Europe, the EU is far better suited to play that role than is NATO.

The Potential Costs of Expansion

The Pentagon has estimated that NATO expansion would cost $27 billion to $35 billion over the next 10 years and has assumed that Washington's share would be about $200 million a year. The RAND Corporation estimated the probable costs of expansion at $30 billion to $52 billion. And the Congressional Budget Office—assuming that the new members would need more military support than they themselves can provide—has predicted that the cost could range as high as $125 billion.[2] (The CBO projections were presumably based on what would be needed in case of a major regional confrontation.)

Recognizing the political outcry that would ensue if the United States was expected to bear a very large share of enlargement costs, Secretary of State Madeleine Albright asserted at a Senate hearing in May 1997 that "NATO enlargement is not a scholarship program" and that new members would have to pay for the modernization of their militaries to meet Western standards.[3] If that is the case, then it is likely that an expanded new NATO will be less adequate as a fighting machine than is NATO in its current form. Neither Poland, Hungary, nor the Czech Republic is likely to be able to bear the expected costs of the expansion.

At a time when both the Clinton administration and the Republican-led Congress are seeking a balanced budget, costs of NATO expansion would doubtless have to be balanced by further cuts in the public sector—excluding, of course, other portions of the defense budget. There is little likelihood that the administration would be willing to raise taxes to pay for expansion. More likely, the costs of new NATO members would come out of further reductions in health care or education.

The Need to Include Russia

To assuage Russian fears of exclusion in a cold peace, the NATO nations and Russia signed on May 27, 1997, the Founding Act on Mutual Relations, Cooperation and Security. The act established a NATO-Russia Permanent Joint Council for consultation on security issues, and NATO assured Russia that it had no intention of deploying nuclear weapons on the territory of any of its new members. The NATO-Russia council can discuss anything from drug trafficking to nuclear defense strategy, but, according to the agreement, neither

Russia nor NATO will have any "right of veto over the actions of the other."[4]

Such linking of Russia to NATO represents recognition of the need not to antagonize NATO's former adversary. But the agreement falls far short of what is needed if the purpose of the new NATO is to provide for the security of the European continent, "to promote greater stability in all of Europe, including Russia," as President Clinton said when he signed the new agreement in Paris.

If the purpose of the new NATO is indeed to meet threats to the peace of Europe that are likely to arise from small conflicts within the European continent rather than from the overweening demands of an expanding or unsatisfied great power, then a pan-European security system that would include both America and Russia is the logical successor to NATO.

Such a military organization would keep the United States tied to Europe, though economic tensions between North America and Europe may worsen once Washington is stripped of its customary (but increasingly residual) leverage over European affairs. Were there a pan-European security organization, the U.S. military presence in Europe could drop to fewer than 50,000 troops.

A European security organization that included the United States and Russia would surely help to ensure a European balance of power. It would act as a counterweight to German power or a regressive Russia, or both; it would more effectively tie the United States to European security by lessening Washington's financial burden. In addition, tying Russia's military forces to a broader European organization would inhibit the Kremlin's sending Russian troops across the new borders of the Russian Federation. Intervention to reestablish Russian authority in Georgia, Azerbaijan, Chechnya, or other parts of the former Soviet Union would be far less likely— though not impossible—if Russia belonged to a European security organization.

The primary purpose of a European security organization would be to preserve the territorial status quo, except where changes were mutually agreed on by both parties. Borders are not carved in stone, but the greatest danger that faces the new Europe is a rectification of borders by force rather than negotiation, as happened in the former Yugoslavia. In addition, a European security organization

could monitor arms control agreements and set up verification procedures, expand conference diplomacy, and create buffer and neutral
zones by establishing peacekeeping capabilities.

Why should the United States not withdraw totally from Europe?
In addition to the long-standing American interest in preventing
any one power from dominating Europe, Europeans appear to want
an American commitment to European security, as was evident in
the Yugoslav war when the Europeans were unable to settle the
conflict without U.S. participation. But under the aegis of a European
security organization, the Europeans would bear by far the greatest
burden for their defense and would offer to Russia and the countries
of the former Soviet bloc true inclusion in an overall European
balance of power.

U.S. Role in the Post–Cold War World

At the end of the 20th century, America is, by all accounts, the
greatest power in the world. The United States has the world's most
powerful military buttressed by a booming economy. With a 1998
defense budget of some $260 billion, the United States spends more
on its military than all the other industrial nations of the world
combined.

But the United States has not yet determined what to do with its
unparalleled military and economic prowess. It is time to ask what
Washington wants to do. What does the Clinton administration see
as America's foreign policy goals in light of its great power? Is NATO
expansion merely a reflex of American hegemony? The evidence
suggests that such may be the case. In 1992 a Pentagon planning
document was leaked to the press; in language intended for the
defense mandarinate, the paper argued that the United States must
"discourage the advanced industrial nations [that is, Germany and
Japan] from challenging our leadership or even aspiring to a larger
regional or global role."[5]

What is good for America, it seems, is good for the world. To fulfill
America's obligations, the United States must "retain the preeminent
responsibility for addressing ... those wrongs which threaten not
only our interests, but those of our allies or friends, or which could
seriously unsettle international relations."[6]

When the Pentagon's thinking became public knowledge, Defense
Department planners were ordered to revise the document. But

today's defense budget bears out the notion that the American military is designed to keep order in the world. "Where the American arsenal was once directed primarily against the Soviet Union," Ronald Steel has written, "it would now be directed against everybody. Whereas it was once intended to contain communism, its goal now is nothing less than the containment of global disorder."[7]

NATO expansion extends America's interests and commitments and in so doing risks stirring up new threats from those countries that are left out. Clearly such an initiative does not advance U.S. interests. The United States must decide where its interests lie and conduct its foreign policy accordingly, not make impulsive commitments that are irrelevant or even dangerous to American national security. It is not enough for Bill Clinton to repeat the mantra that America is "the indispensable nation." In fact, the absence of a grave crisis bearing down upon the United States and the lack of any threat to American power and purpose make it even more essential than in the past to spell out America's role in the world.[8]

It may well be that our task is to perfect our society at home, as both Roosevelts tried to do. It may well be time to show restraint of power now that we have demonstrated in the Persian Gulf, in Panama, in Bosnia, in Haiti, in the Taiwan Strait—interventions that took place in the post–Cold War era—our willingness to use force for limited ends.

Restraint of power does not mean an isolationist or abstentionist America. What it does mean is an America prepared to reexamine its values in a world without an enemy to threaten its security and prosperity. Americans can then focus their considerable energies on completing the Rooseveltian vision of the good society that was so cruelly blocked by almost half a century of German and Soviet power.

Notes

1. See James Chace, "'Managing' Russia's Decline," *World Policy Journal* 13, no. 1 (Spring 1996): 125–27.

2. Congressional Budget Office, "The Costs of Expanding the NATO Alliance," March 1996, p. xiii.

3. Quoted in Alison Mitchell, "Clinton Girding for Stiff Debate on NATO Issue," *New York Times*, May 27, 1997, p. A6.

4. Alison Whitney, "Russia and West Sign Cooperation Pact," *New York Times*, May 28, 1997, p. A10.

5. Quoted in Ronald Steel, *Temptations of a Superpower* (Cambridge, Mass.: Harvard University Press, 1995), pp. 55–56.

6. Quoted in ibid.

7. Ibid., p. 56.

8. See James Chace, "An Empty Hegemony," *World Policy Journal* 14, no. 2 (Summer 1997): 97–98.

13. The Errors of Expansive Realism
Owen Harries

... it is sometimes necessary to repeat what all know. All mapmakers should place the Mississippi in the same location and avoid originality. It may be boring, but one has to know where it is. We cannot have the Mississippi flowing toward the Rockies, just for a change.

—Saul Bellow, *Mr. Sammler's Planet*

In many ways NATO is a boring organization. It is a thing of acronyms, jargon, organizational charts, arcane strategic doctrines, and tired rhetoric. But there is no gainsaying that it has a Mississippi-like centrality and importance in American foreign policy. When, then, proposals are made to change it radically—to give it new (and very different) members, new purposes, new ways of conducting business, new nontotalitarian enemies (or, conversely, to dispense altogether with the concept of enemies as a rationale)—it is sensible to pay close attention and to scrutinize carefully and repeatedly the arguments that bolster those proposals. It is important to get things right, even at the risk of making NATO boring in new ways.

Before getting down to particular arguments, it is worth relating the proposed expansion of NATO into Central and Eastern Europe to the wider context that made it an issue. For nearly half a century the United States and its allies fought the Cold War, not, it was always insisted, against Russia and the Russian people, but against the Soviet regime and the ideology it represented. Indeed, one of the principal reasons for characterizing that regime as evil was its vicious treatment of its own people, most of whom were Russian. An implicit Western objective in the Cold War was the conversion of Russia from a totalitarian to a more or less normal state and, if possible, to democracy.

Between 1989 and 1991, a political miracle occurred. The Soviet regime, steeped in blood and obsessed with total control as it had

187

been throughout most of its history, voluntarily gave up its Warsaw Pact empire, collapsed the Soviet system upon itself, and then acquiesced in its own demise—all with virtually no violence. That extraordinary sequence of events was by no means inevitable. Had it so chosen, the regime could have resisted the forces of change as it had on previous occasions, thus either extending its life, perhaps for decades more, or going down in a welter of blood and destruction. That, indeed, would have been more normal behavior, for as the English scholar Martin Wight once observed, "Great power status is lost, as it is won, by violence. A Great Power does not die in its bed."[1] What occurred in the case of the Soviet Union was very much the exception.

A necessary condition for its being so was an understanding—explicit according to some, but in any case certainly implicit—that the West would not take strategic and political advantage of what the Soviet Union was allowing to happen to its empire and to itself. Whatever is said now, such a bargain was *assumed* by both sides, for it was evident to all involved that in its absence—if, that is, it had become apparent that the West was intent on exploiting any retreat by Moscow—events would not be allowed to proceed along the liberalizing course that they actually took. Further, there seemed to be no basis for the United States' objecting to such a bargain. For, after all, its avowed objective was not the eastward extension of its own power and influence in Europe but the restoration of the independence of the countries of the region. In effect, the bargain gave the United States everything it wanted (more, in fact, for the breakup of the Soviet Union had never been a Cold War objective) and in return required it only to refrain from doing what it had never expressed any intention of doing.

Now, and very much at the initiative of the United States, the West is in the process of reneging on that implicit bargain by extending NATO into countries recently vacated by Moscow. That is an ominous step. Whatever is said, however ingenious and vigorous the attempts to obscure the facts or change the subject, NATO is a military alliance, the most powerful in the history of the world, and the United States is the dominant force in that alliance. And whatever is claimed about spreading democracy, making Europe "whole," promoting stability, peacekeeping, and righting past injustices—all formulations that serve, either consciously or inadvertently, to divert attention from the political and strategic reality of what is now occurring—cannot succeed in obscuring the truth that the eastward extension of NATO represents an unprecedented projection of American power into a sensitive region hitherto beyond its reach—a veritable geopolitical revolution. It is not necessary to accept in its entirety the resonant but overwrought dictum of Sir Halford Mackinder ("Who rules East Europe commands the Heartland: Who rules the Heartland commands the World Island: Who rules the World Island commands the World")[2] to recognize the profound strategic implications of what the U.S. Senate is being asked to endorse.

Why is the Clinton administration acting in this way? And does it serve American interests that the administration is doing so and that its expressed intention is to proceed much further along the same path?

It should be recalled that immediately after the end of the Cold War there was no great enthusiasm either in America or in Western Europe for enlarging NATO. In the United States there was a strong sense of a mission accomplished; of the need to address pressing and neglected domestic problems; and, in the absence of any serious threat, of the wisdom of leaving responsibility for European affairs increasingly in the hands of Europeans. In Europe there was a corresponding concern with assuming more responsibility for the region's own affairs, which meant playing down the hitherto central role of a NATO in which U.S. leadership was unchallengeable. In the early days of the Clinton administration, Secretary of State Warren Christopher; Secretary of Defense Les Aspin; and Ambassador at Large Strobe Talbott, the administration's leading expert on Russian affairs and the newly independent states, were all opposed to adding new members to the alliance; no one was strongly in favor.

How, then, did it come about that by the beginning of 1994 President Clinton was declaring that "the question is no longer whether NATO will take on new members, but when and how"? It was certainly not by a process of ratiocination, vigorous debate, and the creation of an intellectual consensus concerning interests, purposes, and means. To this day there is no such consensus, and no coherent case for NATO expansion on which all of its principal supporters agree. For instance, Talbott, now a convert to expansion, insists that "fear of a new wave of Russian imperialism . . . should not be seen as the driving force behind NATO enlargement,"[3] but Henry Kissinger, the most eminent advocate of expansion outside the administration, maintains that enlargement should take place precisely to "encourage Russian leaders to interrupt the fateful rhythm of Russian history."[4] Such a profound difference over the basic purpose between two leading supporters of a policy is, to put it mildly, unusual. Again, while some supporters insist on NATO's continued character as a military alliance, others go out of their way to play that down, emphasizing such new nonmilitary roles for the organization as democracy promoter and nation builder.

How Enlargement Happened

The Clinton administration's conversion from indifference, or even skepticism, to insistence on NATO expansion as its most important foreign policy initiative owes much less to rational argument than to a combination of disparate events and pressures:

- The strength of the Polish-American vote, as well as that of other Americans of Central and East European origin. For a president as sensitive to poll figures as Bill Clinton (and 1996 GOP presidential candidate Robert Dole), this was certainly a major consideration. To ensure that it was fully appreciated, in 1991 a lobbying group called the Central and East European Coalition was formed; it claimed to comprise 19 national membership-based organizations representing 22 million Americans with ethnic roots in 13 countries of Central and Eastern Europe.
- The enormous vested interests—careers, contracts, consultancies, accumulated expertise—represented by the NATO establishment, which now needed a new reason and purpose to justify the organization's continued existence. What Walter Wriston has written of the World Bank also applies to the post–Cold War NATO: "When an organization's mission has been completed and its presence is no longer required, there are almost no instances of simply liquidating it, turning its lights out and going home. Instead a new mission is invented, since the real objective of bureaucracies—public or private—is survival."[5] That need for a new mission was memorably acknowledged by Sen. Richard Lugar (R-Ind.) in his slogan, "Out of area or out of business."[6]

- The "moral" pressure exerted by East European leaders, especially Czech president Václav Havel, who, simultaneously accusing the West of multiple character failings and claiming the moral superiority of those who had suffered under communism, called on the West to redeem itself by making NATO a "genuinely pan-European security structure."[7] For aspiring members, NATO membership is more important as a symbol that they are fully European, and as a possible means of back-door entry into the European Union, than it is as protection against a hypothetical threat from the enfeebled armies of the east.
- The concern and self-distrust felt by some Germans, and not least by Chancellor Helmut Kohl, at the prospect of their country's being left on the eastern frontier of NATO, adjacent to an area of political weakness and potential instability. This concern may have impressed itself on Richard Holbrooke during his spell as ambassador to Bonn and led him subsequently to influence the administration when he returned to Washington as a very forceful assistant secretary of state for European and Canadian Affairs.
- Growing doubts about democracy's prospects in Russia and fear of the reemergence of an assertive nationalism there. In the December 1993 elections, the party of the cryptofascist Vladimir Zhirinovsky and the Communists together received 43 percent of the vote. While this vote did not put Zhirinovsky in power, and he faded quickly as a serious force in Russian politics, it gave the question of Russia's relations with its neighbors greater salience.
- The need of some American conservative intellectuals for a bold foreign policy stroke to "remoralize" their own ranks after some dispiriting domestic defeats, the enthusiasm of others for "a democratic crusade" in Central and Eastern Europe, and the difficulty yet others had breaking a lifetime's habit of regarding Moscow as the enemy. Support for NATO expansion on the right provided the administration with cover and lessened the likely political costs of such a policy.
- The growing eagerness of some West European governments to grant Central European states membership in NATO as an acceptable price for keeping them out of, or at least delaying their entry into, the European Union.

191

Formidable as that combination of pressures was, it is doubtful that it would have been capable of converting the Clinton administration on NATO expansion had it not been for the addition of one other crucial factor: Bosnia. The war in Bosnia focused American attention on post–Cold War Central Europe, and it did so in a most distorted and emotional way. Bosnia presented the West European countries with a harsh test of their ability to manage events in their own back yard without Washington's direction, long before they were ready for it and when what they needed was to gradually resume responsibility for their own affairs. When, predictably, they failed the test, they reconciled themselves to continued American leadership. Bosnia also raised in acute form the question of the future of NATO, as the alliance's feeble response to the crisis cast doubt on its continued viability, and it raised the question specifically in the context of instability in Central and Eastern Europe.

"Bosnia" was increasingly understood not as referring to a discrete event but as a metaphor for the chronic, historically ordained instability of a whole region. The domino theory, forgotten for two decades, was quickly resurrected and applied. Seen in those terms, Bosnia was used to make the case not only for U.S. intervention in the war but for a permanent American presence in the region. And what better way of establishing that presence than by extending eastward the alliance-in-being that the United States had created and then dominated for nearly half a century?

The Flawed Realist Case for NATO Enlargement

Taken together, such pressures were politically formidable, especially for an administration as sensitive to pressure as Clinton's. But they had very little to do with America's national interests, and the administration's post hoc attempts to make a case for NATO's eastward expansion in terms of those interests have been perfunctory and shallow. A much more serious attempt has been made outside the administration, mainly by commentators of a realist persuasion. The case they have made, however, is badly flawed.

The realist case is based largely on the conviction that Russia is inherently and incorrigibly expansionist, regardless of how and by whom it is governed. Kissinger has warned of "the fateful rhythm of Russian history." Similarly, Zbigniew Brzezinski emphasizes the centrality in Russia's history of "the imperial impulse" and claims that in postcommunist Russia that impulse "remains strong and even appears to be strengthening." Russia's approach to Central Europe is "at the very least protoimperial," and Brzezinski sees an unfortunate continuity between the Soviet era and today in the definition of national interests and the formulation of foreign policy.[8] Another realist, Peter Rodman, speaks in the same vein, explaining the "lengthening shadow of Russian strength" by asserting that "Russia is a force of nature; all this is inevitable."[9]

In arguing in that way, those commentators are being very true to their realist position. But they are also drawing attention to what is one of the most serious intellectual weaknesses of that position—namely, that in its stress on the structure of the international system and on how states are placed within that system, realism attaches little or no importance to what is going on *inside* particular states: what kind of regimes are in power, what kinds of ideologies prevail, what kind of leadership is provided. Hence the well-known realist billiard ball analogy, in which states are treated as if they have no inner life but merely obey the laws of political physics and geometry. For those realists, Russia is Russia is Russia, regardless of whether it is under czarist, communist, or nascent democratic rule.

That approach is enormously counterintuitive, and its weaknesses have been particularly evident in this most ideological of centuries. Did it really make no significant difference to Russian foreign policy whether it was in the hands of a Stolypin, a Stalin, or a Yeltsin? Or to German policy whether Stresemann, Hitler, or Adenauer was in power in that country? In foreign policy terms, was it pointless to have exerted great effort to bring down the Nazi and Soviet regimes?

For most people, merely to ask those questions would seem to answer them. But not so long ago such prominent realists as E. H. Carr and A. J. P. Taylor were prepared to argue an essential foreign policy continuity between the Weimar Republic and Nazi Germany.[10] Indeed, and more seriously, it was the assumption of such a continuity—that Hitler was an ordinary compromising politician in the same mold as the Germans of the 1920s—that led British prime minister Neville Chamberlain fatally astray with his policy of appeasement. So far in this century, then, Western statesmen have created a terrible crisis and allowed an unnecessary world war to happen because they falsely assumed that the foreign policy of a totalitarian regime would be no different from that of the struggling democracy it replaced. It would be inexcusable—and possibly again disastrous—if, at the end of the century, we made the same error in reverse by proceeding on the assumption that the behavior of another struggling democracy will be no different from that of the totalitarian regime that preceded it.

Recognizing Spheres of Influence

If in that one respect those who make the case for NATO expansion err in overemphasizing what is weakest in the realist position, in other respects their mistake has been to forget some of the precepts that are its strength. If realism is about anything, it is about a conscientious effort to try to see things as they really are. One of the ways things are in international politics is that great powers have spheres of influence. It is one of their basic characteristics, one of the features that qualify them as "great," that their power radiates to immediately adjacent regions in the form of significant influence, and that they take a particular interest in those regions. That is a characteristic of democratic great powers as it is of autocratic or totalitarian ones: one of the first important foreign policy acts of the United States, even before it was an authentic great power, was to claim for itself a huge sphere of influence with the Monroe Doctrine.

To embark on a policy whose deliberate aim is to deny Russian influence in Eastern and Central Europe, to corset Russia within its own boundaries, is therefore a policy fraught with danger. It retains what meager plausibility it has for two reasons: first, because of revulsion at the fact that in the communist period the Soviet Union ruthlessly and crudely translated the traditional concept of sphere of influence into a totalitarian one of a sphere of dominance, involving puppet regimes, occupying armies, terror, economic exploitation, and ideological regimentation; and second, because for the time being Russia is exceptionally weak. But as Russia recovers, and even if it becomes a functioning democracy, NATO expansion will become a risk-laden and destabilizing policy—not because extreme Russian nationalists or neocommunists are bound to come to the fore, but because, in the nature of things, Russia will again assert its prerogatives as a great power.

Indeed, if one considers some of the arguments now being advanced forcefully, things could get even worse. At the same time that the United States appears determined to commit itself to denying Russia a sphere of influence, many influential voices are insisting that it should do the same to China. Even as the power of that country increases dramatically, it is maintained that it too should be strictly contained within its borders, and any attempt by it to extend its influence beyond them should be seen as illegitimate, if not sinister, and resolutely opposed—with force if necessary—by the United States. Meanwhile, as those two huge countries are so constrained, the United States itself, armed in virtue, should feel free to treat the rest of the entire globe as *its* sphere of influence, extending its presence and imposing its will as it sees fit. In the long run the implementation of such a policy would amount to a recipe for disaster. For when push came to shove—that is, when other states began to resist its assertive hegemony—the United States would lack the conviction and resolution necessary to fulfill the global imperial role that it is now being urged to assume.

The Gap between Ends and Means

Another of the central tenets of realism is that if the end is willed, so must be the means. The two should be kept in balance, preferably, as Walter Lippmann urged, "with a comfortable surplus of power in reserve."[11] In the case of NATO expansion, that tenet is being ignored. The NATO members are moving to assume very large additional commitments at a time when they have all made substantial cuts to their defense budgets, and when more such cuts are virtually certain.[12] (For example, the French cabinet has announced that the military draft, which dates back two centuries, is to be phased out and that defense procurement expenditure is to be cut by 11 percent.) The irresponsibility of such a course of action raises the question of the seriousness of the new commitments being undertaken. Are existing NATO members really prepared to send their soldiers to die to defend the integrity of countries in Central and Eastern Europe? Bearing in mind that such pledges have often been made in the past, only to be broken—Munich, 1938, was the last occasion on which Western powers guaranteed the security of what is today the Czech Republic—this is not only a legitimate question but a necessary one.

It is not only in terms of power that realists should be concerned with the balancing of ends and means. They should also consider

195

the suitability of the instruments involved—particularly the human instruments—for the tasks at hand. Not to do so is likely to result in unpleasant surprises, and some realist supporters of NATO expansion got such a surprise as a result of the March 1997 Helsinki summit. At that meeting, so many concessions were made to Moscow by the Clinton administration that we now have an almost lunatic state of affairs: in order to make acceptable the expansion of NATO to contain a potentially dangerous Russia, we are virtually making Russia an honorary member of NATO, with something close to veto power.

Some of the initially most ardent supporters of expansion are now deeply dismayed. But surely such an outcome was foreseeable. After all, the realists knew from the start that the policy they were pushing would be negotiated not by a Talleyrand or a Metternich—or an Acheson or a Kissinger—but by Clinton, the man who feels everyone's pain. In that instance he felt Yeltsin's pain—and gave away much of the store. Kissinger has been clear-eyed enough to label that a fiasco and to recognize that there is now an intellectual rift dividing those who advocate NATO expansion: a rift between those who still see the need to preserve NATO as a military alliance against a potential enemy (Russia) and those who now see it in terms of a collective security system embracing a Europe now made whole by the inclusion of Russia.

The image of a Europe "made whole" again after the division of the Cold War is one that the advocates of NATO expansion appeal to frequently. But it is not a convincing appeal. For one thing, coming from some mouths it tends to bring to mind Bismarck's comment: "I have always found the word Europe on the lips of those politicians who wanted something from other Powers which they dared not demand in their own name."[13] For another, it invites the question of when exactly was the last time Europe was "whole." In the 1930s, when the dictators were on the rampage? In the 1920s, when Germany and Russia were virtual nonactors? In 1910, when Europe was an armed camp and a furious arms race was in progress? In the 1860s, when Prussia was creating an empire with "blood and iron"? When exactly? And then there is the simple and undeniable fact that at every step of the way—and regardless of how many tranches of new members are taken in—the actual strategic dividing line will be moved to a different place. Only if and when Russia is fully included in whatever arrangement is still called "NATO" will Europe be whole. Anyone who doubts that should consult an atlas and verify how much of the continent of Europe is part of Russia. But if that inclusion were ever to take place, what would be the point of the alliance?

One final note: During the last few months advocates of expansion have been resorting more and more to an argument of last resort— one of process, not of substance. It is that the United States is now so far committed that it is too late to turn back. That argument is not without some merit, for prestige does count, and undoubtedly prestige would be lost by a reversal now. But granted that, prestige is not everything. When the alternative is to persist in serious error, it may be necessary to sacrifice some prestige early, rather than much more later. To proceed resolutely down the wrong road— especially one that has a slippery slope—is not statesmanship. After all, the last time the argument that it was too late to turn back prevailed was exactly 30 years ago, as the United States was advancing deeper and deeper into Vietnam.

Notes

1. Martin Wight, *Power Politics* (London: Royal Institute of International Affairs, 1946), p. 21.

2. Quoted in Colin S. Gray, "Keeping the Soviets Land-locked: Geostrategy for a Maritime America," *National Interest*, no. 4 (Summer 1986): 27. Since writing this paragraph, what I had assumed to be merely implicit has been made explicit by Zbigniew Brzezinski in his latest book, *The Grand Chessboard* (New York: Basic Books, 1997). He begins the second chapter with the flat assertion, "For America, the chief geopolitical prize is Eurasia" (p. 30), and goes on to quote Mackinder's dictum.

3. Strobe Talbott, "Why NATO Should Grow," *New York Review of Books*, August 10, 1995, p. 29.

4. Henry Kissinger, "NATO Was Basically a Mirror of the Warsaw Pact," *Washington Post*, March 30, 1997.

5. Walter Wriston, Comments on a proposal to privatize the World Bank, *National Interest*, no. 40 (Summer 1995): 19.

6. Quoted in William Odom, "Send in Ground Troops, and Lots of Them," *New York Times*, May 31, 1995.

7. Václav Havel, "A Call for Sacrifice," *Foreign Affairs* 73, no. 2 (March–April 1994): 6.

8. Zbigniew Brzezinski, "The Premature Partnership," *Foreign Affairs* 73, no. 2 (March–April 1994): 72, 76; see also Zbigniew Brzezinski, discussion recorded in *Conference Report on the New Geopolitical Shape of Central Europe* (Washington: Center for Strategic and International Studies, 1997).

9. Peter Rodman, "4 More for NATO," *Washington Post*, December 19, 1994.

10. See E. H. Carr, *The Twenty Years' Crisis: 1919–1939* (London: Macmillan, 1940); and A. J. P. Taylor, *The Origins of the Second World War* (London: Hamilton, 1961).

11. Walter Lippmann, *U.S. Foreign Policy: Shield of the Republic* (New York: Little, Brown, 1943), p. 5.

12. See Charles Truehart, "France to Curtail Military," *Washington Post*, August 21, 1997, p. A24.

13. Quoted in A. J. P. Taylor, *Bismarck: The Man and the Statesman* (London: Hamish Hamilton, 1955), p. 167.

14. NATO Enlargement: To What End?

Eugene J. Carroll Jr.

General of the Army Dwight D. Eisenhower was the first NATO supreme allied commander, Europe. Not long after assuming command he wrote these words: "If in 10 years, all American troops stationed in Europe for national defense purposes have not been returned to the United States, then this whole project [NATO] will have failed."[1]

As the product of an army neglected for 20 years between World Wars I and II, and the leader of an alliance that mounted a brutal reconquest of Europe in 1944, Ike understood the cost of neglecting U.S. defenses and the importance of a stable, peaceful Europe. Nevertheless, he unequivocally declared that American troops should not remain in Europe more than 10 years to secure the peace.

Implausible Motives for Expansion

One wonders what questions he might raise 46 years later about the decision not only to continue a powerful U.S. military presence but to expand NATO's responsibilities and increase the costs and risks of the U.S. presence in Europe. His first question would almost certainly be, What is the threat? It would astound him to learn that there is no military threat to NATO nations or to the security of the new nations to be granted the NATO pledge of protection. That has been made abundantly clear in repeated assurances from President Clinton that NATO expansion is not motivated by fear of Russia. But if Russia is not a threat, who is?

Although his official disclaimer of anti-Russian intent may be motivated more by political expediency than by the truth, Clinton's comments accurately reflect the reality of Russia's military condition today. The nearly total collapse of Russia's offensive military capabilities is undeniable. Moscow has no effective means of projecting military power outside the Russian Federation and only a marginal capability to maintain domestic order within it.

199

The Russian debacle in Chechnya is the most obvious example of the present ineffectiveness of the Russian military. Despite that gross failure, Russian president Boris Yeltsin's response has been to continue major reductions in the armed forces and in military spending. The result is a demoralized force that itself is a growing threat to internal stability. When that is added to the ineffectiveness of law enforcement authorities in Russia, where organized criminal elements are dominating many industries and commercial activities, the ability of the government to carry out economic reform initiatives and maintain civil order is severely taxed.

The next Eisenhower query would logically be, If there is no military threat, why expand a military organization that was created solely to confront the Soviet Union? Here the replies become murky. For example, Clinton gave an Oval Office briefing on NATO expansion for a select group of influential journalists on May 23, 1997. His key words were, "What we've done is to construct a balance of power that both restrains and empowers all the people who come within the framework of the agreement."[2] He was referring to military restraint of Russia and Germany and empowerment of Russia to participate in the economic and political evolution of Europe.

That makes very little sense in practical terms. Germany is already restrained because its leadership is committed to a major political and economic role in the European Union, a goal that would be unattainable if Germany resorted to military adventurism. Russia is equally restrained by its present weakness and need for substantial support from the West to restore its devastated economy. Also, if the objective is to empower Russia to participate in the economic and political evolution of Europe, there are more promising means than NATO expansion for advancing that cause. Russian membership in the European Union and strengthening the Organization for Security and Cooperation in Europe are obvious candidates.

Another assertion of the need for NATO expansion was made at West Point on May 31, 1997. There the president confidently proclaimed, "To build and secure a New Europe, peaceful, democratic and undivided at last, there must be a new NATO, with new missions, new members and new partners."[3] It is not unreasonable to claim that NATO has a role in maintaining peace; it is questionable whether NATO has anything at all to do with democracy; but it is delusory to claim that expanding NATO will unify Europe. Clearly there is no intention to make NATO membership universal. Thus, expanding NATO simply moves the division between NATO and non-NATO nations eastward. NATO costs go up, U.S. risks go up, and movement toward a unified Europe is inhibited by the arbitrary division.

Even former secretary of state Henry Kissinger, who strongly favors NATO expansion, is not willing to support the misleading proposition that NATO expansion is a benign or constructive way to promote unity in Europe. He forthrightly recognizes that the real objective is to divide—not unify. He says that the states seeking membership "are seeking to participate in NATO for reasons quite the opposite of what the Founding Act describes—not to erase dividing lines but to position themselves inside a guaranteed territory by shifting the existing NATO boundaries some 300 miles to the east." Kissinger's only fear is that the ambiguous, conciliatory language of the Founding Act on Mutual Relations, Cooperation and Security between NATO and the Russian Federation may blur that fact by leading Russia to believe that it will have a say in NATO affairs and can thus dilute the powerful Cold War alliance into a toothless, ineffective collective security system.[4]

Will NATO Become Entangled in Domestic Disputes?

There is a remarkable parallel between the disingenuous claim that NATO expansion will create an undivided Europe and the claim that NATO is present in Bosnia to enforce the Dayton agreement and preserve a single Bosnian state. On November 21, 1995, Clinton stated, "The peace plan agreed to would preserve Bosnia as a single state. The state would be made up of two parts ... with a fair distribution of land between the two."[5] Of course the Dayton agreement to maintain a single state by creating two states was also delusory, but NATO forces have done virtually nothing to enforce other provisions that might have ameliorated the situation. It seems now that, if NATO troops withdraw in 1998, the resumption of hostilities is highly likely and the only contribution of NATO to a "peaceful, democratic, undivided" Bosnia will have been to enable both sides to rest and rearm before resuming partisan hostilities. The alternative, a permanent NATO presence in Bosnia, is no more acceptable in the long term than is an expanded NATO military presence in Eastern Europe. Neither measure will truly promote progress toward stable, peaceful political structures in Europe.

The murky mélange of arguments for NATO expansion that confuse military initiatives, political objectives, and economic goals is further compounded by policy contradictions in Washington. Within hours of each other the secretary of defense and the secretary of state gave conflicting testimony to the Senate Armed Services Committee on April 23, 1997. Secretary of Defense William Cohen specifically rejected any role for NATO in domestic disputes, saying, "An internal dispute is something that NATO would not be engaged in."[6] Secretary of State Madeleine Albright suggested a far more intrusive role for NATO by stating, "NATO will continue to maintain itself in a way that it can deal with an outside threat, even though what we are talking about now are primarily those internal threats that are due to instability and problems created by ethnic tension within those areas."[7] A NATO that is responsible for military intervention in the internal affairs of European nations is a far cry from the organization created to defend its members from external attack.

Some Adverse Economic Consequences

Clinton recently introduced even more confusion about the aims of NATO expansion. During his celebratory tour in Europe to sign the Founding Act and to commemorate the 50th anniversary of the Marshall Plan, the president attempted to equate the objectives of NATO expansion with those of the Marshall Plan. Such confusion of military and economic objectives is misleading and illogical. The costs of military expansion will directly inhibit economic development in the new member nations. Far more than strengthened military capabilities, those victims of the Cold War require capital and Western technology to rebuild their infrastructures in order to create the goods and services needed to meet domestic demands. That is exactly what the Marshall Plan brought to Europe. Arms manufacturers are already competing for orders that will divert resources to the purchase of unneeded weapons.[8] Frequent references by U.S. leaders to the prosperity that NATO expansion will create certainly do not apply to the new members, although they may be accurate for the arms industries in the United States and Western Europe.

There is also an ominous precedent that Congress may be inclined to favor funds for military programs over economic development efforts in NATO's new member nations. In 1996 Congress was quick to divert more than $15 million from two economic assistance accounts into Foreign Military Financial Program accounts in order to fund Partnership for Peace military programs within NATO candidate nations. Another $7 million was similarly diverted from economic assistance funds in 1997, bringing PFP military assistance to $113 million for 1996–97.[9] That figure will pale into insignificance if present proposals prevail. Under current plans, the United States will provide as much as $700 million in 1998 to facilitate military programs in the nations approved for NATO membership. Future cost growth is impossible to predict until expansion plans are better defined, but the need for additional military funds will reduce, not increase, the availability of economic development funds for former Warsaw Pact nations.

The Effect on Relations with Russia

At this point Eisenhower would certainly ask about Russia's attitude and possible responses to NATO expansion, knowing that it was the addition of West Germany to NATO in 1955 that produced the Warsaw Pact. Three points would need to be made in response. First, there is broad-based opposition to NATO expansion in Russian political, military, and academic circles. It is not just hard-line nationalists who object. The arbitrary decision to expand NATO without regard for genuine Russian concerns may well create a significant coalition motivated primarily by anti-Western sentiments.

Second, there is absolutely nothing Russia can do militarily about expansion today or in the foreseeable future. Russian leaders are not in a position to form a new alliance to balance the NATO initiative, not even among former states of the Soviet Union, and certainly not by coercing buffer states to join as they did in 1955. The military danger lies, not in the short term, but in the long term when the consequences of expansion may well motivate Russian countermeasures against NATO pressure.

Third, expansion can inhibit positive mutual security measures, both short term and long term, and such inhibition may have undesirable consequences. The most immediate problem is attaining early Russian ratification of START II and progress on further nuclear reductions. "Loose nukes" in Russia pose a grave security problem for the world. Early progress on reducing the numbers of, lowering the alert status of, and increasing internal security measures for both weapons and fissile material are matters of urgent concern. There are many reasons that the Russians would benefit in financial and security terms by progress in nuclear disarmament, but NATO expansion may well make it impossible for Yeltsin to obtain cooperation from the Russian Duma on those issues. Because Russia is tremendously vulnerable in military terms and incensed by the arbitrary expansion of NATO, it is probable that a consensus will emerge that nuclear weapons remain the country's last vestige of military power and political significance as a major participant in world affairs.

That outcome is even more likely if domestic political pressure on Clinton forces him to assert that the Founding Act gives Russia no veto on the timing and future extent of NATO expansion. Such a public posture will make it clear that the purpose of expansion is to confront Russia and exclude that country from constructive participation in European security arrangements.

It is ironic that the expansion of NATO is proclaimed as a contribution to the creation of an undivided Europe. In truth, the eastward movement of NATO's borders has a real prospect of hardening divisions between NATO members and nonmembers and provoking long-term responses from Russia that are the absolute antithesis of what Clinton proclaims as our goals. For example, faced with an expanding NATO that they are powerless to control, Russian leaders, too, may look eastward for an ally: China. They will also have opportunities to exploit the distress of those former Warsaw Pact nations that are denied NATO membership. Left outside the NATO security envelope, they might well accept Russian aid and military assistance rather than be caught between NATO and Russia. There is no way that NATO expansion can be said to unify Europe if the result is a new Russia-China entente or the restoration of Russian influence within non-NATO nations.

Nor can the argument stand that democracy in Europe will be strengthened through NATO expansion if resulting internal political pressures in Russia strengthen the influence of nationalist extremists. There are many members of the Russian political elite who want to turn the clock back to the good old days when the Soviet Union had a powerful military and political voice in Europe. The humiliation of being forced to accept the expansion of NATO will stimulate their resentment and strengthen their resistance to Yeltsin's efforts to continue democratic reform. That danger was foreseen clearly by George F. Kennan, the intellectual father of America's Cold War policy of containment, when he wrote that "expanding NATO would be the most fateful error of American policy in the post cold-war era. Such a decision may be expected to influence the nationalistic, anti-Western and militaristic tendencies in Russian opinion; to have an adverse effect on the development of Russian democracy; . . . and to impel Russian foreign policy in directions decidedly not to our liking."[10]

An Unwise Initiative

Clearly, the United States has important interests in Europe and must remain engaged there, politically and economically. It is far less clear, given the present security conditions in Europe, that we need to sustain, much less expand, our Cold War military presence and responsibilities. There is simply no current or foreseeable military threat that justifies 100,000 American troops and the expenditure of as much as $30 billion per year to provide unneeded security services on the Continent. Our presence is not needed to maintain peace today or for the foreseeable future, and it does not promote democracy or create an undivided Europe. It seems that the real reason the United States is committed to NATO expansion is to maintain Washington's dominant role in European affairs and to hedge against the resurgence of an aggressive Russia. Secretary of State Albright said as much in her testimony to the Senate Armed Services Committee when she confided, "On the off-chance that in fact Russia doesn't work out the way that we are hoping it will, and its current membership wants, NATO is there."[11]

The risks and costs of NATO expansion as insurance against the improbable reemergence of a military threat from Russia in the distant future are burdensome, but the negative consequences are much worse. Our long-term interests in Europe can best be served by the existence of a stable, peaceful order in Europe that includes cooperative participation by Russia. If we want to make a friend of Russia, we cannot treat Russians as enemies. At its heart, NATO expansion is aimed at Russia, and proceeding on this road creates the strong possibility that our actions will produce the very outcome we least desire.

Notes

1. Dwight D. Eisenhower, Letter to Edward John Bermingham, trustee of Columbia University, February 28, 1951, Dwight D. Eisenhower Presidential Library, Abilene, Kansas.

2. Quoted in Stephen S. Rosenfeld, "The New Balance of Power," *Washington Post,* May 30, 1997, p. A25.

3. White House Press Office, "Remarks by the President at the United States Military Academy Commencement, West Point, New York, May 31, 1997."

4. Henry Kissinger, "The Dilution of NATO," *Washington Post,* June 8, 1997, p. C9.

5. "Clinton's Words: The Promise of Peace," *New York Times,* November 22, 1995, p. A21.

6. U.S. Senate Committee on Armed Services, *Hearing on Poland, Hungary, and the Czech Republic in NATO,* 105th Cong., 1st sess., April 23, 1997, p. 38.

7. Ibid., p. 49.

8. "NATO Expansion Boosts Aerospace Opportunities," *Aerospace Daily,* May 29, 1997, pp. 323, 326.

9. Louis J. Samelson, "New Security Assistance Legislation for Fiscal Year 1997," *DISAM Journal* 19, no. 2 (Winter 1996–97): 38–39.

10. George F. Kennan, "A Fateful Error," *New York Times,* February 5, 1997, p. A23.

11. U.S. Senate Committee on Armed Services, p. 49.

PART IV

ALTERNATIVES TO AN ENLARGED NATO

15. Europe's Unhealthy Security Dependence

Doug Bandow

Is there an alternative to NATO? To ask that question is to put oneself out of step with the alliance's bureaucracy, the Clinton administration, and Republican hegemonists. New lobbies have been created—the New Atlantic Initiative, for instance, organized by John O'Sullivan, the British editor of *National Review*—to push for an expanded, and potentially ever-expanding, alliance. In the view of those influential interests there is no alternative to NATO. Indeed, some expansionists insult people who dare ask the question. Zbigniew Brzezinski, President Carter's not-so-successful national security adviser, complains of "carping," which he calls "even comical," by those who oppose NATO expansion.[1]

Yet many Americans today seem to be asking the question. A recent poll by Rasmussen Research found that only Great Britain elicited majority support for a U.S. defense guarantee. France and Spain gained narrow pluralities. Germany, Hungary, Poland, and Latvia won far less support, which declined as one moved further east.[2] Few Americans outside of the Washington Beltway favor risking their loved ones to protect existing, let alone the host of would-be, NATO members.

Alternatives to NATO is not just an elite versus populist issue, however. The giants of American foreign policy who created NATO a half century ago would also be asking the question. After all, Secretary of State Dean Acheson assured Congress that a U.S. troop presence in Europe would be only temporary, intended to protect the war-torn nations until they could stand on their own. In 1951 Dwight D. Eisenhower, NATO's first supreme commander, argued that the United States should "set clear limits" on the length of time it would maintain forces in Europe.[3] A decade later, he warned, "Permanent troop establishments abroad" would "discourage the development of the necessary military strength Western European countries should provide themselves."[4] His granddaughter, Susan Eisenhower, chairman of the Center for Political and Strategic Studies, today criticizes railroading expansion in order to meet the 50th anniversary of NATO's founding: "I cannot imagine we are rushing through a policy that has all kinds of unforeseen consequences."[5]

NATO Expansion and the Politics of Institutional Preservation

Experience has borne out Dwight Eisenhower's fears. Although the Europeans were always far more at risk, they never matched America's defense effort. Even today they devote a much smaller percentage of their gross domestic products to the military, on average about half of the percentage spent by the United States. Washington spends 60 percent more on defense than do all NATO's European members combined, even though the latter possess a larger economy and population.[6]

That is why advocates of an expanded NATO so fear the question, Is there an alternative? Answering it honestly threatens to end the alliance. Indeed, while most people celebrated the fall of the Berlin Wall, NATO enthusiasts fussed. Some seemed to even pine for the "good old days" of the Cold War.

And, as would have been predicted by public choice economists, NATO supporters immediately began a creative search for new justifications to perpetuate their organization, despite its loss of relevance. The earliest claim was "nothing's really changed," or at least "nothing's really changed permanently." The collapse of the Warsaw Pact, the shift in allegiance of the East European states, and the spectacular implosion of the Soviet Union quickly invalidated that argument.

More serious were proposals for alternative missions. Robert Zoellick, State Department counselor under George Bush, explained that the policy planning staff was looking "at how you transform established institutions, such as NATO, to serve new missions that will fit the new era."[7] Many of the proposed tasks were simply ludicrous. Assistant Secretary of State Robert Hormats, who went on to the usual high-paying Wall Street job, suggested that the alliance "expand the range of issues on which NATO engages the common efforts of the European and North American democracies—from student exchanges, to fighting the drug trade, to resisting terrorism, to countering threats to the environment."[8] Not to be outdone, David

Abshire, a former NATO ambassador and now head of the Center for Strategic and International Studies, observed that NATO "could coordinate the transfer of environmental-control and energy-conservation technology to the East, thereby benefiting the global ecology."[9] All that was lacking was a proposal for a NATO literacy initiative, with tanks invading the former communist states to distribute books rather than seize territory.

Other, more serious, suggestions included intervening in out-of-area conflicts, "managing change" in Eastern Europe, and promoting stability in the former Soviet bloc. None of those related ideas ended up looking terribly fruitful: The Yugoslavian civil war demonstrated how difficult it was for outside parties to resolve the ancient hatreds that litter Central and Eastern Europe. What was required for that task was not an alliance but the will to use the military forces already possessed by the major European states. Without that will, NATO was irrelevant.

Finally, expansion became the last refuge of the NATO-forever crowd. Although a variety of justifications is offered for extending Western military ties, the proposal is merely the latest attempt to preserve an alliance whose purpose has disappeared. Explains William Odom of the Hudson Institute, without expansion, "the longer-term dynamics would inevitably fracture the alliance."[10] Similarly, *Washington Post* columnist Jim Hoagland writes, "Expansion provides a new basis for maintaining a militarily significant American presence in Europe beyond the Cold War to project power outside Europe."[11]

It is important to remember that NATO involves a commitment to go to war. Some cynics suggest that the United States need not fulfill the additional defense guarantees—to Poland over its borders with Belarus, for instance—implicit in an expanded alliance.[12] But other countries, especially the new NATO members, are likely to act on their own perception of such a guarantee, especially since the U.S. government has stressed its commitment. One official told the *New York Times*, "We take this every bit as seriously as we took our commitment to Berlin."[13] The president himself told West Point cadets that the alliance was extending its "most solemn security pledge," which meant that they "could be asked to put [their] lives on the line for a new NATO member."[14] In any case, in a crisis, concerns about credibility, honor, and leadership would likely overwhelm the hesitations of any president.

211

America will inevitably bear the brunt of the cost of NATO expansion. The Congressional Budget Office estimates that the potential expense could be as high as $125 billion over 15 years, a far more realistic figure than the $27 billion to $35 billion promoted by the Defense Department.[15] This is not the first time the administration has underestimated military costs. It promised that the mission in Bosnia would cost $1.5 billion; the tab has hit $6 billion and is still running. Nor is there much chance the Europeans will pick up the bill. As Michael Mandelbaum of the Johns Hopkins School of Advanced International Studies points out, "The Eastern Europeans, struggling to fulfill the social welfare obligations they inherited from the communist era, cannot pay. The Western Europeans, under pressure to reduce public spending to pave the way for the single European currency, will refuse to pay. So the U.S. will be stuck with the lion's share of the bill."[16]

Bogus Justifications for Expansion

What conceivable reason is there for maintaining, and expanding, the quintessential anti-Soviet alliance when the Soviet Union no longer exists? Some supporters, especially in the countries hoping to join, see NATO as a panacea for a variety of economic and political ills.[17] Ted Galen Carpenter notes that those politicians and analysts seem to view the alliance as a "mechanism for everyone to gather in the center of Europe for a group hug."[18] But NATO is a *military* alliance, and its relevance should be judged on that basis.

What the formerly communist states really need is access to Western markets, not the presence of Western troops. Yet only now are the West Europeans preparing to invite several former Soviet bloc members (the Czech Republic, Estonia, Hungary, Poland, and Slovenia) to join the European Union. The West Europeans still plan to exclude countries like Romania—which has been desperately lobbying to join NATO—as well as Bulgaria, Slovakia, Latvia, and Lithuania. The European Commission says the door remains open, but those nations would most benefit from immediate membership.[19]

Even more dubious is the claim that expansion will advance democracy, since in none of the three countries invited to join NATO (the Czech Republic, Hungary, and Poland) is democracy in doubt. Were the alliance a mechanism for generating internal stability and protecting fragile political freedom, membership should be offered first to such countries as Albania, Bulgaria, Slovakia, and Ukraine. Indeed, why not ask Russia to join, and even China (make NATO into the North Atlantic North Pacific Treaty Organization, or NANPTO)?[20] But NATO membership per se will do nothing to promote democracy. Indeed, to the extent that participation causes weaker nations to unnecessarily divert scarce resources to the military, NATO expansion could actually impede democratization.[21]

Another argument is that NATO should be enlarged to counteract any revived Russian threat. Anything could happen, of course, but the Russian Humpty Dumpty has broken into many pieces and no one is going to put it back together any time soon. Today a Russian attack on Eastern Europe, let alone on Central and Western Europe, is a paranoid fantasy. Even a revived Russia would face a daunting task: the West Europeans have a vast population advantage, 414 million to 149 million, and an even greater economic edge, with a combined GDP of $7.4 trillion compared to Russia's $1.1 trillion.[22] And that's not counting the resources of the Central and East European nations.

An expanded NATO is also seen by some as a hedge against an aggressive Germany. Deputy Secretary of State Strobe Talbott points to the cost of World Wars I and II: "Let's not do it again."[23] But people who cite history should recognize that circumstances change—often so dramatically that we no longer live in the same world. After all, France was long the leading aggressor in Europe, but we do not guard against a Napoleonic revival. The prospect of a German attack on its nuclear-armed neighbors is about as likely as a landing from Mars. Aggression against smaller states is scarcely more likely, since Germany has become Europe's dominant power peacefully and has an enormous stake in the status quo.

Finally, NATO enlargement is promoted as a means to stabilize Central and Eastern Europe. Czech president Václav Havel, among many others, claims that "a security vacuum in Central Europe exists today."[24] But there is no vacuum, since there is neither an outside threat nor a local imbalance. The former Soviet bloc may still be feeling its way internationally, but those nations possess options for cooperation outside of NATO.

A Blueprint for Endless Entanglements

Many of the former communist states obviously face serious internal challenges, but NATO is a military alliance that derives its meaning from the existence of an outside aggressor, not angry factions within individual states. Again, the events in Yugoslavia demonstrate the limits of NATO's capabilities. The essential ingredient in resolving deep-seated conflicts that go back centuries is not NATO membership but the willingness of the other alliance members to use force. And few countries believe it is worth sacrificing their own soldiers to suppress such disputes, no matter how tragic. Even more limited efforts—attempts to hunt down war criminals and reshuffle the balance of power in the Serbian region of Bosnia, for example—entail enormous risks with virtually no benefits (replacing a hard-line Serb nationalist tainted by war crimes with a more suave and attractive hard-line nationalist is no bargain). The cost of attempting to impose stability by preventing or terminating full-scale civil wars elsewhere in Eastern Europe would be far higher.

Even without expansion NATO is preparing to intervene in a host of potentially brutal, but utterly irrelevant, squabbles. "During the Cold War, there was a central focus and unity among nations" in the southern region, explains Adm. T. Joseph Lopez, commander of NATO's Allied Forces Southern Europe. "Now if you take a macro-look at our theater, it's literally filled with instability and pockets of unrest." His list of potential hot spots includes Albania, Algeria, Armenia and Azerbaijan, Bulgaria, Greece and Turkey, Libya, the Middle East, and Zaire. "With the end of the Cold War, the new enemy is instability," argues Lopez. "Our business and our mission today is to maintain stability."[25]

The mind boggles at the likely consequences of such an open-ended mission. There is little the West can do to promote stability in such cases, absent direct intervention and long-term occupation, which would be in the interest of neither Western Europe nor America. Who knows the solution to the violence in Algeria? And why would it be worth involving NATO in the fighting to impose a solution?

NATO expansion would add to the number of potential conflicts in which America could find itself enmeshed. By admitting Poland, for instance, the alliance would become guarantor of Poland's border with Belarus, a country sinking into dictatorship even as it establishes extensive political and military ties to Russia.[26] The admission of three Central European countries, however, may be only the beginning. Although the Clinton administration insisted on limiting the first round of expansion to the Czech Republic, Hungary, and

Poland, a majority of NATO members, including the particularly insistent French, desire to bring in Romania and Slovenia. Moreover, influential Americans advocate expanding membership still further. Rep. Benjamin Gilman (R-N.Y.), chairman of the House Committee on International Relations, argues that "it is essential that everyone understand that the first round of enlargement . . . will not be the last round. Aspiring candidates for NATO membership must be assured that their omission from the first round does not mean that they will never get in."[27]

The potential for conflict, especially confrontation with the Russians, increases as one moves farther east. Admitting the Baltic states and Ukraine, for instance, would incorporate nations with large Russian populations and a variety of ongoing disputes with Moscow. The House Republican Conference observes that "the fundamental geopolitical reality in Central and Eastern Europe is the inherent imbalance of power between Russia and its immediate and near neighbors" and cites a number of squabbles among the various parties.[28] That situation, argues the organization, warrants NATO expansion. But by the conference's own logic, Washington should stay out. Expansion into the lands of the former Soviet Union would inject the United States into areas of traditional and significant Russian interest but scant strategic value to America. Moreover, the costs of intervening would prove staggering. Observes columnist Patrick Buchanan, "There is no way America or NATO could defend or liberate these four nations [the Baltic republics and Ukraine]— without risking a nuclear exchange with Moscow."[29]

Thus, NATO expansion is unlikely to make Central and Eastern Europe more stable. Rather, it will ensure that any effects of instability are transmitted to Western Europe and America. The lesson of World War I, in fact, is that nonintervention is a better strategy for preserving continental stability. In 1914 every major power was willing to go to war over a conflict started in the Balkans. Alliances acted as transmission belts of war. In 1991 civil war erupted in Yugoslavia and the conflict lasted longer than did World War I, without spreading, because the major powers created firebreaks to war by refusing to intervene as they had seven decades before.

Expanding NATO, however, would itself be destabilizing. Enlargement is seen as bad faith by the Russians. They believe, with good reason, that at the time of Germany's reunification the United

States promised not to expand NATO.[30] Russia's perception matters because moving the borders of an alliance that has always been directed against Moscow closer to Russia naturally looks threatening. Of course, the Founding Act on Mutual Relations, Cooperation and Security between NATO and the Russian Federation, signed in May 1997, stated that "Russia and NATO do not consider each other as adversaries."[31] But few Russians take such diplomatic pablum seriously. Secretary of State Madeleine Albright complained to Russian foreign minister Yevgeny Primakov during her trip to Moscow in May 1997, "Your intellectuals have been berating me for the past hour" over the NATO enlargement issue.[32] Anywhere between 70 percent and 85 percent of Russians, according to recent polls, harbor similar misgivings.[33]

True, Moscow formally accepted NATO expansion, but for a reason. One diplomat told the *Washington Post*, "What we're seeing is the influence of [Deputy Prime Minister Anatoly] Chubais and the financial elites. They are not interested in confrontation with the West. They want stability with the West, and they want to avoid remilitarization of the economy."[34] But that sentiment would discourage Russian coercion in Central and Eastern Europe irrespective of alliance enlargement.

Unfortunately, NATO expansion is likely to create countervailing nationalistic pressures. Domestically, allied policy will strengthen anti-Western political factions in a system that remains both unstable and volatile. Enlargement is also influencing Russian foreign policy for the worse. For instance, the Duma has balked at approving START II, which would significantly cut America's and Russia's nuclear arsenals. NATO's actions have also encouraged Russia to dramatically strengthen ties with China. Providing security guarantees to Central and Eastern Europe may affect the conduct of countries in those regions as well, making them more willing to play political and military games of chicken with each other and with Russia. In short, by expanding NATO Washington risks losing a far larger and more important geopolitical game.

Ending the Opportunity for More European Free Riding

It is not in America's interest to defend, not only populous and prosperous states that can defend themselves, but a host of other nations that, only a few years ago, were arrayed on the other side of the international divide—especially when there are alternatives to NATO.

America's goal should be to encourage the development of a new, comprehensive European security system managed by the Europeans themselves. Admittedly, that is no simple task. But the difficulty of doing so in part reflects the dominant role of the United States— Europe sees no reason to do more in the security realm when it can rely on America. However much a nation like France may gripe about "excessive U.S. influence," Washington's presence reduces the need for the Europeans to spend more on defense or grapple with difficult regional problems. Moreover, the very lack of a serious threat, the usual justification for an alliance, has reduced the need for the Europeans to act on their own behalf.

The result is brazenly exploitive European behavior. In 1993 German chancellor Helmut Kohl told an audience that included U.S. secretary of defense Les Aspin that his country intended to cut its military forces by 40 percent over the following three years, but that America, naturally, should maintain its troop presence in Germany. French policy is equally hypocritical. Paris has long complained about Washington's dominant role in Europe and around the world. According to Prime Minister Lionel Jospin, "We see a certain tendency toward hegemony, which is not necessarily identical with exercising the global responsibilities of a great power, even if it is a friend."[35] Yet the new socialist government announced significant military cuts shortly after taking office. It plans to cut spending on military procurement alone by 11 percent next year.

American disengagement would eliminate today's perverse incentive structure. The United States should phase out its troop presence and withdraw from NATO. The Europeans obviously have the resources to defend themselves, with combined economies and populations far greater than those of either America or Russia. Today Britain, France, and Germany alone spend more than Moscow on defense. The Western European Union, EuroCorps, and the Organization for Security and Cooperation in Europe all provide potential frameworks for a security organization organized, funded, and manned by Europeans.

The exact form of such a post-NATO security structure should be up to the Europeans. In particular, the West Europeans should decide what commitments they want to make to Central and Eastern

Europe. No longer would they be able to blackmail the United States, as they did when they stated that an American withdrawal from Bosnia means a European withdrawal. "One out, all out," observed British foreign secretary Robin Cook.[36] (Perversely, Washington currently discourages any independent European action. For instance, in July 1995 Assistant Secretary of State for European Affairs Richard Holbrooke opposed proposals that the WEU include as members the former communist states, since doing so would "deeply damage Western institutions and especially NATO.")[37]

In any case, the most important need of the former Soviet bloc countries is economic integration with prosperous Western Europe. However, America's dominant defense role has so far allowed the West Europeans to act irresponsibly, in essence denying market access to the new democracies while offering U.S. security guarantees. Only now, eight years after the fall of the Berlin Wall, is such an economically insensitive policy toward Central and Eastern Europe finally starting to change.

More intensive Continent-wide cooperation would also fulfill the role currently attributed to the United States, that of forestalling any renationalization of European politics. America's involvement is far less important today than it was in the aftermath of World War II. European integration in many fields is obviously far advanced—much further advanced than it was earlier this century. Without the United States, the Europeans would have an incentive to extend that cooperation to military matters. The time for the Europeans to design an alternate security structure is now, before a crisis arises. Should the kinds of passions capable of causing a major war nevertheless emerge in the future, they would likely be strong enough to sweep aside any U.S. stabilizing presence as well.

Of course, Washington should help ease the transition to European security self-sufficiency. For instance, the United States should push the Europeans to Europeanize the Balkans occupation force, that is, the Stabilization Force in Bosnia. Doing so, writes John Hillen of the Council on Foreign Relations, would "foster a wider sense of responsibility for security affairs."[38]

America should also remain involved economically, politically, diplomatically, and culturally in Europe. But in the security realm Washington should merely remain watchful for the development of a potential hegemon that cannot be contained by the Europeans.

"We cannot turn a blind eye to Europe," admonishes Sen. Mike DeWine (R-Ohio), a strong proponent of NATO expansion.[39] But no one is advocating that. Remaining interested in European affairs does not require guaranteeing the security of populous and prosperous nations capable of defending themselves. It also does not preclude the United States from returning to the role of a normal country.

Is there an alternative to NATO? Yes. In fact, there are several. It is time for Europe to choose one.

After World War II the United States abandoned its traditional foreign policy, that of a republic, in order to contain the Soviet Union. Americans spent some $13 trillion (in 1997 dollars) and sacrificed more than 100,000 lives (in Korea and Vietnam) to win the Cold War. They now deserve to reap the benefits of their victory. Washington should drop foreign military commitments that are no longer relevant.

The apparent organizational immortality of NATO demonstrates how, despite a drastically changed world, interventionist American foreign and military policies remain the same. The Cold War has ended, but the United States retains a Cold War–sized military. Defense spending, adjusted for inflation, is roughly what it was in 1980 and 1975 and almost as much as it was in 1965—in the midst of the Vietnam War. Force levels exceed those necessary to protect America from any plausible threat.

By enlarging NATO Washington would be undertaking even more expansive commitments than it did during the Cold War—defending at least three Central European states to start, as well as attempting to impose an artificial Bosnian state on three warring ethnic groups committed to separation. And there's no logical limit to new commitments. Even Uzbekistan is currently attempting to build ties with NATO.

It is time to move in the other direction. NATO was created for a reason: to shield Western Europe from an expansionist totalitarian superpower. It has fulfilled its objective. Rather than search for new justifications for an old organization, the United States should encourage the Europeans to create new institutions for new purposes. Best would be some form of NATO without the United States, a continental security architecture with neither American forces nor American security guarantees.

219

Notes

1. Quoted in Martin Sieff, "Repeat Effort for Eastern Europe Unlikely in Different Era," *Washington Times*, May 29, 1997, p. A12.

2. Rasmussen Research, "Most Think U.S. Defense Obligations Should Include Only Three Countries—Canada, Mexico, and Great Britain," Press release, August 8, 1997.

3. Quoted in Stephen E. Ambrose, *Eisenhower: Soldier, General of the Army, President-Elect* (New York: Simon & Schuster, 1983), p. 506.

4. Dwight D. Eisenhower, "Let's Be Honest with Ourselves," *Saturday Evening Post*, October 26, 1963, p. 26.

5. Quoted in Martin Sieff, "Experts Hit Hard at NATO Expansion," *Washington Times*, June 27, 1997, p. A22.

6. International Institute for Strategic Studies, *The Military Balance 1996–1997* (London: Oxford University Press 1996), pp. 19–76.

7. Quoted in Doug Bandow and Ted Galen Carpenter, "Preserving an Obsolete NATO," *Cato Policy Report* 12, no. 5 (September–October 1990): 10–11.

8. Robert D. Hormats, "Redefining the Atlantic Link," *Foreign Affairs* 68, no. 4 (Fall 1989): 86.

9. David M. Abshire, "Don't Muster Out NATO Yet: Its Job Is Far from Done," *Wall Street Journal*, December 1, 1989, p. A14.

10. William Odom, "Maintaining Status Quo Spells Death for NATO," *Foresight* 1, no. 8 (August 1997): 3.

11. Jim Hoagland, "The End of Armies," *Washington Post*, September 18, 1997, p. A21.

12. Author's conversations with U.S. officials, June and July 1997.

13. Quoted in R. W. Apple Jr., "Europe's New Order: Making a Club, Not War," *New York Times*, May 18, 1997, p. E1.

14. Quoted in Alison Mitchell, "Clinton, at West Point, Says Bigger NATO Lessens Chance of War," *New York Times*, June 1, 1997, p. 12.

15. See Ivan Eland, "The High Cost of NATO Expansion: Clearing the Administration's Smoke Screen," Cato Institute Policy Analysis no. 286, October 28, 1997.

16. Michael Mandelbaum, "Bigger Isn't Better," *Wall Street Journal*, July 9, 1997, p. A14.

17. See, for example, Jane Perlez, "Joining NATO: Central Europe Sees a Cure-All," *New York Times*, June 11, 1997, pp. A1, A14.

18. Ted Galen Carpenter, "The Folly of NATO Enlargement," *World & I*, July 1997, p. 77.

19. For a detailed discussion of the debate surrounding expanded EU membership, see "Eastward Ho, They Said Warily," *The Economist*, July 19, 1997, pp. 43–44.

20. Columnist Thomas Friedman sarcastically suggests including Chile, using arguments eerily similar to those advanced by advocates of NATO expansion. Thomas Friedman, "Chile, First and Forever," *New York Times*, June 26, 1997, p. A37.

21. NATO's military requirements are already causing serious political difficulties even in the Czech Republic. See, for example, Jane Perlez, "Pentagon Aide Warns Czechs to Upgrade Military for NATO," *New York Times*, October 1, 1997, p. A7.

22. International Institute for Strategic Studies, pp. 49–76, 113.

23. Quoted in Ben Barber, "Talbott Predicts NATO Approval," *Washington Times*, July 3, 1997, p. A10.

24. Václav Havel, "NATO's Quality of Life," American Enterprise Institute On the Issues, May 1997, p. 2.

25. Quoted in James Kitfield, "Danger Zone," *National Journal*, May 10, 1997, p. 924.

26. Ted Galen Carpenter and Andrew Stone, "NATO Expansion Flashpoint No. 1: The Border between Poland and Belarus," Cato Institute Foreign Policy Briefing no. 44, September 16, 1997.

27. Benjamin Gilman, "How to Expand NATO," *Washington Times*, April 23, 1997, p. A17.

28. House Republican Policy Committee, "NATO Expansion," Report to the Conference, May 23, 1997, p. 2.

29. Patrick Buchanan, "Too Clever by Half . . . and Chancy?" *Washington Times*, May 28, 1997, p. A12.

30. Michael Gordon, "The Anatomy of a Misunderstanding," *New York Times*, May 25, 1997, p. E3.

31. Quoted in "Consultations Will Not Extend into the Internal Matters," *Washington Times*, May 27, 1997, p. A8.

32. Quoted in Michael Dobbs, "For Clinton, Sticking with Yeltsin Sealed Agreement on NATO," *Washington Post*, May 27, 1997, p. A11.

33. Vladimir Raskin, "Barring Russia from NATO Would Be Mistake," Letter to the editor, *New York Times*, May 11, 1997, p. E14.

34. Quoted in David Hoffmann, "For Yeltsin, Business Prospects Outweighed NATO Threat," *Washington Post*, May 27, 1997, p. A1.

35. Quoted in Paul Taylor, "Clinton's Talk in Denver Angers French Premier," *Washington Times*, May 25, 1997, p. A11.

36. Quoted in Melinda Liu, "Now It's Cohen vs. Albright," *Newsweek*, June 9, 1997, p. 47.

37. Quoted in R. T. Davies, "Not NATO's Day," *Washington Post*, July 21, 1997, p. A21.

38. John Hillen, "After SFOR—Planning a European-Led Force," *Joint Force Quarterly* (Spring 1997): 79.

39. Mike DeWine, "The Cost of Not Expanding NATO," *Washington Post*, August 19, 1997, p. A13.

16. A Strong OSCE for a Secure Europe

Jonathan G. Clarke

In discussing alternatives to NATO, it is important to note what most of the critics of NATO expansion are *not* advocating. We are not talking about dismantling the areas in which NATO has a comparative advantage. Some of those are interoperability of equipment, shared procurement programs, sharing of intelligence, joint training, and combined operations. All of those capabilities have been established over time and should not be lightly discarded. Whatever form alternative security arrangements may take in Europe, NATO's comparative advantages need to be retained—both among the existing NATO membership and as part of any new collaborative structures that may be established.

Any discussion of an alternative to NATO needs to be chiefly about the form of organizational structure that is best suited for dealing with the foreseeable problems of European security. It is important that we get that structure right. European instability and conflict have a nasty habit of embroiling the United States. What has happened in Bosnia shows that the United States will tend to get sucked into European problems even in the face of widespread congressional and popular opposition. The Bosnia example also shows that, if the organizational structure is deficient, American intervention will be untidy and ineffective.

Important though it is, the debate about NATO's future appears to be becalmed in a fog of limp conventionality. For reasons that no one can articulate clearly and at costs that no one can estimate, NATO is set to expand, almost by inertia. New guarantees are being extended about which no one is certain, which will not be supported by real resources, and which the advocates of expansion expect will never be invoked. Czech president Václav Havel, a tireless campaigner for NATO expansion—at least to the Czech Republic—expressed the rather dreamy conventional wisdom when he said that "there was no alternative" to NATO.[1]

In examining Havel's assertion, we need to remind ourselves that, for the United States, the key question is whether NATO continues to make military sense as the organization that "first and foremost" guarantees American security interests in Europe. That is a question of credibility. With the drawdown of U.S. troops in Europe continuing as if by stealth (units that went from Europe to the Persian Gulf War never returned), there is already some question about how effective NATO is as a military organization.

Much of the discussion about expansion of NATO, which has concentrated on the political objectives expressed in article 4 of the treaty rather than the military guarantees in article 5, reflects that doubt. Havel, for example, urges that NATO redefine its mission as one almost entirely outside the military sphere. He calls for NATO to act as the "guarantor of Euro-American civilization."[2] American sources have echoed that approach. The 1997 official Defense Department report to Congress, for example, stresses that the primary rationale for the expansion of NATO is that it "contributes to the broader goal of a powerful, undivided, and democratic Europe."[3] Amplifying that theme in testimony to the Senate Armed Services Committee, Secretary of State Madeleine Albright explained that the fundamental goal of NATO expansion was to "build for the very first time a peaceful, democratic and undivided transatlantic community."[4]

There is nothing wrong with such objectives, but it is a profound mistake to make NATO bear a disproportionate political load at the expense of its military role. NATO's success in devising new relevance for itself must be judged against a military yardstick, not by how well it duplicates or substitutes for other organizations such as the European Union. The consolidation of democracy in the former Warsaw Pact nations is, of course, a very desirable objective. Whether it comes about or not will have much more to do with economic development, through links with the EU, than with NATO membership. Short of a military justification, American support for a Cold War era organization brings no advantage.

Principles of an Alternative European Security Design

A weakness of much of the criticism of NATO expansion has been a reluctance to put forward any alternative. That is a serious weakness, given that the NATO-based status quo is demonstrably inadequate. Alternative designs for European security should not, however, start from ground zero. The United States must safeguard the following principles:

- The United States must retain the capability to resist any potential European hegemon. Although a potential hegemon is low on the list of potential threats at present, that central need must not be forgotten.

- The new security structure must be inclusive. Disputes on Europe's outer boundaries, such as the conflict between Armenia and Azerbaijan and the continuing tension over Cyprus, have implications for the rest of Europe. They are connected, in the former case, with the flow of oil and gas from the Caspian basin and, in the latter case, with the potential for hostilities between two existing NATO members, Greece and Turkey. The new structure must not be narrowly focused on just a few favored nations, nor should it draw new dividing lines in Europe.

- The new structure must develop an alternative security doctrine. NATO's traditional philosophy of collective defense against an onslaught from the Soviet Union was necessarily and judiciously based on the premise that "an attack on one is an attack on all." That principle was, in fact, the core of article 5 of the North Atlantic Treaty. That emphasis was necessary to signal to the USSR that it could not probe NATO's defenses on the periphery, for example in Turkey, without encountering the full weight of the alliance. Such an approach is not suitable for smaller regional problems such as those in Albania and Abkhazia or ethnic disputes such as the conflict in Bosnia. Those problems are of local or regional significance. As noted above, they may have potentially wider implications, but they nevertheless are not the kind of all-out challenge to NATO's integrity envisioned in article 5. To include such problems within NATO's competence without a revision of NATO's defense doctrine can only lead to confusion, frustration, and disarray.[5]

- Mediation capability, rather than static defense against invasion or high-tech military intervention, must be a central mission. Unlike the cross-border, war-fighting scenarios envisioned under NATO's traditional defense doctrine, today's security problems in Europe are predominantly domestic or intrastate in nature. Such disputes require civilian mediation rather than military intervention.

- Regional responsibility and responsiveness should be given a high priority. An example is the Italian-led intervention in Albania. That mission benefited from the strong leadership provided by the two countries with the most at stake in Albania, namely, Italy and Greece. Forces, including police units, were marshaled quickly. Political follow-up, including economic aid, was properly coordinated, with much of the load being taken by the private sectors in Italy and Greece.
- The United States should encourage European initiative. For example, interesting discussions are taking place within the Western European Union. The 1997 Amsterdam Treaty made provision for an eventual defense role for the European Union. In May 1996 WEU governments agreed to strengthen their military cooperation through the Combined Joint Task Force system under which European forces would be available for missions in which the United States did not wish to participate.[6]
- NATO should not seek to take on nonmilitary, developmental tasks. They dilute the military capabilities of the alliance by diverting resources. Instead, such tasks should be left to the appropriate agencies, such as the EU or the U.S.-sponsored Southeast European Cooperation Initiative—and whenever possible to the private sector.

The OSCE as an Initial Model

No existing security structure in Europe fully meets those criteria, and it is important that, in designing new structures, policymakers not confine themselves solely to organizations that already exist. Nonetheless, a possible starting model is the Organization for Security and Cooperation in Europe. That organization has many of the desired attributes, especially if they are combined with some of the cooperative features of the Partnership for Peace and other European structures such as the WEU, and if OSCE procedures and capabilities are upgraded.[7]

That may seem a surprising assertion, given that, since the OSCE's inception, the United States has maneuvered to keep it in the background and to discourage it from challenging NATO's primacy among European defense structures. In the run-up to the Paris conference of December 1990 (at the time the OSCE was still called the Conference on Security and Cooperation in Europe), the Bush administration was determined not to allow the OSCE to supplant NATO as Europe's principal security organization.[8] Similarly, the PFP was seen as an interim measure in the lead-up to NATO expansion, not as a possible alternative to expansion.

During the Cold War, insistence on NATO's primacy may have been the correct policy in the face of the threat of Soviet invasion. But changed circumstances mean that the time has come to take a less negative look at the OSCE and a more creative look at the PFP.

The OSCE's record in managing the Cold War endgame and in interbloc reconciliation was excellent. Its performance in post–Cold War security has been mixed. On the positive side, it has enjoyed some success in mediating disagreements between the Baltic nations and Russia on the pace of Russian troop withdrawals and questions of citizenship. In Kosovo OSCE monitors played some part in defusing tensions between the Serbian authorities and the predominantly Albanian population. Former secretary of state Warren Christopher praised those successes, stating that "OSCE's innovative work on crisis management and conflict prevention is one of the most promising security experiments underway in Europe today."[9]

More recent successful OSCE initiatives include the mission, championed by former Spanish prime minister Felipe Gonzalez, to Serbia in January 1997. That mission played a key role in persuading President Slobodan Milosevic to recognize the municipal election results, which included major victories by opposition political forces. Similarly, in September 1997 OSCE provided the crucial administrative infrastructure for the municipal elections in Bosnia-Herzegovina. In the Caucasus, the OSCE Minsk group, which includes the United States, is performing useful work in mediating the dispute between Armenia and Azerbaijan over the latter's breakaway Armenian-dominated enclave of Ngorno-Karabakh. On the debit side, the OSCE performed no better than anyone else in the early stages of the conflict in the former Yugoslavia.

The organization does, however, enjoy some significant conceptual and structural strengths that, if developed, would allow it to make a major Continent-wide contribution to European security and become the key organization for tackling what Christopher termed "the root causes of European security problems."[10] Its membership includes all NATO members as well as all of the countries of the former Warsaw Pact and the former Soviet republics. It is developing specialized expertise in arms control, confidence-building measures, and conflict mediation and resolution. It continues to consolidate its infrastructure—Secretariat in Prague, Conflict Prevention Center in Vienna, and Office for Democratic Institutions and Human Rights in Warsaw.

Changes to the OSCE

That is a promising foundation, but it still leaves the OSCE vulnerable to the criticism that it remains stuck at the "talking-shop" stage. Imaginative U.S. policy could help change that. The OSCE now needs to develop structures that will enable it to exert significant influence over the behavior of its members. Three steps in ascending order of complexity might be considered.

Procedure

The OSCE has traditionally operated by consensus. There are good reasons for that, but the requirement has also proved a weakness. Both the Soviet Union and the federal government of Yugoslavia, for example, were able to block substantive discussion of and mediation efforts in the impending Bosnian conflict. A procedure that enabled discussion to proceed at the will of a qualified majority (that is, something less than unanimity but still substantially in excess of a simple majority and with safeguards for regional and large-country interests—a system that already exists in the European Council of Ministers) would address that weakness. At the very least, none of the parties to a dispute should be allowed to block mediation procedures.

Such a reform still falls short of the proposals for legally binding arbitration that have been discussed within the OSCE but never agreed to. Enforcement would remain a problem, with contravening states able simply to ignore OSCE resolutions.

Benefits and Responsibilities

A way around the problem of noncompliance would be to enhance the benefits of OSCE membership, particularly in the military sphere. That could be done by expanding the OSCE's responsibilities to include such operational matters as joint planning, coordinated exercises, and common procurement policies. An international military staff along NATO lines would be required to carry out those tasks. The lessons derived from both NATO's long experience in this regard and the PFP's more recent experience may be able to help. OSCE membership would thereby confer significant military benefits. It would also make suspension or exclusion a more potent threat.

Armed Forces

As the concept of the OSCE as an increasingly powerful executive agency took root, it might become desirable to have armed forces that would be answerable to the OSCE Council of Ministers for Foreign Affairs. NATO has already indicated its willingness to undertake military missions at OSCE's behest. The logical next step would be to enhance and empower the OSCE Secretariat to carry out such tasks directly rather than through a subsidiary organization that does not include the full OSCE membership.

The issue of OSCE military forces requires careful definition. The goal should not be to perpetuate NATO under another name by creating a new collective defense structure or wider security commitments for any current NATO member. Nor should the OSCE be turned into a war-making organization to the detriment of its central mission of conflict prevention and resolution. Instead, this proposal to create OSCE forces is intended to place in the hands of the Council of Ministers an instrument with which, in the last resort, it can back up its resolutions.

Implications of Changes

Equipped with those extra abilities, the OSCE would be transformed into a "one-stop" mediation and peacekeeping institution. If, as the Bosnia example indicates, there is going to be a growing need for long-term "peace protectorates" to address ethnic conflict in former communist lands in Eastern Europe and elsewhere, then an OSCE force would provide the required troops. Likewise, as the pace of negotiations on Cyprus accelerates, there will be a need for a postsettlement troop presence on the island. In Cyprus and other problem areas, troops from a Europe-wide organization rather than a specifically Western group would be likely to be both more acceptable and more effective than NATO-provided intervenors.

A greater emphasis on the OSCE would enable the United States to strengthen an organization that is much more finely calibrated to respond to today's problems in Europe than is any other existing organization. An additional benefit to American interests would accrue from the fact that reliance on the OSCE would enable the

United States to transcend the debilitating discussions over the Europeanization of NATO and the involvement of the alliance in "out-of-area" issues.

On the Europeanization question, the United States should encourage EU moves toward a defense and security dimension. That objective by the EU was incorporated for the first time in a treaty at the June 1997 Amsterdam EU summit.[11] That is a positive development from the U.S. perspective.

On the out-of-area issue, the OSCE is better suited than NATO to assume such responsibilities. If operational responsibility were transferred to the OSCE, of which all NATO countries are members, the legal and treaty difficulties between in- and out-of-area security missions might be smoothed away.

Within the OSCE, it would make sense for the United States to promote the creation of regional subgroups. The challenges in southern Europe and the eastern Mediterranean are, for example, very different from those in the Baltic republics.[12] Such problems need regional or sometimes even subregional solutions, not an all-purpose approach from the center, as would be the case with an enlarged NATO. Luckily, there are many regional initiatives under way, notably the Balkan foreign ministers' conferences led by Greece and similar initiatives in Central Europe and the Black Sea region. The Black Sea Economic Cooperation Organization, for example, brings together all of the states in the Black Sea area.

Moving beyond a NATO-Centric Policy

By adapting a less NATO-centric policy, the United States would move its security relations with Europe firmly into the new age. Of course, the OSCE does not by itself provide the Holy Grail of a new generation of peace. There are too many entrenched hatreds, claims, and counterclaims for that to be a realistic prospect. In addition, the OSCE, like NATO, will be only as effective as its membership wishes it to be. Nonetheless, in putting more muscle behind the OSCE, or a new security mechanism based on its structure, the United States would be helping to develop a real organization to deal with the real problems of the Continent. In that way the United States would break away from the current sterility of clinging to an obsolescent institution that is addressing phantom problems.

A new security structure, which incorporates the OSCE membership and organization and includes elements of the PFP and other European organizations, will provide a more promising base than NATO for handling future European crises. It will have the advantage both of allowing the United States to approach the whole spectrum of European security issues under one roof and of providing regional means of preventive diplomacy and, if necessary, effective intervention. In many de facto ways that is the direction in which actual European security structures are evolving. It would be better to acknowledge that reality and initiate a purposeful, not a piecemeal, evolution than to seek to keep NATO on life support.

Notes

1. Václav Havel, "NATO's Quality of Life," *New York Times*, May 13, 1997, p. A12.
2. Ibid.
3. U.S. Department of Defense, "Report to the Congress on the Enlargement of the North Atlantic Treaty Organization: Rationale, Benefits, Costs and Implications," February 24, 1997, p. 1.
4. Madeleine Albright, Statement before the Senate Armed Services Committee, April 23, 1997, U.S. Department of State *Dispatch* 8, no. 3 (March–April 1997): 16–20.
5. This point is developed at greater length in Jonathan G. Clarke, "Beckoning Quagmires: NATO in Eastern Europe," in *The Future of NATO*, ed. Ted Galen Carpenter (London: Frank Cass, 1995), pp. 42–60.
6. See the WEU Birmingham Declaration of May 7, 1996, at http://www.flo.gov.uk/weu.
7. A useful account of the OSCE may be found in Daniel Nelson, "America and Collective Security in Europe," in *The Future of NATO*, pp. 105–24.
8. An account of U.S. attitudes toward the CSCE and the OSCE may be found in Catherine McArdle Kelleher, "Cooperative Security in Europe," in *Global Engagement: Cooperation and Security in the 21st Century*, ed. Janne E. Nolan (Washington: Brookings Institution, 1994), pp. 293–352.
9. Warren Christopher, Intervention at the North Atlantic Council Ministerial Meeting in Athens, Greece, June 10, 1993, U.S. Department of State *Dispatch* 4, no. 5 (June 21, 1993): 448–51.
10. Warren Christopher, Intervention at the North Atlantic Council Ministerial Meeting at Noordwijk, Netherlands, May 30, 1995, U.S. Department of State *Dispatch* 6, no. 23 (June 5, 1995): 471–74.
11. Article J7 of the Amsterdam Treaty reads in part: "The common foreign and security policy shall include all questions relating to the security of the Union, including the progressive framing of a common defense policy, in accordance with the second subparagraph, which might lead to a common defense, should the European Council so decide." European Union document conf/4001/97, June 17, 1997.
12. This point is developed in Ted Galen Carpenter, "The Mediterranean Cauldron," *Mediterranean Quarterly* 8, no. 2 (Spring 1997): 45–64.

17. Political Alternatives to NATO Expansion

Amos Perlmutter

Numerous problems and dangers are associated with the enlargement of NATO. Critics have addressed many of them at length, including the likelihood that expanding the alliance to the borders of the Russian Federation will fatally undermine pro-Western democrats in Russia and poison Russia's relations with the West; that enlargement may create a new division of Europe; and that enlargement may increase the danger of NATO's becoming entangled in parochial quarrels among the various Central and East European countries—a possibility not unlike that of a war between NATO members Greece and Turkey.

Those serious problems should not be ignored. It is important to examine even more fundamental issues, however, such as the rationale for NATO expansion and whether extending the alliance's borders eastward is the best means of achieving the desired objectives. Close examination of the rationale for NATO enlargement as described in Pentagon planning documents suggests that NATO is the wrong institution for the job. Other institutions and arrangements would likely advance the Clinton administration's objectives far more effectively, without the exorbitant costs and risks associated with NATO enlargement.

The Administration's Rationale for NATO Enlargement

The rationale for NATO expansion presented by the Pentagon's "Report to the Congress on the Enlargement of the North Atlantic Treaty Organization: Rationale, Benefits, Costs and Implications" is overwhelmingly political. There is hardly a military cause, reason, motive, or purpose offered. The Pentagon argues that NATO enlargement is one part of a much broader, post–Cold War strategy to help create a peaceful, undivided, and democratic Europe.[1] The other elements of the strategy include support for German reunification; encouragement of reforms in Russia, Ukraine, and the new independent states; enhanced negotiation and adaptation of the Conventional Forces in Europe Treaty; and the evolution and strengthening of European security and economic institutions, including the European Union, the Organization for Security and Cooperation in Europe, the Council of Europe, and the Western European Union. All of those activities are political in nature, as is the overall objective of creating a "peaceful, undivided, and democratic Europe."

NATO, however, is a military alliance. As such, it is not particularly well suited for fulfilling essentially political objectives. NATO entails all of the costs and risks normally associated with military alliances, and expanding military commitments is an inherently expensive and risky endeavor. An organization that is primarily political in nature, such as the EU, is a more natural candidate to fulfill the political objectives the administration seeks to achieve with NATO enlargement. The Pentagon, however, has said it would be "unwise" to delay NATO enlargement until the EU expands. Why? "Doing so would unnecessarily postpone measures that are worthwhile and possible today, and it would diminish America's voice in current efforts to build the security of the Euro-Atlantic region."[2] Washington is championing NATO enlargement so that the United States can sustain a leading role in formulating European and Atlantic policies.

The Clinton administration, because it is using NATO enlargement primarily for political purposes, has sought to minimize the associated risks and costs. Consequently, the Pentagon has dreamed up a plan for enlargement "on the cheap." According to that plan, NATO enlargement will cost from $27 billion to $35 billion over the next 10 years; the U.S. share of those costs will be approximately $1.5 billion to $2 billion. Most experts agree that that sum is impossibly low to support a military strategy and, despite the administration's equivocation, no military alliance exists in the abstract without at least an implicitly identified rival or adversary.

In this case, the implicit adversary is Russia. Even a democratic Russia has national interests, which may include a sphere of influence beyond its western borders. Moreover, a nondemocratic or revisionist Russia is still a possibility. An enlarged NATO must view Russia as its potential adversary for military planning purposes.

With that in mind, credible security guarantees to Central and Eastern Europe require military restructuring and the enhancement of the alliance's regional reinforcement capabilities, which will entail costs, such as those for harmonizing control and communications systems, over and above direct enlargement costs. It is impossible to predict with any precision what the total cost of enlargement could be, but credible security guarantees to new members would almost certainly cost at least $125 billion—four times the administration's estimate.[3] The administration realizes that neither Congress nor the American people are likely to support such expenditures, which is one reason the Pentagon offered a less expensive alternative. Enlargement "on the cheap," however, will result in paper guarantees as useless as those extended to Poland by Great Britain and France in 1939. At best, such guarantees offer a false sense of security. At worst, they invite disaster.

Even if an enlarged NATO had at its disposal the resources that would allow it to extend a viable security guarantee to new members, the array of NATO institutions that has sprung up since the end of the Cold War calls into question the alliance's military effectiveness. Henry Kissinger has issued warnings about that problem even though he is a supporter of NATO expansion. He has noted with concern the plethora of institutions that

> soon will compete for NATO consultation: the existing NATO Council, composed of the current 16 NATO members; the NATO-Russia Council, composed of NATO members plus Russia; the North Atlantic Cooperation Council, grouping NATO and most former Eastern Bloc countries; and the Partnership for Peace, composed of NATO and 11 Eastern countries, extending as far as Kazakhstan. Since all these institutions are served by the same staffs and attended by the same NATO representatives, *a dilution of traditional NATO purposes is inevitable.*[4]

In a subsequent article, Kissinger has specifically warned about the dangers inherent in the Founding Act on Relations, Cooperation and Security between NATO and the Russian Federation. In criticizing the act, he made the following points: (1) "The language of the Founding Act is that of collective security not of alliance. Article 2 speaks of the parties' 'shared commitment to build a stable, peaceful and undivided Europe, whole and free.' Article 6 refers to the parties'

'allegiance to shared values, commitments and norms of behavior.' "
(2) The act would turn NATO into a mini–United Nations. (3) "The
most worrisome aspects of the Founding Act however, are its unambiguous provisions, specifically the consultative machinery for
which it provides. Article 12 calls into being, side by side with
existing NATO institutions, a new Permanent Joint Council composed of the same ambassadors who form the existing NATO Council plus a Russian full member."[5]

How, then, will Russia, as a permanent member of the Joint Council, deal with a Poland that Russia, as a nation, may threaten? Kissinger ends with the point that new members of NATO, the three
Central European states or others who are admitted later, "are clearly
joining in a second-class status." In the end, Kissinger confesses,
"Had I known the price of NATO enlargement would be the gross
dilution of NATO, I might have urged other means to achieve the
objective."[6] The Founding Act would mean a Russian veto over
NATO. Thus, the price paid for NATO expansion is Russia's entry
through a back door. As a result, "the NATO council in which the
allies conduct their most sensitive consultations is to be diluted by
the creation of a competing NATO-plus-Russia forum," Kissinger
argues.

The Pentagon's report on enlargement states correctly that "the
end of the Cold War has created a new security environment."[7]
The administration's conclusion that NATO enlargement is the best
response to the new strategic environment, however, is misguided
and potentially dangerous.

Alternatives to NATO Expansion

The European Union

What, then, are the alternatives to NATO expansion? The expansion of the EU is one possibility, particularly if the military aspect
of NATO is to take a back seat to NATO's political identity. The
EU, not NATO, is the proper European institution to guide the
transition to democracy of the former Warsaw Pact states. As Marybeth Peterson Ulrich, assistant professor at the U.S. Air Force Academy, has written,

> The establishment of a security community in Europe whose
> members expect peaceful change and have developed norms

that "members will not fight each other physically, but will settle their disputes in some other way" is the goal of post-communist Europe. The development of these norms and expectations is dependent on the success of political, economic, and social ties—*ties which are more likely to develop through the expansion of the EU.*[8]

Ulrich further argues that "the democratization and integration of the former Eastern bloc into European political, economic, and security structures is the solution to the security problem of post–Cold War Europe."[9] A proper and democratic civilian-military relationship must prevail if democracy is to be consolidated in Central and Eastern Europe, and such a relationship does not exist even in the Visegrad countries.[10]

The EU, the Council of Europe, and the Western European Union have contributed significantly to peace and stability in Western Europe and could do the same in Central and Eastern Europe. The Council of Europe promotes democratic values. Another institution connected with the EU, the European Political Cooperation, coordinates the foreign policies of EU members. Together, such institutions could provide Central and Eastern Europe with the benefits the Clinton administration maintains will come from NATO enlargement. EU enlargement is also advantageous in that the Russians are not opposed to Central and Eastern Europe entering the EU.

It is important to reverse the administration's position and make the case that NATO enlargement, if it is to occur at all, must follow enlargement of the EU. In all likelihood, EU enlargement would make NATO enlargement unnecessary. The administration is unwilling to, and should not, relinquish America's primary role in the security of Europe. As political scientists James Sperling and Emil Kirchner have argued, however, "There is no compelling logic to dictate that all EU members must belong to NATO or that all European NATO member states must belong to the EU."[11]

The Clinton administration's rationale for NATO expansion clearly lies within the realm of the EU's responsibility. The EU is essentially a political and economic entity, not a military organization. But the security of Europe today has more to do with economic and political development than with traditional military concerns. EU enlargement, by addressing the economic and political needs of the Central and East European countries, would likely provide greater security benefits than would NATO enlargement. NATO expansion promises only the enlargement of a military infrastructure. It does not promise the political and economic benefits that EU enlargement would entail.

Mittleuropa Security Structures

Admitting the Central and East European countries to the EU would offer them indirect security benefits. Their security could be further enhanced by the creation of some type of regional security organization. The Central and East European states could join the EU to fulfill their political and economic aspirations but seek protection against a potential Russian threat in a security structure that guaranteed their security without threatening Russia. As long as Russia's future remains in doubt, European stability—political, economic, and military—would be enhanced by such a separation of purposes.

The creation of a Mittleuropa bloc would thus enhance the security of Central and Eastern Europe without triggering a security dilemma for Russia, as an enlarged NATO would. Historically, NATO has been seen as a threat to Russia, and NATO expansion only strengthens Russians' concerns about a long-time adversary on their borders. A separate Mittleuropa security structure would be a lesser threat— especially if it were to seek some sort of relationship with the Russians to parallel its ties to the EU. (Such an arrangement would also absolve NATO from granting Moscow special concessions to compensate for Russian concerns about NATO enlargement.)

A Mittleuropa organization would take one of two forms. One would revolve around a Polish-Ukrainian axis, and the other, an elaboration of the first, is reminiscent of Churchill's Danubean Confederation.

The concept of a Polish-Ukranian axis is very promising in view of the historical relationship between the two countries. We should remember interwar Polish president Joseph Pilsudsky's idea of a federal Poland. Poland between 1919 and 1939 was composed of 60 percent Poles and some 20 percent Ukrainians. Ukraine and Poland have been allies and antagonists throughout the centuries. The post-1989 conditions create favorable conditions for both Ukraine and Poland, now liberated from the Soviet Union. The two states have established close security relationships with one another, supported by the United States and NATO.

The formation of such a Central-East European, or Mittleuropa, regional security organization would fulfill all the security, strategic, and military needs of the Visegrad states and others who would possibly join it later. To those who would argue that a Ukrainian-Polish axis would be a threat to Russia, one can point out that it is certainly less threatening to Russia than is NATO enlargement.

The second possible form is an updated version of Winston Churchill's concept of the confederation of the Danube, which would have linked Poland, Czechoslovakia, and Hungary. Churchill, realizing at the end of World War II that the rest of Europe was vulnerable to Soviet pressure, viewed a confederation of Central and East European states as a means of ensuring that the history of 1919–39 would not be repeated. Although Churchill's idea was related to his fear of Stalinist aggression, the concept of a Central and East European political or security arrangement is as practical and beneficial in the post–Cold War era as it was in 1945. A Danubean confederation that included the Czech Republic, Hungary, Romania, and Slovenia could provide a firm security structure for at least two of the Central European states. That confederation could be complemented by the Polish-Ukrainian security arrangements, and the threat of an unstable and insecure Central and Eastern Europe would thereby be overcome. Such an arrangement would satisfy the needs of the Central and East European countries for security and reassurance that Europe would no longer be divided and that a powerful, aggressive, and interventionist power would be unable to gain dominance without opposition.

A Mittleuropa bloc would render obsolete the most powerful argument advanced by proponents of NATO expansion—that the unstable "gray zone" between Russia and Germany, prey to Hitler and Stalin, could once again prove vulnerable to a would-be hegemon. One should not underestimate the historical insecurity of those who are worried about the reemergence of that gray zone. The Polish experience is detailed in Norman Davies's book on the history of Poland, *God's Playground*.[12] The innate hostility between Poles and Russians is not new; it goes back to the three partitions of Poland, the Stalin-Hitler Pact of 1939, and the post-1944 Soviet occupation of Poland. The Czechs also recall that their country was divided by Hitler, and although Czechoslovakia never had a common border with Russia, it fell into the Soviet sphere of domination during the

Cold War. All of that may be history, but national interest is fed by national memories.

For states concerned about the perils of the gray zone, Mittleuropa should actually be more reassuring than membership in a NATO diluted by the Founding Act or, especially, enlargement that admits Poland, the Czech Republic, and Hungary but excludes the rest of Central and Eastern Europe. Mittleuropa would also be anchored—formally or informally—in an American-supported regional strategic enterprise in Europe. It would benefit psychologically from the continued existence of NATO in its current configuration. A combination of EU enlargement and a Mittleuropa security structure should reassure Central and East European countries that they would not go undefended against a future Hitler or Stalin.

Mittleuropa vs. a Stronger OSCE

Mittleuropa would also be preferable to an enhanced Organization for Security and Cooperation in Europe, which some experts have proposed. The OSCE, with 54 member states, is too large and unwieldy to effectively provide for European security. James Madison's persuasive arguments about the weaknesses of an enlarged executive committee are instructive. Furthermore, the OSCE would at best be a collective security structure, not a NATO-style military organization.

A Central and East European regional military alliance with parallel relationships with the West and Russia would be a better European security system than OSCE if the intent is to stabilize and make secure the most vulnerable Central and East European states. Mittleuropa would be a more efficient organization for addressing their specific needs, which are different from those of Western Europe.

The U.S. Role in Europe

The United States should continue to play a key role, in fact, a primary role, in the security of Europe. Over the long term, the existence of a Mittleuropa would be more conducive to significant U.S. involvement in Europe—and would also serve American strategic purposes better—than any form of NATO enlargement. NATO enlargement is an open-ended proposition that does not serve U.S. interests. There are already 11 states in line to join NATO. Once the first wave of enlargement is complete, there will be great pressure to add Romania and Slovenia—which many European NATO members wanted to include in the first group of new members—and the Baltic states.

The administration is playing cat and mouse with Congress and the public, refusing to name the next candidates for NATO membership once the Visegrad states join. It is no secret that the White House has explored the idea of a Baltic security pact to placate a domestic constituency. As Michael Dobbs has written in the *Washington Post*, "To reassure the Baltic nations, and the politically influential network of Baltic ethnic groups in the United States, the Clinton administration has said repeatedly that the first wave of new entrants into NATO will not be the last."[13] Diplomats from the Baltic states have mounted a multimedia campaign for recognition of the "aspiration" of the Baltic states to NATO membership. Estonion ambassador Hendrik Ilves has noted that his country has been "encouraged by American assurances on the eligibility of the Baltic states for eventual membership."[14]

NATO would then become a regional League of Nations or a mini United Nations. The impotence of such organizations when it comes to matters of security is well established. NATO is distinguished from the collective security organizations by three key capabilities, as Kissinger has pointed out: rapid, secure, and frank consultations among like-minded nations about critical international issues; effective crisis management; and a credible system of deterrence under an effective integrated military command.[15] The creation of a Mittleuropa security organization would allow NATO to remain a robust military alliance, without leaving Central and Eastern Europe out of the European security system. That would serve U.S. interests better than would an enlarged NATO that amounted to little more than a European UN.

Conclusion

In conclusion, it is quite clear that the raison d'être for the integration of the Visegrad and other East European states into NATO could be better achieved in the various forums that the EU provides. The EU is replete with economic, financial, intellectual, and security organizations. Turning NATO into a system of collective security, if that idea is to be taken seriously, would be at enormous cost to the United States. If NATO is to continue to exist, it must remain in its current form, and my proposal for two frameworks for European regional security makes NATO expansion unnecessary. The rationale for NATO enlargement could be less costly and better served by existing European organizations.

With the expansion of the EU and, eventually, the achievement of a more perfect union among Europeans, the expansion of NATO, a military organization that has lost its mission and purpose, would indeed be a political error. It could cost the American people dearly, and it would buy no real security for Central and Eastern Europe. NATO expansion would call into question the integrity and purpose of the alliance and could even render it obsolete.

Notes

1. U.S. Department of Defense, "Report to the Congress on the Enlargement of the North Atlantic Treaty Organization: Rationale, Benefits, Costs and Implications," February 24, 1997, p. 6.

2. Ibid., p. 31.

3. Congressional Budget Office, "The Costs of Expanding the NATO Alliance," March 1996, p. 26.

4. Henry Kissinger, "Helsinki Fiasco," *Washington Post*, March 30, 1997. Emphasis added.

5. Henry Kissinger, "The Dilution of NATO," *Washington Post*, June 8, 1997, p. A24.

6. Ibid.

7. U.S. Department of Defense, p. 31.

8. Marybeth Peterson Ulrich, "Nato and Partnership for Peace: Building Democratic Partners?" Paper presented at 38th Annual Meeting of the International Studies Association, Toronto, Canada, March 18–22, 1997. Emphasis added.

9. Ibid.

10. For a comprehensive analysis of civil-military relations in the Visegrad states, see Jeffrey Simon, *NATO Enlargement and Central Europe: A Study in Civil-Military Relations* (Washington: National Defense University, 1996).

11. James Sperling and Emil Kirchner, *Recasting the European Order* (New York: Manchester University Press, 1997), p. 262.

12. Norman Davies, *God's Playground. A History of Poland*, vol. 1, *The Origins to 1795* (New York: Columbia University Press, 1982).

13. Michael Dobbs, "White House Explores Baltic Security," *Washington Post*, March 28, 1997, p. 24.

14. Quoted in ibid.

15. Kissinger, "Helsinki Fiasco."

18. Beyond NATO

Ronald Steel

To expand, or not to expand. That is the question for NATO. Or so it would seem from the noisy argument now shaking policy circles about whether to admit new members to the hoary Cold War alliance. But the membership question is—like a married couple's squabbles over which route to take to the grocery store—only the tip of the iceberg of contention. Beneath it lie issues that go to the very heart of America's relationship with Europe and to the place of postcommunist Russia in the world. What may look on the surface like little more than a bureaucratic detail is a matter of enormous potential impact.

The debate over NATO is hard and noisy, with passionate advocates of one position or the other lined up along the great divide. But the debate is also remarkably narrow, focusing only on the question of taking in new members, as though that were simply a mechanical arrangement, like adding new seats to a sports arena. Yet it is more akin to the question of whether or not a couple should have children. To move from being a couple to being a family is not only a change of size. The whole entity is transformed. The full consequences of the decision are only dimly glimpsed at the time, and mostly ignored.

Focusing on the expansion issue alone, as if it did not affect everything else about the purpose and the value of the alliance, is easy. It gives the debate an air of deceptive simplicity. We owe it to the East Europeans to bring them into the transatlantic club, the expansionists argue. The East Europeans were, after all, treated so badly at Yalta, a point that prospective members have not hesitated to raise. Polish deputy defense minister Andrezj Karkoszka's comment, "The smell of Yalta is always with us," is representative.[1] NATO may have come into being as a result of the Cold War, but now that that conflict is history, why keep the club confined to the original members? Why not let the sun shine in on all the East

243

European states once under Moscow's yoke? It's just a matter of equity, advocates maintain. And anyway it would—or so they hope—give a boost to market-loving, democracy-embracing politicians in the formerly communist states.

Couched in those terms, NATO expansion sounds like a sure winner that will make everybody feel happier, safer, and more virtuous. That is the approach the Clinton administration is using as it prepares to push the Senate into ratifying an expanded membership list for NATO. In the first round, Hungary, Poland, and the Czech Republic are up for approval. But the rest of the East European nations, including the Baltic states that not long ago were part of the Soviet Union, are eagerly pressing their claims. And once the decision is made to expand, it will be hard to draw the line anywhere west of the Russian border. Indeed, as Secretary of State Madeleine Albright said in May 1997, "No European democracy will be excluded because of where it sits on the map."[2] But she did not mean Russia itself.

That pleases many observers, particularly traditional Russophobes, who believe that the best offense is a good defense. But it alarms others. Skeptics fear that pushing NATO east will discredit Russian reformers who are building a democratic, market-oriented society and provide fodder for nationalists who are smarting badly under Russia's calamitous fall from global status. The critics also warn that the whole complex of arms control accords, including the dismantlement of nuclear missiles, could be jeopardized if a more nationalist regime came to power in Moscow. Why risk a Cold War settlement that has given the West everything that it has asked for, and more, particularly at a time when Russia poses no threat to its western neighbors?

Underlying Motives for Expansion

If those opposing positions seem to give the whole debate a surrealistic character, so be it. In many ways it is surreal. Both sides have valid arguments, but they are dancing around the central issue. It is true, as expansionists insist, that NATO's current boundary line seems arbitrary and capricious. If there are no longer two hostile economic and political systems in Europe, why should there still be a Cold War dividing line in the military realm? Since the very concept of "Europe" is moving east, shouldn't NATO?

While on the surface that seems merely a matter of tidying up old membership lists, the problem is deeper. The eastern states may talk about the joys of inclusion, and want to be invited into the clubroom with their western neighbors, but they are pushing for membership for a far more practical reason. They want the United States to protect them should they get into a fight with their neighbors or, more important, should the Russians once again become menacing. NATO came into being as an anti-Russian military alliance, and that is the way the prospective new members still see it.

This is the simple truth that lies behind all the window-dressing about "inclusion," and "fairness," and "overcoming Yalta": The states of the defunct Warsaw Pact do not need NATO membership to be in Europe. They are there and always have been. What they want is the automatic guarantee of American protection that membership provides.

Understandably, neither they nor the Clinton administration focuses on that aspect of the expansion argument. Nor do they mention that there are other clubs, like the European Union, that the former communist states could be asked to join if they simply seek "inclusion." Instead, advocates, especially in Washington, press for NATO expansion as though it hardly concerns Moscow at all and will have no effect on Russian policy in other critical areas, such as arms control, technology transfers, international peacekeeping operations, and policy toward rogue states. Albright has even said, "NATO is a defensive alliance that . . . does not regard any state as its adversary, certainly not a democratic and reforming Russia."[3] But that is disingenuous and hardly explains why East European elites (though not in most cases the general public) are pressing for admission and the promise of U.S. protection. Even in politics it is sometimes best to call things by their proper names.

American officials are tiptoeing through the entire expansion process. They hope that they can keep the Russians mollified with space shuttle stunts and deliberately vague proposals like the Founding Act on Mutual Relations, Cooperation and Security between NATO and the Russian Federation; delay the Balkan and Baltic states' pressing their demands; soothe the resentments of the West Europeans, who have their own ideas about the extent and speed of expansion; and conceal the real cost of what is an open-ended operation. Cost estimates range all the way from $21 billion to $125 billion, depending on how missions are assigned and threats are gauged. The administration claims, in what is widely viewed as an act of wishful thinking, that the price tag can be kept to around $35 billion and that the Europeans will pay 94 percent of the cost.[4]

The problem confronting Washington, as officials ultimately admit when seriously pressed, is not that Eastern Europe is in danger but that NATO itself is. It has become an alliance without a clear sense of mission or even, in the absence of any discernable threat, a compelling reason for being. It is living mostly on inertia. Yet for quite different reasons both Americans and Europeans are reluctant to let it expire.

West European governments like it because it means an American subsidy of their defense. They can chop away happily at their military budgets, as they have been doing, knowing that in a pinch the Americans will fish them out of trouble. Why turn down a free lunch, particularly when it does not involve any inconvenience to their commercial activities? Their membership in NATO has not in any noticeable way impeded their pursuit of lucrative contracts with regimes—such as those of Cuba, Iran, and Iraq—that Washington deems pariahs. The beauty of NATO membership is that it provides the reality of military protection, should the need arise, without the imposition of any serious economic or political inconveniences. No wonder everyone wants to join.

American policymakers, for their part, also like it—but more for political than military reasons. And military contractors, who provide the hardware for perpetual new generations of U.S.-designed equipment for the allies, like it best of all. Indeed, the defense industry, which hopes to equip the East European armies with all the latest high-tech gear, is one of the biggest domestic lobbies for an expanded NATO.[5]

But it is hard to justify a bigger NATO as a subsidy for the arms industry. And the anemic present state of the Russian military—which has cut its forces and its budget to a small fraction of their Cold War size—makes the defense argument sound a bit abstract. Russia, after all, could not subdue even a rag-tag band of Chechen rebels in its own territory. That is why American policymakers are concerned, with good reason, that NATO, having run out of tasks to perform, may be losing not only its reason for being but, more seriously, its constituency.

Officials believe that unless NATO finds new tasks to perform it may go into a terminal decline. Its problem, to quote Sen. Richard Lugar (R-Ind.), is that it must either "go out of area or go out of business."[6] The Bosnian mess took NATO out of its usual geographic area, but that is only a short-term solution. Incorporating much of the old Warsaw Pact would, it is assumed, give NATO a new lease on life. Undeniably, new members would give it new scope along with new bureaucracies and new headaches.

But does NATO deserve a new lease on life? Yes, the argument goes, because NATO is good for the United States. It is good because it gives the United States not only a continued military presence in Europe but also (so policymakers believe) political leverage over Europe. In the past, the reality of a powerful Soviet Union kept the prideful West Europeans in America's military and political orbit. To be sure, the allies sometimes went their own ways on economic issues, as evidenced by the fracas in the 1980s over their contracts for Soviet natural gas. But on the items that really counted, such as support during military showdowns and summit bargaining, they could be counted on to fall into line.

Lately, however, they have been more willful, particularly in the commercial realm, where they challenge U.S. trade policy and forge new deals with pariah countries like Cuba, Iran, and Iraq. Peace may be good for business, but it is leaving NATO rather on the sidelines. Yet without NATO, which institutionalizes Europe's military dependence, how can the United States hope to influence its allies' economic and political decisions?

Thus NATO is now being assessed less for its ability to hold back the Russians than for its utility in reining in the allies. Some U.S. officials have been disarmingly specific about that. Lugar, one of the best informed legislators on foreign policy issues, warned that unless Washington provides a solution for the problems of the European states, "they will ultimately seek to deal with these problems either in new alliances or on their own."[7]

Whether an expanded NATO will be able to prevent that, and indeed whether such an objective is really in America's interests, is, of course, another matter. Nevertheless, it is clear that what would on the surface seem to be merely a parochial issue of whether the NATO club should grow a little larger is really a much broader one. It goes to the heart of what kind of post–Cold War diplomacy the

United States ought to pursue. That is why the great expansion debate has gained the ardent, even noisy, attention of the foreign policy community—though not, to be sure, of the wider public, which understandably treats it as arcane and largely irrelevant.

Interestingly, the great NATO debate has not taken place among the usual suspects: nostalgic cold warriors on one side and starry-eyed peaceniks on the other. The lines cut across both extremes and through the middle, forming a postideological crazy quilt. On the side of the expanders, anti-Russians like Zbigniew Brzezinski and realpolitikers like Henry Kissinger line up with Wilsonian liberals like Anthony Lake. On the other side, former Reagan hard-liners like Fred Iklé and Edward Luttwak make common cause with centrists like Michael Mandelbaum for keeping the alliance as it is.

The opponents of expansion are not, for the most part, anti-NATO. Rather, they are foreign policy professionals who fear that a bigger alliance might create huge headaches for the United States. They point out that most of the current NATO members do not really want expansion. Nor are the high brass at the Pentagon enthusiastic about enlargement; they are going along only because the White House has made doing so a test of loyalty. What concerns opponents of enlargement most of all is the effect it may have on a Russia still grappling with the results of its economic and political collapse and trying to engage with the West without being humiliated by its fall from status. Viewed in that light, today's NATO may be a Cold War anachronism, but it is less dangerous than an expanded alliance. Pushing it east into the old Warsaw Pact territories, with no built-in limitations short of the Russian border, could unleash some extremely unpleasant consequences.

What makes the situation so frustrating is that the debate is taking place on several different planes. The East Europeans say they deserve membership to demonstrate that they are just as European as anyone else. But what they really care about is an American insurance policy against the Russians, and even against their own neighbors. The West Europeans think the whole thing is unnecessary but are going along not to annoy the Americans. Administration proponents claim that an expanded NATO is just a latter-day version of the Marshall Plan, a way to make the old continent "united and free." But what actually animates them is the fear that, devoid of new members and new missions, NATO—as a means of exerting political pressure on the Europeans—will become about as relevant as a treaty governing migratory birds.[8]

Clearly, NATO does have problems. And now, almost a decade after the collapse of the Berlin Wall, is hardly too soon to address them. Maintaining the current structure while adding new members is one kind of reform, but certainly not the only one that can be imagined. The following options are among the others that have been discussed:

- Expand all the way and bring Russia into the alliance. That would, in Charles de Gaulle's famous phrase, unite Europe "from the Atlantic to the Urals," and a good deal beyond. What would be left of the original NATO, and the special European-American connection, in an alliance extending to the frontiers of China is another matter.
- Delete the treaty's key provision, article 5, which obliges every member more or less automatically to come to the aid of any other in case of attack. That would reduce the danger of being in an alliance with regimes and ethnic groups that hate each other and want to expand their borders. But it would also transform NATO into a traditional—and conditional—defense pact. It would be a friendship, not a marriage.[9]
- Make NATO more continental by turning over key command posts to Europeans. As it is, the Americans almost totally run the show. Europeanizing NATO would take the pressure off the United States and presumably encourage the Europeans to take more responsibility for their own defense. The result would likely reduce American influence over Europe, and, from Washington's perspective, that is not an appealing outcome.
- Tell the East Europeans to forget about NATO and instead put pressure on the European Union to let them into that rich man's club. A rapid expansion of the EU should take care of their concerns about "inclusion" and being treated as "real Europeans," although it won't do much to persuade them to love the Russians.
- Build a true European army based on the national forces of the present and future European members of NATO, and expand the existing defense entity, the Western European Union, from a shell into an effective military organization.

None of those alternatives can resolve all the problems affecting Europe. But neither will expansion of the alliance, as it is now structured, to the east. Expansion will not, as many proponents assume, make Europeans more subject to control from Washington. Even during the Cold War, military dependence could not be translated into compliance on economic and political issues; such U.S. "leverage" is even less likely today.

Expansion will not bring tranquillity to countries that have unstable, unrepresentative, or demagogic governments. More likely, it will involve all of NATO's members, including the United States, in quarrels that were masked, but not resolved, by the Cold War. And to move the alliance east without incorporating Russia into a wider security network—one in which it exerts influence proportionate to its interests—is to make Europe less, not more, stable.

Doing the Right Thing about NATO

It is indeed, as the current argument assumes, time to do something about NATO. But expansion into Eastern Europe is not in itself a solution; rather, it would quite likely be an exacerbation of the problem. Instead, what is required is to rethink the meaning of the Atlantic alliance and to work out between the United States and Europe a relationship that is more appropriate than the one that evolved during the Cold War. That relationship served its purpose. It has now become an impediment both to Europe's evolution and to America's own interests.

The energy being expended in Washington on making NATO bigger could be better spent devising alternatives to an alliance in radical need of redefinition. The Europeans, after decades of willing dependence on the United States, are capable of establishing their own defense organization and should be encouraged to do so. NATO, for its part, should be changed from an integrated, multinational army effectively under American direction into a mutual defense pact between the United States and the Western European Union or a new and more comprehensive European security organization. The Americans, and ideally the Russians as well through treaty arrangements, would become guarantors, ready to come to the aid of Europeans in the event of unprovoked aggression that threatened the balance of power. But the United States would no longer be the financier of Europe's defense, nor the gendarme automatically pulled into every quarrel among Europeans.

This means a refocusing and a redefinition of American policy. The United States is not a European power, any more than it is an Asian power. That is a mischievous Atlanticist exaggeration. The United States is a global power that has very serious concerns in Europe, as it does in Asia, with maintaining favorable relations with the dominant powers of the region. It also should seek to prevent any single major actor from upsetting the balance of power in a way that is detrimental to American interests. That was one of the original functions of NATO. But NATO was created in another time and under a different set of circumstances.

By adjusting our diplomacy to the present circumstances, we could finally, a decade after the end of the Cold War, begin to define our role not as Europe's overseer but as a global balancer. That requires not only military strength but a realistic, and parsimonious, interpretation of our interests. The argument over NATO expansion takes us in the wrong direction and, if pursued, could have unfortunate results. But if it induces us to undertake an overdue reassessment of our relations with Europe, it will have served a useful purpose.

Notes

1. Quoted in Paul Goble, "NATO: Analysis from Washington—'The Smell of Yalta,'" Radio Free Europe/Radio Liberty, March 18, 1997, at http://www.rferl.org.

2. Quoted in Michael Dobbs, "U.S. Indicates Preference for Just 3 New NATO States," *Washington Post*, May 30, 1997, p. A30.

3. Quoted in Charles A. Kupchan, "Doing the NATO Shuffle," *Washington Post*, August 31, 1997.

4. On the dispute over estimates, see Steven Erlanger, "Rancorous Debate Emerges over Cost of Enlarging NATO," *New York Times*, October 13, 1997.

5. For an account of the defense industry's pro-enlargement lobbying efforts, see Jeff Gerth and Tim Weiner, "Arms Makers See a Bonanza in Selling NATO Expansion," *New York Times*, June 29, 1997, p. A1.

6. Richard G. Lugar, "NATO: Out of Area or Out of Business: A Call for U.S. Leadership to Revive and Redefine the Alliance," Remarks delivered to the Open Forum of the U.S. Department of State, August 2, 1993, p. 7.

7. Ibid.

8. For a discussion of the various motives of the parties supporting NATO expansion, see Ted Galen Carpenter, "Conflicting Agendas and the Future of NATO," in *The Future of NATO*, ed. Ted Galen Carpenter (London: Frank Cass; 1995) pp. 143–64.

9. For a similar proposal, see Charles A. Kupchan, "Reviving the West," *Foreign Affairs* 75 (May–June 1996): 92–104.

19. James Madison vs. Madeleine Albright: The Debate over Collective Security

Stanley Kober

The expansion of NATO is typically presented as a way to end the division of Europe and to prevent the creation of unprotected "gray" areas stuck in some sort of security limbo that would invite aggression. Enlargement of NATO will achieve neither ambition. First, since NATO is not going to replace the United Nations—indeed, it was created because the United Nations could not fulfill the collective security function its Western founders envisioned for it—NATO cannot be a universal organization. Therefore, it must end somewhere. Unlike that of the United Nations, NATO's purpose is to protect the "ins" from the "outs."

That is an inescapable reality. Even if NATO were to ultimately embrace all of Europe, including Russia, what would be the Chinese reaction? After all, at that point all the permanent members of the UN Security Council save China would be members of NATO. What could Beijing possibly conclude other than that the expansion of NATO was directed against China? Indeed, one suspects that it is precisely that concern that has prompted "Chinese diplomats [to] advise their Russian colleagues to assume a tougher stand in the dialogue with the West on NATO eastward enlargement."[1] In other words, unless NATO is meant to replace the United Nations, it must create divisions; and if the argument for expanding NATO is that division is bad, then it must be concluded that NATO expansion is a misguided solution to the underlying problem.

Second, the history of the Cold War demonstrates that gray areas are *not* a cause of instability. There was no brinkmanship over Switzerland. Rather, the danger of world war was the result of the military confrontation of the forces of East and West, notably in Germany. And the most dangerous moments of the Cold War in

Europe were the result of the isolation of West Berlin—an enclave totally surrounded by the Soviet bloc. By bringing the forces of NATO and Russia into direct contact, NATO expansion would re-create the dangerous confrontation of the Cold War. Worse, expansion of NATO into the Baltic states would re-create in reverse the Cold War situation in Berlin by separating the Russian enclave of Kaliningrad from the rest of Russia. That may help explain why the Russian ambassador to the United States has warned that Russia's reaction to the admission of the Baltic states to NATO would be "very fierce."[2]

Indeed, if there is a potential flashpoint for major war in Europe, it is Kaliningrad. The Baltic states feel squeezed between a militarized Kaliningrad (as they see it) and the rest of Russia. The Russians, on the other hand, see Kaliningrad, part of their territory, cut off from the rest of their country. Even without NATO expansion, that would be an issue that would need defusing, but NATO expansion will only make matters worse. If NATO does expand, Russia will probably react by increasing its military presence in the area, particularly in Kaliningrad.[3] Arms control agreements will also be in jeopardy. Even if the Russian executive branch is inclined to go forward, it is difficult to see the Duma consenting to further arms reductions.[4]

Any Russian remilitarization of the Baltic region would understandably alarm the Baltic states, who would then want some tangible sign that the NATO guarantee will not prove to be another empty Locarno gesture. The Locarno Treaty was the NATO of the interwar period, providing a security guarantee by France (and by extension, Britain) to Poland and Czechoslovakia. There was initially a "spirit of Locarno" because Germany was a signatory to the treaty; similarly, Russia would be made a partner in NATO expansion through the Founding Act on Mutual Relations, Cooperation and Security between NATO and the Russian Federation. But the spirit of Locarno faded, and when Germany under Hitler began to violate the treaty, Britain and France capitulated, leaving us with the legacy of Munich. Even when they formally honored their obligations and declared war against Germany after it had invaded Poland, their effort was feeble and militarily irrelevant.

That is a history we should certainly not repeat. Yet if NATO (read the United States) responds to a Russian buildup next door to the Baltic republics, a new arms race will ensue, reversing the progress toward arms reduction that has characterized the post–Cold War world. Perhaps deterrence would work in that case the way it worked during the Cold War, when the Berlin crises never escalated into outright conflict. But that is not a sure thing: Russian passions about the Baltic republics (with their Russian minorities) and Kaliningrad are much deeper than they were about Berlin, which was merely the capital of a defeated enemy. And if war occurs, it is difficult to see how NATO will be able to prevent vast destruction from being visited upon the Baltic countries even if nuclear weapons are not used, and even if NATO ultimately "wins" the war.

Misplaced Confidence in Alliances

The logic of NATO expansion is that deterrence, which helped keep the peace in Europe during the Cold War, can also maintain peace indefinitely into the future. That is a questionable assumption. Although Henry Kissinger is now a fervent proponent of expansion, he expressed very different views before the Cold War ended:

> If it were not for nuclear weapons it is likely that there would have been a war between us and the Soviets. So it is almost certainly true that nuclear weapons have preserved the peace. It is also true that *if we continue the strategy that has got us these 40 years of peace,* that *some catastrophe somewhere along the line is going to happen* and therefore the big problem of our period is to build on this long period of peace we have a structure that is different from the preceding one.[5]

Whatever NATO expansion represents, it is not "a structure that is different from the preceding one." Rather, the Clinton administration's position is eerily reminiscent of American policy in the 1950s, which saw a proliferation of U.S.-sponsored alliances. According to Secretary of State Madeleine Albright, we should take "strong measures to forge alliances, deter aggression and keep the peace."[6] But that is exactly what we did when we created the Central Treaty Organization and the Southeast Asia Treaty Organization (SEATO), as well as NATO. For some reason, that history has been forgotten. "In the last half century, America has never been called upon to go to war to defend a treaty ally," Secretary Albright told the Senate Armed Services Committee in April 1997. "Alliances make the threat of force more credible and therefore the use of force less likely."[7]

The secretary clearly has forgotten about Vietnam. On March 4, 1966, the State Department's legal adviser, Leonard C. Meeker, released a memorandum that argued, "The United States undertook an international obligation to defend South Vietnam in the SEATO Treaty."[8] Indeed, when SEATO was established, Secretary of State John Foster Dulles used language that parallels Secretary Albright's. "We have come here to establish a collective security arrangement for Southeast Asia," he said in a press release. "We are united by a common danger.... The danger manifests itself in many forms. One form is that of open armed aggression. We can greatly diminish that risk by making clear that an attack upon the treaty area would occasion a reaction so united, so strong and so well-placed that the aggressor would lose more than it could hope to gain."[9]

If alliances make the threat of war less likely, then Secretary Albright has to explain why the North Vietnamese were not deterred by our SEATO commitment. She might also want to explain why the Locarno alliance—for that is what it was—failed to deter World War II. And while she is at it, she might explain why powerful alliances—which involved automatic commitments to a threatened member—also failed to deter World War I.

Indeed, if there is one similarity between our present period and that preceding World War I, it is the conviction that war—major war, at least—is unthinkable. "How extraordinary it was that none of us had any inkling that all hell was just about to be let loose in Europe," Lord Ismay, NATO's first secretary general, wrote about the summer of 1914.[10] The complacency of Ismay and his friends was widely shared. Even so insightful an observer as *The Economist*'s editor, Walter Bagehot, contended that modern society had moved from a "fighting age" to an "age of discussion."[11] Instead of the current belief that instability was the cause of World War I, there was a misplaced confidence that the absence of major war for so long meant that major war could not happen.

The Real Cause of Wars

In short, by placing its faith in alliances, the administration is seriously misreading history. It is also betraying the legacy of the principal framer of the U.S. Constitution, James Madison. Responding to an essay in which Jean-Jacques Rousseau had advocated a collective security system for Europe, Madison insisted that Rousseau had his priorities backwards. "Instead of beginning with an external application, and even precluding internal remedies, he ought to have commenced with, and chiefly relied on, the latter prescription," Madison wrote. "As the first step towards a cure, the government itself must be regenerated. Its will must be made subordinate to, or rather the same with, the will of the community."[12]

In other words, the main cause of war is tyrannical government. "Whilst war is to depend on those whose ambition, whose revenge, whose avidity, or whose caprice may contradict the sentiment of the community," Madison explained, "the disease must continue to be *hereditary*, like the government of which it is the offspring."[13] For Madison, the first prerequisite of a more peaceful world was legislative control of the war power. "In no part of the constitution is more wisdom to be found than in the clause which confides the question of war or peace to the legislature, and not to the executive," he wrote a year later in Helvidius no. 4. "The executive is the department of power most distinguished by its propensity to war: hence it is the practice of all states, in proportion as they are free, to disarm this propensity of its influence."[14]

Unfortunately, the emphasis on alliances and collective security has undermined Madison's approach. After World War I, concern that Congress's constitutional authority would be abridged played a large part in the Senate's rejection of the League of Nations. As Professor Arthur Schlesinger Jr. of the City University of New York has noted, there was a *"constitutional* obstacle: how to reconcile the provision in the constitution giving Congress exclusive power to declare war with the dispatch of American troops into hostilities at the behest of a collective security organization?"[15]

That constitutional concern is now typically derided as "isolationist," a criticism that merely indicates how far we have come from the founding vision of the United States. Although the administration's objective in advocating NATO expansion is the enlargement of the community of democracies, U.S. officials do not seem to recognize that the pursuit of alliances has the effect of undermining what Madison regarded as the single most important characteristic of American democracy. The confusion is evident in the administration's insistence that countries entering NATO have civilians in control of the armed forces. Although civilian control of the armed forces is preferable to an uncontrolled military establishment, it does not provide much of a restraint on dictatorial wars. Adolf Hitler, after all, was a civilian.

The administration also misunderstands the relationship between democracy and war. As Madison pointed out in his response to Rousseau, it is possible for wars to accord with the public will: in other words, it is possible to have democratic wars. And precisely because such wars have the support of the people, Madison acknowledged, they "are less susceptible of remedy." Those wars "can only be controlled by subjugating the will of the society to the reason of the society," and therefore he proposed that "each generation should be made to bear the burden of its own wars, instead of carrying them on at the expense of other generations."[16]

Madison, of course, lived in a time of imperial wars—what might be called wars of plunder. Such wars might well be affected by the remedy Madison provided. The problem, however, is that the nature of warfare has changed. Modern warfare is less about plunder and more about identity. The failure to understand that transformation has been one of the great intellectual shortcomings of the 20th century. Just before World War I, Sir Norman Angell demonstrated that the belief that war could provide economic advantages to the victor is a "great illusion."[17] He was absolutely right, but his observation was utterly beside the point. As the Balkan Wars that immediately preceded World War I make clear, wars of identity are very different from wars of plunder because they are characterized by popular hatreds, with little or no consideration of economic gain or loss. "War is waged not only by the armies but by the nations themselves," reported a commission sponsored by the Carnegie Endowment for International Peace that examined the Balkan Wars. "The populations mutually slaughtered and pursued with a ferocity heightened by mutual knowledge and the old hatreds and resentments they cherished."[18]

In such a situation, Madison's remedy can have little effect. People who believe they are avenging historical wrongs will not stop to consider how they will pay for their savagery. The only remedy is to create a political relationship that submerges those passions and a political and legal system that views people as individuals, rather than as members of groups. Indeed, that was a major reason behind the change in language from the Articles of Confederation to the

Constitution, from "between the states" to "we the people." "The great and radical vice in the construction of the existing Confederation is in the principle of LEGISLATION for STATES or GOVERN-MENTS, in their CORPORATE or COLLECTIVE CAPACITIES, and as contradistinguished from the INDIVIDUALS of whom they consist," Alexander Hamilton stressed in Federalist no. 15. In Federalist no. 20, he and Madison added, "A legislation for communities, as contradistinguished from individuals . . . is subversive of the order and ends of civil polity."[19]

The Illusory Benefits of NATO Expansion

Viewed in that light, some of the expected "triumphs" of NATO expansion appear highly questionable. For example, the treaties between Hungary and Romania and Hungary and Slovakia—which attempt to resolve historical difficulties, particularly with regard to ethnic minorities—have been hailed as an indication of how the desire of those countries to enter NATO is already having a healthy effect on their relationships. To be sure, treaties are preferable to disagreement, and those countries should be commended for their efforts to put historical troubles behind them. But those treaties have legitimized the idea that states can have a special interest in the fate of their national minorities in other countries.[20] That sort of thinking has led to tragedy in the past. After all, it was Hitler's claim that he spoke for all Germans that "legitimized" his concerns about the ethnic Germans in the Sudetenland. Once we start down that road, where do we stop? More to the point, having encouraged the treaties between Hungary, Romania, and Slovakia, how shall we respond if Russia invokes those agreements as precedent for claiming a special interest in the status of ethnic Russians in neighboring countries? With a precedent established, how can we tell Moscow that Hungary has such a right but Russia does not?

The other problem with that approach is that, although it may satisfy the diplomats, it is likely to be ignored by ordinary people. "I'll survive the Romanian-Hungarian treaty, but so will our problems," one Hungarian Romanian observed. "The treaty? Nothing but a piece of paper," echoed a pub mate. "Politicians will sign it and we will read it. So what?"[21] The best instrument for affecting the lives of ordinary people, for preserving their rights while making them all equal citizens, is not treaties between countries but guarantees of fundamental rights within countries. For example, Americans of Hungarian descent do not look to Hungary to protect their rights; they look to the U.S. Constitution and the courts, just as other Americans do. If there is a problem with minority rights in the newly independent countries, Americans would do better to advise those countries to look to the American practice of ensuring the protection of fundamental rights through an independent judiciary, rather than through treaty arrangements with their neighbors.

Similarly, advocates of democracy as a means of resolving conflict should recognize that the Europeans' identification of the nation with the state is at the root of their problems. The American conception, expressed by Abraham Lincoln in his first inaugural address, is very different: "A majority, held in restraint by constitutional checks, and limitations, and always changing easily, with deliberate changes of popular opinion and sentiments, is the only true sovereign of a free people."[22] In a nation-state, especially one obsessed with its national identity, the majority is not based on public opinion and therefore cannot change easily. That was the reason Lebanon and Yugoslavia blew up. As a Yugoslav academic put it, in such a situation, guarantees of minority rights by the majority are inadequate, for they merely give rise to the question, Why should we be a minority in your state, when you can be a minority in our state?[23] NATO expansion does not address that problem; on the contrary, it creates the danger that, if minority problems emerge as a cause of instability in the future, all sides will look, not to their judicial systems, but to the United States as NATO's leader to preserve their rights and will feel betrayed if we do not come to their aid. Anyone who doubts that outcome should consider the current American predicament in the Middle East, where both sides in the Israeli-Palestinian dispute expect the United States to pressure the other party but resent any pressure on themselves.

In short, if the new enemy is "instability," we should identify the source of that instability, rather than assume that NATO is a universal cure for war. Although President Clinton has acknowledged that NATO expansion "means that we are committing the people who wear the uniform of our nation to go and fight and die" for the new members if they are attacked, he has argued that "it's a pretty good gamble, because no NATO nation has ever been attacked, ever, not once."[24] But if solving the problem of war were that simple, it would have been solved already. Indeed, one would think that someone who protested the Vietnam War would want to examine why deterrence did not work there. In short, Clinton's argument fails to recognize that deterrence worked during the Cold War when the identity of the parties to the conflict was not challenged. By the same token, the two major failures of deterrence during the Cold War—Korea and Vietnam—both involved issues of identity (i.e., whether the Korean and Vietnamese nations would live in one or two states).

It is not true that NATO membership automatically reinforces democratic tendencies, as supporters of NATO expansion repeatedly argue. NATO's support of the Greek junta during the Cold War is a historical fact, and we should not ignore it. Even more troubling, because it took place while the process of NATO expansion was under way, has been the recent change of government in Turkey. At the same time NATO has been insisting on civilian control over the armed forces as a condition of NATO membership for the Central European countries, it has ignored (and possibly even encouraged) military pressure to change a legitimately elected civilian government in a current member. "The generals began to take policy into their own hands, according to interviews with political analysts and officials close to Turkey's generals," the Associated Press reported on June 21, 1997. "The West got the message. When foreign visitors came through Ankara, including U.S. deputy secretary of state Strobe Talbott, they unfailingly met with the chief of staff, Gen. Ismail Karadayi, or his outspoken deputy, Gen. Cevik Bir." The AP quoted a columnist for the Turkish newspaper *Hurriyet*, Zeynep Atikkan, who described the change of government as "a kind of post-modern coup," to distinguish it from the military coups of 1960, 1971, and 1980.[25] Significantly, that characterization was not disputed by Turkey's new prime minister, Mesut Yilmaz. "When asked whether the Turkish army had carried out a post-modern coup, which had facilitated the current government's establishment, Yilmaz said that the military had had an inevitable role in the establishment of the 55th government," the *Turkish Daily News* reported. "He continued, explaining that, as the civil institutions in Turkey were not so effective yet in the political sphere, the military's influence had been much more apparent in establishing the new government."[26]

The Turkish drama has two consequences. First, it demonstrates that NATO membership does *not* necessarily promote democracy.

"The current coalition was put together by the influence of the army, but also under threat from it," wrote Peter Millar in the *European* in July 1997. "Rumors of a coup have been rife and, significantly, gone undenied. *This is not democracy,* in the sense we are accustomed to praising it."[27] His opinion was echoed by an editorial in the *Turkish Daily News*. "Democracy has been forgotten and once again we hear even those who championed democratic ideals in the past telling us freedom and liberties are a luxury 'under current conditions,'" lamented Ilnur Cevik. "Turkey is still far from being a country where democracy, freedom and human rights are a norm of the society and are not regarded as a luxury."[28]

The second consequence is the deterioration in relations between Greece and Turkey. "U.S. officials are distressed over the prominence in Turkey's government of Deputy Prime Minister Bulent Ecevit, a hard-liner on Cyprus and Greece who as prime minister sent Turkish troops to occupy the northern third of Cyprus in 1974," the *Washington Post* reports. "Turkish Foreign Minister Ismail Cem, an ally of Ecevit, took exception when his Greek counterpart, Theodoros Pangalos, recently said he could not negotiate with 'the bandit, the murderer and the rapist.'"[29] The Turks have replied in kind. "The Greeks were described by our ancestors as barbarians and they are still barbarians," an unsigned article in the *Turkish Daily News* declared. "Turkey has to see that building close relations with Greece is an impossibility."[30]

The growing tension between Turkey and Greece challenges one of the central reasons for NATO expansion: that NATO eliminates the threat of war among its members. "For centuries, virtually every European nation treated virtually every other as a military threat," Secretary Albright told the Senate Foreign Relations Committee in its inaugural hearing on NATO expansion. "That pattern was broken only when NATO was born, and only in the half of Europe NATO covered."[31] But has the pattern been broken? When asked whether improving ties between Turkey and Israel were inspired by the closer relations between Greece and Syria, a Turkish diplomat did not deny it, but he stressed that Turkey's concerns did not lie with Damascus. "Why would we have to fight with Syria?" asked Ayden Alagakaptan, a former Turkish ambassador to Syria. "But with Greece, there is always a potential for a conflict to arise any time." Explaining Turkey's policy, he stressed that "Israel has an advanced arms industry and Turkey needs military hardware, and since the U.S. has imposed an embargo on military supplies to Turkey, we were told that Israel was our final resort."[32]

The ambassador's language begs the question, Told by whom? If this is part of Secretary Albright's effort to prevent war by forging alliances, it could have disastrous consequences not only for Europe but also for the Middle East. When the *Turkish Daily News* reported a plan by Turkey and Israel to jointly develop missiles, the Egyptian reaction was immediate. "These policies will lead to an arms race and the return of tension," warned Egyptian foreign minister Amr Moussa.[33] Just as in physics every action prompts a counterreaction, so in international politics every alliance prompts a counteralliance. "A rapprochement of sorts is already under way between Iran and Egypt, Saudi Arabia and Syria," notes the semiofficial Egyptian newspaper *Al-Ahram*. "Such a rapprochement could serve as a signal to the Americans of a possible establishment of an Egyptian-Syrian-Iranian alignment, to counter the Israeli-Turkish-U.S. alliance."[34]

In short, the philosophy behind NATO expansion—that alliances preserve peace by deterring aggression—is suitable in some situations but not in others. In this case, the language that is used to justify NATO expansion—that the prospective members belong to the West—implies that the rest of the world belongs to a different and inferior civilization. The consequences transcend relations with Russia. "The underlying notion of 'racial' and 'cultural' harmony is also used, and more forcefully, by advocates of Cold War values who are clearer in providing a conceptual framework for a dividing line based on a nation's readiness to conform to Western cultural and economic values," observes a recent article on NATO expansion in *Al-Ahram*. "Such statements echo a divisive view of the world that brings back to mind Samuel Huntington's controversial theory of an inevitable 'Clash of Civilizations.' Although American officials have never publicly espoused Huntington's ideas, the repeated stress on shared values and the emergence of Euro-centric policies follow the trend."[35]

In other words, promoters of expansion, as evidenced by their emphasis on integration of prospective members into the "West," do not appreciate the resentment their policies and language are stirring in the rest of the world. Not only are those promoters betraying the legacy of America's Founders, who intended our values to be universal (the Declaration of Independence does not read that all *Western* men are created equal), but they are clumsily provoking other countries to find common interests in opposition to the United States. That situation is eerily similar to the one that preceded World War I, when Germany's effort to build an alliance prompted the development of a countervailing alliance. The result was not peace but the greatest war in history up to that time.

Alliances—whether the Triple Alliance or NATO—seek to preserve peace through deterrence, and deterrence assumes a bloodless rationality. But modern wars, which are typically wars of identity rather than plunder, are more the product of unrestrained emotion than of rational calculation. "All my libido is given to Austro-Hungary," Sigmund Freud enthused at the outbreak of World War I.[36] Deterrence in such a situation is virtually useless. To prevent wars of identity, it is more important to establish political institutions and cultures that reduce the significance of identity. If the problem of post–Cold War Europe is ethnic rivalry, it can only be solved if the legitimacy of the state is based on something other than its synonymy with the nation. As Michael Ignatieff, who has chronicled post–Cold War nationalism in the BBC series *Blood and Belonging*, has pointed out, "A society anchored in a culture of individual rights and liberties is more easily returned to the practice of toleration than one where social allegiance is invested in ethnicity."[37] The United States, by its history and traditions, is uniquely placed to provide the rest of the world with an example of the benefits of such a culture. The United States should deal with any dangers of ethnic instability now confronting Europe by continuing to set an example, not by assuming that an alliance that arguably prevented a Soviet invasion of Western Europe will prevent all kinds of war in Europe forever.

Notes

1. Yury Savenkov, "Moscow and Beijing for Partnership Based on Trust," *Izvestia*, April 24, 1997, at www.ria-novosti.ru/products/dr, April 24, 1997.

2. Quoted in Reuters, "NATO Chief Consoles Russia over Enlargement," at www.centraleurope.com, July 24, 1997.

3. In September 1997, for example, Russian defense minister Igor Sergeyev indicated that Russia would reinforce its defenses in Kaliningrad if the Baltic states joined NATO. See "In the Event the Baltic Countries Join NATO Moscow May Take Adequate Steps," at ria-novosti.russianet.ru/products/hotline, September 4, 1997.

4. See, for example, Alexei Arbatov, "As NATO Grows, Start 2 Shudders," *New York Times*, August 26, 1997, p. A23.

5. "An Interview with Henry A. Kissinger: 'We Were Never Close to Nuclear War,'" *Washington Post*, August 11, 1985, p. L8. Emphasis added.

6. Madeleine K. Albright, Commencement address at Harvard University, June 5, 1997, at http://secretary.state.gov/www/statements.

7. Madeleine K. Albright, Statement before the Senate Armed Services Committee, April 23, 1997, U.S. Department of State Transcript, p. 3.

8. Leonard C. Meeker, Memorandum, U.S. Department of State *Bulletin* 54 (1966): 474. The memorandum may also be found in John Norton Moore, *Law and the Indo-China War* (Princeton, N.J.: Princeton University Press, 1972), pp. 603–32.

9. U.S. Department of State, Press release 492, September 6, 1954, reprinted in William Appleman Williams et al., eds., *America in Vietnam: A Documentary History* (New York: Doubleday, 1985), p. 172.

10. Hastings Lionel Ismay, *The Memoirs of General Lord Ismay* (New York: Viking, 1960), p. 19.

11. Quoted in Asa Briggs, *A Social History of England*, 2d ed. (London: Weidenfeld & Nicolson, 1994), p. 273.

12. James Madison, "Universal Peace," *National Gazette*, February 2, 1792, in *The Mind of the Founder*, ed. Marvin Meyers, rev. ed. (Hanover, N.H.: University Press of New England, 1981), p. 192.

13. Ibid.

14. Helvidius no. 4, in ibid., pp. 212–13.

15. Arthur Schlesinger Jr., "Back to the Womb?" *Foreign Affairs* 74, no. 4 (July–August 1995): 3. Emphasis in original.

16. Madison, "Universal Peace," pp. 192–93.

17. Norman Angell, *The Great Illusion* (New York: G.P. Putnam's Sons, 1910).

18. Carnegie Endowment for International Peace, *The Other Balkan Wars* (1914; Washington: Carnegie Endowment for International Peace, 1993), p. 148.

19. Alexander Hamilton, James Madison, and John Jay, *The Federalist Papers* (New York: New American Library, 1961), pp. 108, 138.

20. For example, in February 1997 Hungarian foreign minister Laszlo Kovacs complained that the issuance in ethnic Hungarian schools of reports written only in Slovak was inconsistent with the terms of the Slovak-Hungarian treaty, the Slovak constitution, and "the spirit and the wording of other legal standards." See "Fear of a 'War of Statements' between Slovakia and Hungary," CTK-Czech News Agency, distributed by Central Europe Online at www.centraleurope.com, February 14, 1997.

21. Quoted in "Romanian-Hungarian Pact Will Ease, Not Cure Enmity," *New Europe* (Athens), September 15, 1996, p. 48.

22. Abraham Lincoln, *Speeches and Writings: 1859–1861* (New York: Library of America, 1987), p. 220.

23. Vladimir Gligorov, "Is What Is Left Right? (The Yugoslav Heritage)," in *Transition to Capitalism: The Communist Legacy in Eastern Europe*, ed. Janos Matyas Kovacs (New Brunswick, N.J.: Transaction, 1994), p. 158.

24. William Clinton, Press conference, July 9, 1997, *Washington Post*, July 10, 1997, p. A25.

25. Associated Press, America Online, June 21, 1997.

26. "Yilmaz: 'Military Helps Democracy Function,'" *Turkish Daily News*, October 11, 1997.

27. Peter Millar, "A Nation Torn between Two Continents," *European* (London), July 3, 1997. Emphasis added.

28. Ilnur Cevik, "Can Democracy Survive without the Democrats?" *Turkish Daily News*, October 10, 1997.

29. Thomas W. Lippman, "U.S. Envoy Holbrooke to Visit Turkey," *Washington Post*, October 11, 1997.

30. "What Is Greece After?" *Turkish Daily News*, October 18, 1997.

31. Quoted in Thomas W. Lippman, "Senators Lukewarm on NATO Expansion," *Washington Post*, October 8, 1997.

32. Quoted in "Ankara Downplays Cooperation with Israel," *Al-Ahram Weekly*, September 11, 1997.

33. Associated Press, America Online, October 19, 1997.

34. Galal Nassar, "Clouds over the Mediterranean," *Al-Ahram Weekly*, May 22, 1997.

35. Lamis Andoni, "Europe Goes American," *Al-Ahram Weekly*, July 24, 1997.

36. Quoted in Ernest Jones, *Sigmund Freud: Life and Work*, vol. 2, p. 192, cited in Daniel Pick, *War Machine: The Rationalization of Slaughter in the Modern Age* (New Haven, Conn.: Yale University Press, 1993), p. 241.

37. Michael Ignatieff, "Nationalism and Toleration," in *Europe's New Nationalism*, ed. Richard Caplan and John Feffer (New York: Oxford University Press, 1996), p. 219. See also Michael Ignatieff, *Blood and Belonging* (New York: Farrar, Straus and Giroux, 1993).

Contributors

Doug Bandow, a nationally syndicated columnist, is a senior fellow at the Cato Institute. He is a frequent contributor to a number of publications, including the *New York Times,* the *Wall Street Journal,* the *Washington Post, USA Today, National Review, New Republic,* and *Foreign Policy.* He has written and edited several books, including *Tripwire: Korea and U.S. Foreign Policy in a Changed World* (1996) and *Perpetuating Poverty: The World Bank, the IMF, and the Developing World* (coedited with Ian Vásquez). Bandow also appears regularly on radio and television programs. Before joining the Cato Institute in 1984, he was a special assistant to President Reagan. Bandow has a J.D. from Stanford University.

Ted Galen Carpenter is vice president for defense and foreign policy studies at the Cato Institute. He is the author of *The Captive Press: Foreign Policy Crises and the First Amendment* (1995), *Beyond NATO: Staying Out of Europe's Wars* (1994), and *A Search for Enemies: America's Alliances after the Cold War* (1992) and the editor of numerous other books. Carpenter's work has appeared in various policy journals, including *Foreign Affairs, Mediterranean Quarterly, Foreign Policy, World Policy Journal, Journal of Strategic Studies,* and the *National Interest.* His articles have also been published in the *New York Times,* the *Washington Post,* the *Wall Street Journal,* the *Los Angeles Times,* and many other newspapers and magazines. He is a frequent guest on radio and television programs. Carpenter holds a Ph.D. in diplomatic history from the University of Texas.

Eugene J. Carroll Jr. is deputy director of the Center for Defense Information, where he is actively engaged in research and analysis of major defense issues. He writes and speaks frequently on the need for rational military programs that will meet the long-term national security interests of the United States. Before joining CDI, Carroll had a long and distinguished career with the U.S. Navy. He attained the rank of admiral and served as assistant deputy chief of naval operations for plans, policy, and operations; director of U.S. military operations for all U.S. forces in Europe and the Middle East; and commander of Task Force 60, the carrier striking force of the Sixth Fleet. Carroll earned an M.A. in international relations from George Washington University.

James Chace is editor of *World Policy Journal* and the Henry Luce Professor in Free Inquiry and Expression at Bard College. He has served as director of the Program on International Affairs and the Media at Columbia University's School for International and Public Affairs, international affairs editor of the *New York Times Book Review*, and managing editor of *Foreign Affairs*. Chace's articles have appeared in the *New York Review of Books, New York Times Magazine, Foreign Affairs*, and other prominent publications. He is also the author of numerous books, including *The Consequences of the Peace: American Foreign Policy after the Cold War* (1992). His forthcoming book, *Acheson, Architect of the American Era: A Biography*, will be published by Simon & Schuster in 1998. Chace has a degree from Harvard University and studied at l'Ecole de Sciences Politiques in Paris.

Jonathan G. Clarke, a research fellow in foreign policy studies at the Cato Institute, is a writer, lecturer, and consultant on international issues. He is a former career diplomat in the British Diplomatic Service whose areas of expertise include political, economic, and development issues related to Europe, sub-Saharan Africa, the Middle East, and East Asia. Clarke is the coauthor (with James Clad) of *After the Crusade: American Foreign Policy for the Post Superpower Age* (1995). In addition, he writes a syndicated column for the *Los Angeles Times* and has contributed articles to *Foreign Affairs, Foreign Policy*, the *Atlantic Monthly*, the *Washington Post*, and numerous other publications. Clarke is heard frequently on radio and television. He has an M.A. from Oxford University.

Barbara Conry is an associate foreign policy analyst at the Cato Institute, where she writes extensively on European security, the Middle East, and other defense and foreign policy issues. She is the author of several Cato policy papers, including "U.S. Global

Leadership: A Euphemism for World Policeman" and "The Western European Union as NATO's Successor." Conry has also contributed articles to a number of journals and newspapers, including *Mediterranean Quarterly,* the *Chicago Tribune,* the *San Francisco Chronicle,* and the *Philadelphia Inquirer.* She frequently provides expert analysis of foreign policy issues for broadcast and print media. Conry holds an M.A. in national security studies from Georgetown University.

Jonathan Dean has served as adviser on arms control and international security to the Union of Concerned Scientists since 1984. Before that, he had a long career in the U.S. Foreign Service, working primarily on East-West relations, European security, and international peacekeeping. Dean is the author of several books on European security, including, most recently, *Ending Europe's Wars* (1994), which examines post–Cold War security problems and the institutions established to deal with them. He has also published many newspaper and journal articles on national security, European security, nuclear disarmament, and multilateral peacekeeping. Dean has a Ph.D. in political science from Georgetown University.

Hugh De Santis is a professor of international security affairs at the National War College. Previously, he was a senior staff member of the RAND Corporation and a senior associate at the Carnegie Endowment for International Peace, where he directed the European Security Project. As a career officer in the U.S. Department of State, he served on the policy planning staff of Secretary of State George Shultz in 1983–84. He has also worked as legislative assistant to Sen. Jeff Bingaman (D-N.Mex.) for foreign policy and arms control. De Santis is the author of *Beyond Progress: An Interpretive Odyssey to the Future; The Diplomacy of Silence,* an award-winning study of the origins of the Cold War; and numerous articles on international affairs. He holds a Ph.D. in international relations from the University of Chicago.

Susan Eisenhower is founder and chairman of the Center for Political and Strategic Studies and president of the Eisenhower Group, Inc., a Washington-based consulting firm. Before founding her consulting business, she was a senior staff member in the Washington office of Burson-Marsteller. Eisenhower gives regular news analyses on foreign affairs for the radio, television, and print media. She has appeared on a number of major programs, including *This Week with David Brinkley, Good Morning America, The Today Show,* and *CBS Evening News.*

Owen Harries is the editor of the *National Interest.* He has also served as Australia's ambassador to UNESCO, senior adviser to Australian prime minister Malcolm Fraser, and director of policy planning in the Australian Department of Foreign Affairs. Harries's articles have appeared in *Foreign Affairs, Commentary, New Republic, Harper's, National Review,* the *New York Times,* the *Washington Post,* the *Wall Street Journal,* and the *Times* of London. He also edited *America's Purpose: New Visions of U.S. Foreign Policy* (1991). Harries was educated at the University of Wales and Oxford University.

William G. Hyland, an adjunct professor at Georgetown University, was editor of *Foreign Affairs* from 1984 to 1992. He also worked in the U.S. Department of State and served on the National Security Council during the Nixon and Ford administrations. Hyland is the author of numerous books and articles on international affairs, including *Mortal Rivals* and *The Cold War.* He earned degrees from Washington University, St. Louis, and the University of Missouri, Kansas City.

Stanley Kober is a research fellow in foreign policy studies at the Cato Institute. His articles have appeared in a number of prominent publications, including the *New York Times,* the *Washington Post,* the *Wall Street Journal,* and *Foreign Policy.* Kober is also a frequent lecturer for the United States Information Agency. Before joining the Cato Institute, he worked on defense issues for several other public policy research organizations, including the Hudson Institute and the Center for Naval Analyses. Kober holds a Ph.D. from the Fletcher School of Law and Diplomacy, Tufts University.

Christopher Layne is a visiting associate professor at the Naval Postgraduate School in Monterey, California. During the 1995–96 academic year, he was a residential fellow at the Center for Science and International Affairs at the Kennedy School of Government, Harvard University. He was also a visiting lecturer in the Department of Political Science at UCLA from 1991 to 1995. Layne's articles have appeared in numerous journals and newspapers, including *International Security, Foreign Policy,* the *National Interest, Orbis,* the *Atlantic Monthly, New Republic,* the *New York Times,* the *Washington Post,* the *Wall Street Journal,* and the *Los Angeles Times.* He holds a Ph.D. in political science from the University of California at Berkeley.

Anatol Lieven is a correspondent in Budapest for the *Financial Times* (London). He has also served as a correspondent for the *Times* in Moscow, the Baltic states, Eastern Europe, Pakistan, and Afghanistan. His articles have appeared in a number of other publications as well, including the *Economist,* the *Atlantic Monthly,* and the *National Interest.* Lieven is the author of *The Baltic Revolution: Estonia, Latvia, Lithuania and the Path to Independence* (1993), which won the 1993 George Orwell Prize for Political Writing and the 1995 Yale University Press Governors' Award and was a *New York Times* Notable Book of the Year for 1993. His two forthcoming books, *Flaying the Bear: The Chechen War and the Collapse of Russian State Power* and *Trouble in the House of Rurik: The Ukrainian-Russian Relationship* will be published in 1998.

Amos Perlmutter is a professor of political science and sociology at the American University and editor of the *Journal of Strategic Studies.* He is the author of numerous books, including *Making the World Safe for Democracy: The Legacy of Wilsonianism and Its Challengers* (1997). Perlmutter's articles have appeared in such leading publications as the *New York Times,* the *Washington Post,* the *Los Angeles Times, Harpers, Foreign Affairs, Foreign Policy, New Republic,* the *Wall Street Journal,* the *National Interest,* and the *International Herald Tribune.* He has also made numerous media appearances.

Benjamin Schwarz is executive editor of *World Policy Journal* and a senior fellow at the World Policy Institute. He is also a contributing editor of the *Atlantic Monthly.* He was for six years a staff member of the International Policy Department of the RAND Corporation. Schwarz's articles have appeared in numerous newspapers and journals, including the *New York Times, Foreign Policy,* and the *Atlantic Monthly.* He is also a frequent guest on radio and television programs. Schwarz was educated at Yale and Oxford Universities.

271

Ronald Steel is a professor of international relations at the University of Southern California. A former fellow of the Woodrow Wilson International Center for Scholars and the Institute for Advanced Study in Berlin, he has taught as a visiting professor at a number of American universities. He has also served in the U.S. Army and Foreign Service. Steel is a columnist for the *New Republic* and a frequent contributor to numerous other publications. He is also the author of numerous books, including, most recently, *Temptations of a Superpower* (1995), and the recipient of several book awards, including the Bancroft Prize, the National Book Award, and the National Book Critics Circle Award. Steel holds degrees from Northwestern and Harvard Universities.

Alan Tonelson is a research fellow at the U.S. Business & Industrial Council Educational Foundation. He has served as a fellow at the Economic Strategy Institute and as associate editor of *Foreign Policy*. Tonelson's articles on American politics and foreign policy have appeared in numerous publications, including the *Atlantic Monthly*, the *New York Times*, the *Washington Post*, the *Wall Street Journal*, *Foreign Policy*, and the *National interest*. He is coeditor of *Powernomics: Economics and Strategy after the Cold War*. He is also a frequent commentator for radio and television.

Index

Brandt, Willy, 65
Britain
 defense spending of, 2, 217
 position on German reunification, 33
Brzezinski, Zbigniew, 5, 145, 192–93,
 209, 248
Buchanan, Patrick, 215
Bulgaria
 as candidate for NATO membership,
 122
 fractured economy of, 165–66
 instability in, 214
 relations with Russia, 7, 166–67
Bundy, McGeorge, 26
Burden sharing, 181–83
Bush, George, 38, 107
 on German reunification, 117
 relations with Gorbachev, 110, 112
 vision of revamped NATO, 106
Bush administration
 creation of North Atlantic
 Consultative Council, 35
 policy toward OSCE, 226–27
 position on NATO expansion, 35,
 78–79
 unified Germany as NATO member,
 33–34
 world without American dominance,
 76–77

Carpenter, Ted Galen, 95, 212
Carr, E. H., 193
Caspian basin, 225
Ceausescu, Nicolae, 89
Cem, Ismail, 262
Central European countries
 current U.S. interests in, 63–64
 EU membership potential, 237–40
 geopolitical vulnerability, 47–48
 NATO membership potential, 2, 4,
 19–20
 need for investment, 50
 perceived role of, 48–49
 perception of Partnership for Peace,
 160
 potential for conflict in, 10, 56–59
 in proposed Mittleuropa bloc, 238–40
 See also Former Soviet Union
Central Treaty Organization, 255
Cevik, Ilnur, 262
CFE. See Conventional Forces in
 Europe (CFE) Treaty.
Chamberlain, Neville, 193
Chechnya, 46, 55, 150–51, 200, 246

Chen Qimao, 138
Chernomyrdin, Viktor, 126, 167
China
 with enlarged NATO, 253
 military cooperation with Russia,
 136–39, 171
 policy toward Taiwan, 137–39
 potential power of, 148
 relations with Russia, 6–7, 24, 66,
 136–38, 170–71, 204, 216
 relations with United States, 138–39
 U.S. policy of containment toward,
 195
Chirac, Jacques, 2
Chisinau, 172
Christopher, Warren, 35, 189, 227
Chubais, Anatoly, 145, 162
Ciorbea, Victor, 165, 167
Clinton, Bill
 on building a new NATO, 18
 concessions to Russia, 196
 East European policy of, 5
 equating NATO with Marshall Plan,
 64, 66–67, 202
 on NATO as defensive organization,
 18
 on NATO enlargement, 17–18, 42–43,
 49, 54, 56, 60, 68 n. 5, 86, 199–200,
 211, 260–61
 on NATO's peacekeeping role, 4, 17
 on NATO's use of nuclear weapons,
 37
 on partnership with Russia, 38
 on preservation of Bosnia, 201
 on provision of security for new
 NATO members, 27–28, 49
 on Russian elections, 44
Clinton administration
 advocacy of NATO enlargement, 5,
 31, 35–36, 44, 64, 66–67, 78–80, 109,
 116, 121, 178, 188–92, 234, 237,
 248–49, 255–58
 Bosnia mission viewed by, 18
 concessions at Helsinki to Russia, 196
 European policy of, 51, 64–66
 foreign policy of, 72
 lack of endorsement for policy in
 Bosnia, 57–58
 Partnership for Peace initiative, 159–
 60
 position on Russian membership in
 NATO, 133
 proposal to offer NATO membership
 to three countries, 13

274

of United States in Europe, 44
See also START II nuclear arms
treaty; START III nuclear arms
agreement

Odom, William, 21, 58–59
Organization for Security and
Cooperation in Europe (OSCE)
as framework for European security
organization, 217, 226–28
member countries, 227
proposals for changes in, 228–31
proposed strengthening of, 12, 124,
200
Osgood, Robert E., 60
Oslo peace accord, 108
O'Sullivan, John, 209

Palous, Martin, 134
Paris summit (1997), 103
Partnership for Peace (1994)
as compromise, 35–36
military cooperation under, 178–79
NATO military cooperation under,
109
political-military dialogue under, 161
proposed building on, 124
rationale for, 159–60
Sea Breeze-97 exercises, 172
U.S. appropriations for military
program of, 203
Peacekeeping
NATO's role, 4, 17, 34, 172, 174, 178
U.S. role in, 4, 46, 212
Peoples Liberation Army, China, 171
Persian Gulf
U.S. intervention, 77
U.S. military assets in, 170
PFP. *See* Partnership for Peace.
Poland
border disputes with neighbors,
56–57
EU membership potential, 124
financial problems of, 2
move to democracy, 58
NATO membership potential, 1, 4,
13, 17, 58, 121, 125, 159–60, 178,
214
relations with Belarus, 94–96
risks for NATO, 85
as Visegrad country, 36
See also Kaliningrad
Portugal, 180

Primakov, Yevgeny, 22, 116, 130–31,
170
Pushkov, Alexei, 109, 112, 131, 132

Qian Qichen, 137, 138

Rakhmaninov, Yurii, 139
Regional stability
as argument for NATO expansion,
56–59
threats to European, 79–80
Rodionov, Igor, 170
Rodman, Peter, 147, 192
Rogov, Sergei, 132
Romania, 25, 37
ethnic Hungarians in, 88–90
fractured economy of, 165–66
NATO membership potential, 122,
179, 215
political parties in, 171
reaction in Scenario 3 NATO
expansion, 165
relations with Hungary, 4, 89–90, 259
reorientation to West, 167
Transdniester region interests of,
171–72
Ruehe, Volker, 174
Rusk, Dean, 74–75
Russia
circumstances for alienation of, 160
competition with Iran, 171
concerns related to NATO
enlargement, 6–7, 22, 36, 103,
110–14, 116, 122–24, 130–32,
143–50, 203–4, 216, 238, 254
as consultant to NATO, 38–39
containment of, 200, 205
early policies of Yeltsin, 107
economic problems of, 55, 107–10,
171, 200
enemies of, 149–50
impact of NATO enlargement on,
5–6, 66
implications of Founding Act on
actions of, 23–24, 38, 110–12
as implicit adversary, 234
interests in Eastern Europe, 3
as member of NATO consultative
council, 38–39
military cooperation with China,
136–39, 171
as military force, 49–50, 199–200
as military threat, 27, 203–4

War
  cause of, 256–59
  NATO to eliminate threat of, 262
  relation between democracy and, 258
Warsaw Pact
  factors influencing creation of, 203
  Gorbachev's opinion of, 131
  views of during its existence, 110
Warsaw Pact states
  expectations of NATO membership, 19–20, 41–43, 204, 245
  liaison missions at NATO headquarters, 35
  proposed EU guidance toward democracy, 236–38
  unilateral abandonment of, 111–13, 188
Washington, George, 139
Western European Union (WEU), 126, 217–18, 226
West European countries
  changing policies toward Central and Eastern Europe, 218
  impact of U.S. Cold War foreign policy on, 73–78
  instability of, 50–51
  lowered military spending of, 2
  management of Bosnian problem, 192
  with NATO enlargement, 173–74
  position on NATO enlargement, 2–3, 248
  position on U.S. NATO troop deployment, 27
  reduced sources of conflict among, 4–5
  scale-back of welfare programs, 2
  U.S. Cold War security guarantees to, 21
  U.S. interest in, 49

as welfare states, 2
Whitney, Craig R., 86
Wight, Martin, 188
Will, George, 147
Wilson, Woodrow, 49, 60, 72, 129
Woerner, Manfred, 81
Wriston, Walter, 190

Yabloko Party, Russia, 113
Yastreshembsky, Sergei, 133
Yavlinsky, Grigory, 113, 162
Yeltsin, Boris
  on cooperation with neighbor countries, 136
  early policies of, 107
  eroded power of, 116
  interest in Russia's NATO membership, 126
  meeting with Jiang Zemin, 136
  on NATO expansion, 46, 144
  on NATO obligation, 45
  overtures to CIS states, 172–73
  relations with Clinton, 115–16
  signing of Founding Act, 6
  on U.S. protectionism, 108
Yeltsin administration
  acceptance of Founding Act, 143
  free-market reforms of, 147
  policies related to military, 200
  policy related to China, 24, 171
Yilmaz, Mesut, 261
Yugoslavia
  breakup of former, 57, 93–94
  civil war in, 178, 211, 215
  NATO role in former, 34

Zaire, 214
Zeman, Milos, 164
Zhirinovsky, Vladimir, 152, 191
Zoellick, Robert, 210
Zyuganov, Gennady, 113, 169

Cato Institute

Founded in 1977, the Cato Institute is a public policy research foundation dedicated to broadening the parameters of policy debate to allow consideration of more options that are consistent with the traditional American principles of limited government, individual liberty, and peace. To that end, the Institute strives to achieve greater involvement of the intelligent, concerned lay public in questions of policy and the proper role of government.

The Institute is named for *Cato's Letters*, libertarian pamphlets that were widely read in the American Colonies in the early 18th century and played a major role in laying the philosophical foundation for the American Revolution.

Despite the achievement of the nation's Founders, today virtually no aspect of life is free from government encroachment. A pervasive intolerance for individual rights is shown by government's arbitrary intrusions into private economic transactions and its disregard for civil liberties.

To counter that trend, the Cato Institute undertakes an extensive publications program that addresses the complete spectrum of policy issues. Books, monographs, and shorter studies are commissioned to examine the federal budget, Social Security, regulation, military spending, international trade, and myriad other issues. Major policy conferences are held throughout the year, from which papers are published thrice yearly in the *Cato Journal*. The Institute also publishes the quarterly magazine *Regulation*.

In order to maintain its independence, the Cato Institute accepts no government funding. Contributions are received from foundations, corporations, and individuals, and other revenue is generated from the sale of publications. The Institute is a nonprofit, tax-exempt, educational foundation under Section 501(c)3 of the Internal Revenue Code.

CATO INSTITUTE
1000 Massachusetts Ave., N.W.
Washington, D.C. 20001